FIXIN' TO GIT

JIM WRIGHT

DUKE
UNIVERSITY
PRESS

DURHAM
AND LONDON
2002

FIXIN' TO GIT

One Fan's Love Affair with NASCAR's Winston Cup

Printed in the United States of

America on acid-free paper ⊗

Designed by Rebecca Giménez

Typeset in Adobe Minion by

Tseng Information Systems, Inc.

Library of Congress Cataloging-

in-Publication Data appear on

the last printed page of this book.

First printing in paperback, 2003

To my racing family:

The old Cowboy, now departed. May he rest in peace.

My sister, Nancy, and my brother, Kelley,
boon companions at Indy and in life.

My race-fan in-laws Neil, Denise, Elaine, and Ed.
To everyone, my thanks for everything.

And my beloved Chris, who's not much for racing
but thinks the people-watching's a hoot.

Prelude: On the Road to Charlotte, 1

1. Car Culture and the American Dream, 17

Daytona Pilgrimage, 46

2. Deconstructing NASCAR, 57

Back Home Again in Indiana, 87

3. Racin' Basics, 98

Lost in the Land of Cotton, 132

CONTENTS

4. The NASCAR Subculture, 144

Short-Track Showdown, 170

5. The Yankee Invasion, 180

Nantahala Interlude, 204

6. Alcohol, Tobacco, and Firearms, 217

Grand Finale in Atlanta, 254

7. We Are Family, 263

Notes, 281

Index, 293

ACKNOWLEDGMENTS

For various kindnesses large and small while this book was being written, I am pleased to thank Charlie Brody, Rhonda Coignet, Leigh Anne Couch, Laura Dail, Alison Dennis, Joel Devine, Joyce Deloach, Dave and Toni Fox, Rebecca Giménez, Ed Herbert, Jay Joyner, Neil Maller, Becca Matteo, Buz McKim, Patricia Mickelberry, Fetzer Mills, Steve Nock, John Shelton Reed, Laura Sanchez, Dwayne Smith, Daphne Spain, Teri Vail, Sondra Vogel, and Bill Wetherell. I also thank my dean at Tulane University, Teresa Soufas, for granting me the sabbatical that made this book possible, two anonymous readers for their enthusiasm and careful reading, and a large number of editors and publishers whose inability to spot a winner even as they held it in their hands eventually led me to Miriam Angress and her capable staff at Duke University Press, who have been delightful.

Prelude: On the Road to Charlotte

◼◻◼◻ On the 22nd of May 1999, I found myself sitting with my wife,
◻◼◻◼ Chris, in the Turn Two grandstands at the Lowe's Motor Speedway in Charlotte, North Carolina, not quite halfway up and just past the
middle of the turn. You won't run into many college professors at the
racetracks, but there we were, hunkered down for a night of action that
would climax with The Winston, a seventy-lap, all-star event for competitors in NASCAR's premier series, the Winston Cup. The May races in
Charlotte are run at night, and the air was uncommonly cool, almost
sweater weather, but the action on the track was hot as only NASCAR
action can be.

We were in Charlotte for "speed week," a ten-day extravaganza of
stock-car racing that has the Winston Cup drivers in town for two consecutive weekends, first for The Winston, then for the Coca-Cola 600,
NASCAR's longest race. Most Winston Cup teams are headquartered in or
around Charlotte, so Lowe's is the home track for most drivers and speed
week is NASCAR's equivalent of a home stand. Because the two races occur
on back-to-back weekends, the second of which includes Memorial Day,
thousands of fans come early and camp out for the duration. No matter
where you park, getting to the track brings you through or past immense
RV villages that stretch for miles up and down all the access roads. These
vast encampments are unique in all of sports.

The Lowe's speedway is north of Charlotte, in the town of Concord, about halfway to Kannapolis (known to race fans as the late Dale Earnhardt's hometown). As you turn off the interstate, the track suddenly rises up out of the flat Carolina piedmont, an immense monument to automobile racing. (The track accommodates 155,000 fans in the grandstands and another 45,000 in the infield.) From the outside, it is improbably large, oddly attractive, very modern in appearance and amenities — the only track of eight I visited in 1999 with a concession stand that sold premium cigars. To be in Charlotte, the state's largest city, is to be at the epicenter of big-time championship stock-car racing, and if you go to the places in Charlotte where NASCAR fans hang out, the air crackles with excitement for days leading up to the race.

From the track's opening in 1960 until the spring of 1999, it had been called the *Charlotte* Motor Speedway, but owner Humpy Wheeler had decided to sell the track's naming rights to Lowe's, the home improvement giant. This $35-million, ten-year deal was unpopular with fans everywhere and especially with fans from the Charlotte area. I overheard one fan wondering out loud, "Good Lord, how much money does that old man need?" *Sports Illustrated* ran a piece on the name change under the headline, "Goodbye, Sweet Charlotte," reporting that "the most commercially saturated sport in the U.S. has begun to sell off the last piece of its soul."[1] I'll bet old Humpy cried all the way to the bank.

At one and a half miles, Lowe's Motor Speedway is an average-sized NASCAR track, and we could see the entire track from our Turn Two vantage point (just as the ticket agent had promised). But the pits at Charlotte, as at most tracks, are along the main straightaway, and various infield structures (garages, pit stands, first aid stations, concessions, team transporters) kept the action on Pit Road hidden from our view. It was also nearly impossible to see the cars as they dropped off Turn Four and headed down the front stretch. But much of the night's wreckage, which was plentiful, took place right in front of us, and we had a great view of the racing action down the back straightaway. I was surprised at just how squirrelly the cars were as they came out of Turn Two and blasted down the back stretch: they'd wiggle and waggle, then snap to straight-line attention as their drivers mashed on the gas. Considering the acceleration provided by these 750-horsepower V-8 engines, it's amazing that anybody gets through the corners in one piece. And yet, most do.

Lowe's Motor Speedway offered up four separate races the night of May 22 for our enjoyment. The first, a Legends Car race, featured small-scale reproductions of classic race cars powered by four-cylinder engines. At Charlotte, part of the main straightaway and Pit Road are used to create a quarter-mile Legends track. From our vantage point out in the Turn Two boondocks, we were unable to see any of this action, although we could easily hear the high-pitched whine of the cars.

The Legends race was followed by ARCA's EasyCare 100. ARCA is the Automobile Racing Club of America, a sanctioning body that sponsors lower-echelon stock car races. Since ARCA cars are, basically, used Winston Cup cars, the qualifying speeds for the ARCA event (just under 180 mph) were only 8–10 mph slower than the qualifying speeds for the main event. Most ARCA races are run on short tracks, and most ARCA drivers have limited experience racing on high-banked superspeedways like Charlotte. The resulting combination of high speeds and relatively inexperienced drivers makes the average ARCA superspeedway race wild as all get out. That night's race was no exception: a succession of spin-outs and crashes littered the track with broken race cars, and four caution periods kept the field tightly bunched to the very end. (A caution period is called whenever there are unsafe conditions on the track—a wreck, debris, rain, and so on. During caution periods, all the cars slow down and get into line behind the pace car. No passing is allowed, so the effect is always to bunch up the field.) Rookie Mario Gosselin, a former champion in the USAR Hooters Pro Cup Series (another of the sport's minor leagues), successfully picked his way through the rubble and racked up his first ARCA win. Shawna Robinson, one of the sport's few female competitors, also had a strong run and finished fourth. (In June 2001 Robinson became the first woman since 1989 to start a Winston Cup event.)

Following the EasyCare 100 were the two Winston Cup races: a preliminary event called the Winston Open and the night's main event, The Winston itself. The Winston is NASCAR's all-star event, not a regular points race. Still, there are bragging rights and plenty of money on the line. (That night, for example, the total purse amounted to $1,338,000, with the winner guaranteed at least $200,000.) Twenty top drivers are invited into The Winston field, with slots automatically given to all drivers and car owners who have won a race in the current or preceding year; to all former Winston Cup champions who are still active; and to any active driver who has won The Winston in the previous five years. If these criteria produce a field of fewer than twenty, race winners from previous seasons are also invited in, until a field of twenty is achieved. The remaining Winston Cup drivers — twenty or twenty-five of them — compete in the Open, the winner of which then becomes the twenty-first and final starting entry for The Winston.

The Open proved to be the most interesting race of the evening. Californian Mike Skinner, driving the Chevrolet sponsored by Lowe's Home Improvement Warehouses, sat on the pole and was the odds-on favorite to win the race and with it the twenty-first starting position in The Winston. Getting the Lowe's entry into the first-ever Winston to be run at the re-christened speedway would certainly have pleased Skinner's sponsor and might be seen, at least by some fans, as somehow vindicating the sale of the naming rights to Lowe's. Ironically, rookie Tony Stewart, driving the Home Depot Pontiac, started beside Skinner on the front row. Day in and day out, Lowe's and Home Depot compete head to head for the business of American do-it-yourselfers. That night, they'd go head to head at the Charlotte — sorry, Lowe's — Motor Speedway at speeds near 190 mph for the final starting spot in NASCAR's annual all-star contest. That front-row line-up was surely symbolic of *something*.

Stewart had begun his day in Indiana qualifying for the Indianapolis 500, then had jetted to Charlotte to compete in the Winston Open. When the green flag dropped, Skinner jumped into the lead, but Stewart overtook him on the second lap and never looked back, leading every subsequent lap and winning the race by a five-second margin. (As Winston Cup racing goes, a five-second winning margin is huge.) Skinner's car handled poorly, and he finished well back in the pack.

Considering that Stewart was a rookie and a Yankee to boot (he is one of several young Indiana drivers making waves in the Winston Cup), you'd not expect him to have much of a following at a venue like Charlotte, at least not that early in the season (or so early in his career). Yet the crowd around us cheered wildly lap after lap as Stewart barreled through the second turn at the front of the field. Chris, who retains her maiden name Stewart and who was therefore a natural Tony Stewart fan, asked what was going on, why all the boisterous enthusiasm for the young Hoosier? I didn't get it either, until about midrace, when a local fan sitting next to me leaned over to say with delight, "Ain't it good to see that

Home Depot car runnin' so strong at the LOOOOWE's Motor Speedway?!"
(Humpy, are you listening? Racing traditions mean something to your
average NASCAR fan.)

The Winston Cup season begins each year with the Daytona 500
in mid-February, and by that weekend of May 22, eleven of the season's thirty-four points races had been completed. Jeff Gordon, NASCAR's
hottest star and the 1995, 1997, and 1998 Winston Cup champion, had already notched three victories, and while some early-season DNFs ("did
not finish") had him languishing in fifth place in the points, he'd been
running strong and was clearly the man to beat. Virginian Jeff Burton,
with two wins, was the only other multirace winner of the year. Burton's teammate Mark Martin, points leader Dale Jarrett, and drivers Terry
Labonte, Rusty Wallace, Dale Earnhardt, and John Andretti all had a
win apiece. That amounted to eight different winners in the first eleven
races — which meant that 1999 was already looking to be a very competitive season.

The Winston features a unique format, three races in one. Cars start in
order of qualifying position and run an initial thirty laps. The leader at the
end of the first thirty laps wins $50,000. Then, the front-runners (on that
night, the top six cars) are "inverted" — the first-place car goes to sixth,
the second-place car to fifth, and so on — and the field races another thirty
laps. Again, the driver leading at the end of the second thirty laps wins
$50,000, the front-runners are inverted, and then there is a ten-lap dash
to the finish and the winner's purse of $200,000. Jeff Gordon picked up
$100,000 for leading the race at the end of both thirty-lap segments. 1996
Winston Cup champion Terry Labonte won the ten-lap finishing dash
and pocketed a cool two hundred grand. Stewart drove through the field
to finish second; Gordon, the most successful of the young Hoosiers and
the dominant force in Winston Cup racing in the 1990s, ended up third.

The race was a NASCAR wreck-fest. Perhaps due to the racing residue
deposited in the preliminary events, the track was slick all night. In a
regular Winston Cup race, adjustments are made during pit stops to improve handling or to compensate for track conditions, but a thirty-lap
dash allows for none of that. So the drivers were stuck with their original
set-ups and nobody had guessed right. Boom! A big wreck on Lap 11 took
seven cars — a third of the field — out of the race, leaving only fourteen
cars to complete the remaining fifty-nine laps. Fourteen race cars look

mighty forlorn out running by themselves in single file around a mile-and-a-half oval. So The Winston was less exciting than the usual Winston Cup race. But the ten-lap finishing dash was all I expected it to be: a dozen fast stock cars running nose-to-tail, fender-to-fender, with the outcome in doubt to the last lap.

Not all the night's interesting action took place on the track. A serious fist fight broke out about ten rows down and a bit to the left of where we were sitting (the only fan altercation of any significance I witnessed all season). It started as a harmless little punching contest between two seriously drunk and heavily tattooed long-haired country boys (to borrow a famous phrase from the Charlie Daniels Band), but friends on both sides quickly joined the fray and, in a matter of seconds, six or eight rednecks were whomping on each other with fists, empty beer coolers, and whatever else was ready to hand. A bloody cut over the eye of one combatant was the only damage I saw, and the incident was over by the time security guards arrived. Still, the two lads who had started it all were escorted unceremoniously to the gate. I never did figure out just what the fight was about, but the peripheral involvement of two foxy little GRITS (that's Southspeak for "Girls Raised in the South," a character type as much as a regional origin) made me think it was a disputation about women, not race cars.

About a half hour later, we saw an obese and evidently besotted fan roll down a grassy slope between our grandstand and the next, stopping only when he piled into the trackside wall. He sat on his duff for a while, looking bewildered, then staggered to his feet and waved, much to the delight of the assembled NASCAR masses. A track ambulance came to investigate and, with some assistance, our roly-poly race fan finally made it back to his seat.

There were many drunken fans at the Charlotte speedway, more than we saw at most other races—although there weren't too many sober people sitting around us at the July event at Daytona, either. Both of these are night races, and while nighttime Winston Cup racing is a spectacular visual experience, it gives fans way too much time to get liquored up before the racing begins. On the other hand, the Richmond event that I attended in the fall was also a night race, and with one exception (a fan about two rows down from us whose only friends in life were apparently Jack Daniels and Jim Beam), the fans seated near us in Richmond were all

A view of the infield campers from our seats at The Winston in Charlotte, the first event on the 1999 *Fixin' to Git* Road Tour. It is a few hours before race time at this point, thus the many empty seats. There is a grassy incline (just visible at the far right of the photo) between the Executive Suites and the East Grandstand where we were seated. We watched a drunk fan roll down this hill and up against the trackside restraining wall.

sober as judges. (Okay, some were a bit tipsy, but we're talking Winston Cup racing here, where the standard for drunkenness is high — way higher than the six-pack or two that I go through during a hot summer race.)

The night's biggest disappointment was my new race scanner, a shortwave radio that is used to listen in on conversations between drivers, spotters, and crews. (Outfitted with a proper set of headphones, my rig had been a $300 birthday present from Chris.) Each team broadcasts on its own frequencies, with most teams using two or three, so there are several dozen frequencies you have to program into your scanner before the race begins — a tedious process. Still, I thought listening in on the drivers and pit crews would add to the enjoyment. But you never know just which driver you should listen to, and to my surprise, driver-to-pit communications are infrequent and usually terse, if you manage to pick one up. Driving a race car at 190 mph requires intense concentration, and drivers do not chatter away on their radios while the race is under way. I'd listen in to a particular driver for a couple of silent laps, then hear him say something like, "We're loose in two." That's it. "We're loose in two." Another silent lap would go by, and then the crew chief would respond, "We'll fix it with air pressure at the stop." And that would be it.

Granted, the format of The Winston leaves little time for drivers and crew chiefs to "dial in" the car; basically, the race team either gets the setup right on the first try or lives with its mistakes for the rest of the night. And there was a bit more car-to-pit communication at some of the other races I attended later in the season. Still, as I flitted haplessly from frequency to frequency and driver to driver, trying in vain to find an interesting conversation—I was looking for something like, "Did you see what that bastard Andretti did to me on the last lap?" or "Jesus Christ, they're NUTS out here tonight!"—I realized that fiddling with my high-tech gizmo had caused me to lose track of the action on the speedway. What I learned at Charlotte and elsewhere is that the best use of the scanner is to listen in on the Motor Racing Network radio broadcast—far more informative than listening to the drivers themselves. But you can do this with a $20 radio. Oh well.

Serious Winston Cup fans know that everything about a race weekend can be a struggle: obtaining tickets, securing accommodations, getting to and from the track, parking once you get there. But that particular trip was a logistical triumph for me and Chris. I had purchased two over-the-counter tickets to the race by telephone for $65 apiece about a month before, a pleasant surprise, since I had been warned that Winston Cup events are always sold out months in advance. And, while a hundred and thirty bucks might seem a lot to spend on four hours of entertainment, these were in fact the cheap seats. The best seats at a stock-car race are those at the top of the grandstand (the higher up, the better the view) and near the start-finish line. With our tickets, we were nowhere close to the top and were a long way from the start-finish line to boot. On the other hand, if you compare the price of Winston Cup tickets to the cost of going to rock concerts, the races don't seem quite so pricey.

By the time I had my tickets, all the hotel and motel rooms within a ten-mile radius of the track were booked. Near the Charlotte airport, about twenty-five miles from the track, I found a hotel that still had rooms, but they were going for $275 a night, with a three-night minimum. I'm no piker when it comes to race weekends, but I wasn't anxious to pay Manhattan rates for Charlotte hotel rooms, so I called my buddy Dwayne Smith at the University of North Carolina in Charlotte and he hooked us up with a guest room in a UNC–C dorm for $23 a night, not five miles from the track. The dorm was empty, the room Spartan but clean, comfortable, and convenient. The school could do a brisk trade renting these rooms to NASCAR fans on race weekends.

We'd spent the day before the race scouting out traffic patterns and parking possibilities — logistical details that fans ignore at their peril. Regardless of the posted starting times, fans begin showing up at the tracks five or six hours before the races begin, but everyone wants to leave as soon as the race is over, so Winston Cup races invariably end with massive traffic jams as hundreds of thousands of fans all try to leave at the same time. With the average Winston Cup gate now approaching 180,000, getting fans away from the tracks and onto the nearby interstates is the logistical equivalent of evacuating, in a couple of hours, a city the size of Dayton, Ohio.

Race-day traffic control limits your freedom in leaving the track. Basically, you go where you are made to go, then loop back around miles later if that's what it takes to get headed in the right direction. So the trick is to park such that the direction you'll be made to go is the direction you'll *want* to be going, not always an easy feat. Usually, this requires avoiding the trackside lots altogether in favor of "quick getaway" spots in the surrounding neighborhoods. We found a $10 parking spot that seemed to fit the bill, and, sure enough, we scampered back to the dorm room after Saturday's race in under half an hour. We talked the next day to fans who'd parked trackside, and they'd spent the better part of two hours escaping the postrace traffic knot.

We had headed to Charlotte at the front end of speed week, hoping to take in both events and fill up the intervening week by visiting friends, giving a couple of talks, and traveling around North Carolina. But tickets to the Coke 600, as it's popularly known, never materialized. A week before the race, scalpers were asking $150 for $95 tickets. (In May I was unwilling to pay the scalper's price; by August I had learned to accept the street market in tickets as a necessary element in the serious fan's repertoire.) So, after Saturday's running of The Winston, we spent some time with friends, I gave a talk about homelessness (my area of research) to a group of forty or fifty academics and social-service workers, and we headed home midweek.

I'd been an earnest Winston Cup fan since the early '90s, but aside from an annual trip to Daytona for the July Pepsi 400 with my brother-in-law Ed, I kept up with the sport through television, books about stock-car racing, and semiregular forays into the sport's fanzines (*Inside NASCAR, Stock Car Racing, NASCAR Winston Cup Illustrated*—just the thing to get a race fan through extended airport layovers). Charlotte was my first look at what Winston Cup racing had to offer besides Daytona. It would not be my last: the trip to Charlotte was the inaugural event in a half-year odyssey that would take me to eight of the Winston Cup's legendary venues and result in the book you now hold in your hands.

Since I had first started following the Winston Cup action, championship stock-car racing had become America's fastest-growing sport. How, I wondered, did that happen? NASCAR, its stars, and its fans seemed (and still seem) to be everywhere. Charlotte was the opening gambit in my effort to figure out why. In February 1999, three months before the Charlotte trip, I was standing on the corner of Napoleon and St. Charles Avenues in uptown New Orleans watching Bacchus, one of the oldest and most spectacular of the city's many splendid Mardi Gras parades. On the inside of that corner sits Copeland's Restaurant, and looming above the restaurant, taller and more imposing than any of the surrounding buildings, was a giant billboard featuring an immense visage of Jeff Gordon with a white stripe over his lip and the query, "Got Milk?" If you've watched much TV, you'll know that Gordon also promotes the Living Word, Pepsi-Cola, microwaveable nachos, Chevrolet Monte Carlos, and a score of other products. What is it about this guy—what is it about his sport?—that has entities from General Motors to the American Dairy Association paying him a king's ransom to hawk their wares?

Gordon is not the only NASCAR star whose face beams down from the billboards or flickers across the TV screen. You've probably seen Dale Jarrett on the tube, paired with football announcer John Madden, pitching Outback Steakhouses (John goes for the "big juicy steaks," Dale wants that "shrimp on the barbie"); Mark Martin shilling for Winn-Dixie supermarkets or Discount Auto Parts; Bill Elliott urging his fans to chow down at McDonald's and spend their nights on the road in Super Eight Motels;

Tony Stewart and Bobby Labonte peddling Chef Boy-Ar-Dee canned spaghetti products. These guys are *race-car drivers,* not rock-and-roll celebrities, models, television personalities, or movie stars. What has turned them into cultural icons whose endorsements command millions?

Have you ever been motoring down the highway when you noticed a car going past with a numeral displayed in the rear window, or maybe on the bumper? Just a numeral, no text or explanation: a 2 perhaps, or a 5, maybe an 88, usually in some iridescent Day-Glo color. Or a pickup truck with a cartoon graphic showing Calvin (of "Calvin and Hobbes") with his pants down, a naughty arc of pee splashing off a number 24? Did you ever wonder what that was all about? Well, it's a NASCAR thing: the people who display those puzzling numerals are stock-car racing fans, and they do it to identify themselves and their preferences to other fans. It's a species marker, a secret code, a clan totem, mysterious to outsiders but instantly recognizable to those in the know: 2 identifies a Rusty Wallace acolyte, 5 a follower of Terry Labonte, 88 an enthusiast for Dale Jarrett. And the Calvin decal? It translates, "Piss on Jeff Gordon" (24 being the number of Gordon's car).

Early in the spring 2000 Winston Cup race at the Texas Motor Speedway, the TV coverage cut away to a live interview with General Colin Powell (now the U.S. Secretary of State), who was attending his first motorsports event and enjoying it, too, he claimed. Powell was at the race to promote America's Promise, his nonprofit foundation dedicated to building character among the nation's youth, and to appeal to NASCAR fans to get involved with kids as mentors, Big Brothers, teachers, and friends. Who'd ever think that NASCAR fans would be attractive as role models for children? Or that a racetrack would be a good place to troll for America's Promise volunteers? A church—sure. A college campus— no doubt about it. But the Texas Motor Speedway on a NASCAR weekend?

An acquaintance of mine who knew of my interest in stock-car racing sent me an article about one of my favorite drivers, Ricky Rudd. It recounted Rudd's problems with his former sponsor (Tide laundry detergent), his hook-up with Robert Yates Racing, his arduous physical fitness regimen, his courageous 1998 victory at Martinsville. It was a nice piece, laudatory, informative, the sort of driver story I've come to expect in *Stock Car Racing* magazine. But this item didn't turn up in *Stock Car*

NASCAR flag cartoon. © 2000 *Atlanta Constitution.* Permission of Mike Luckovich and Creators Syndicate, Inc.

Racing or even in the *Charlotte Observer* (the newspaper of record for motorsports). It ran in the *New York Times.* Since when did readers of the *New York Times* develop an interest in NASCAR?

NASCAR has even insinuated itself into the national political discourse. There was a controversy that seethed for years in South Carolina (and in a number of other Southern states) over the Confederate battle flag that once flew above the state capital. Cartoonist Mike Luckovich suggested we resolve this by swapping out the discredited Stars and Bars for "a flag that isn't racist . . . but preserves white Southern heritage" — a NASCAR checkered flag. Luckovich draws for the *Atlanta Journal Constitution,* and you'd expect Georgians to get the joke. But the cartoon also ran in *Newsweek* without comment or explanation, and I'm sure *Newsweek's* mostly Yankee readers got it, too.

I'd set out for Charlotte that late weekend in May 1999 to see if I couldn't get some answers to these questions or at least develop some sort of adequate take on the NASCAR phenomenon. NASCAR was born in Charlotte a half century ago. The organization's first stock-car race was run on a three-quarter-mile dirt track in Charlotte on 19 June 1949, and championship stock-car racing has been a continuous presence in the city ever since. Nearly all the current Winston Cup teams and NASCAR itself are headquartered in Charlotte, and during the fifty-plus years of competition, more drivers, race winners, and annual champions have hailed from North Carolina than any other state. If you want to figure out NASCAR, where better to begin than Charlotte—the womb, the Earth Mother, of the sport?

I had been granted a sabbatical that freed me of classroom responsibilities from May through December. Chris had arranged with her employer to take off as much time as she wanted. Our nest had been empty since 1993, and with a handful of graduate students willing to tend to our pets, there was nothing to prevent us from traveling around the country to check out as many races and venues as our marriage could withstand. And if I could say I was writing a book based on these experiences, I could even deduct a share of the expense on my income tax return. From these opportunities, the 1999 *Fixin' to Git* Road Tour had been conceived.

Dozens of books have been written about stock-car racing, and I've read many of them over the years. I can't say I ever read a racing book I didn't enjoy, but none seemed to capture the essence of the sport as I had come to know it or to do justice to the phenomenon that NASCAR has become. Most NASCAR books are insiders' accounts that take the reader "behind the scenes" of championship stock-car racing, and while it is fascinating back there, it is not part of the experience of the typical fan. Unlike other NASCAR authors, I was not interested in interviewing drivers, owners, and crew chiefs, or in crafting an exposé, or in following the fortunes of this team or that through the season—these had been done before. No, I wanted to experience and write about the Winston Cup spectacle itself—the fans, the pageantry, the history, the subculture— and, where possible without being pedantic, to connect my observations to larger themes in American history and culture. I was less interested in hanging out in the Winston Cup garages than in the bars, restaurants, parking lots, juke joints, motels, and campgrounds where race fans congregate; less interested in insiders' opinions about the sport than in the views, enthusiasms, and prejudices of the people sitting around me in the grandstands. Most of all, I wanted to experience then convey the rich, erotic sensory overload—the sights, the sounds, the smells, the *feel*—of weekends at Winston Cup racetracks. I wanted to know NASCAR in the biblical sense.

As I've mentioned, no city in America is more closely associated with NASCAR than Charlotte (Daytona Beach being the only possible exception). In Charlotte and the surrounding towns, there are constant reminders that you're in NASCAR country. WELCOME RACE FANS! banners start flying about thirty miles out, and once you near the track, most of the billboards, signs, and banners have something to say about racing. Home to the Sandwich Construction Company, perhaps the best-known stock-car theme restaurant in America (you may have seen photos—it has race cars on the roof), Charlotte boasts any number of other sports bars, restaurants, and souvenir shops catering to NASCAR fans. Travelers through the Charlotte airport can stop for a beer and a burger at the NASCAR Cafe, the first, I believe, of what is now a large national restaurant chain. (It is right down the concourse from the airport cigar store.)

With a city population of 400,000 and a total metropolitan area population of 1.5 million, Charlotte self-consciously bills itself as a major urban center of the New South.[2] None of the young urban professionals I met while I was there (academics from the university and human services workers who attended my talk on the homeless) were race fans, although most of them were aware that it was a race weekend in Charlotte. (It is easy to tell: all the restaurants are packed.) Most of these young, bright, attractive, upwardly mobile New Southerners seemed vaguely embarrassed by their city's NASCAR connections, dumbfounded that I was in town mainly to go to the race, and taken aback to learn I was writing a book about the Winston Cup. They were more interested in comparing notes about Charlotte's new sushi bars than in stock-car racing.

With the exception of a few areas of historical renovation, there is little about the city that looks or feels Southern or that would distinguish it from recently built sections of Omaha, say, or Rochester. The city has none of the antebellum grace of a Charlestown or a Savannah, none of the seamy decadence of a New Orleans, none of the down-home country feel that makes Nashville or Memphis unmistakably *Southern* cities. A first-time visitor would scarcely know that the city was incorporated in 1768. In fact, most of Charlotte looks like it was built sometime in the past ten or fifteen years. Large knots of suburban development have sprung up everywhere on the urban fringe, and with extensive development has come the predictable slurry of malls, chain restaurants, coffee shops, factory outlet stores, and the related ticky-tacky of suburban America. You can still get grits with your morning eggs in Charlotte, but if you're not careful, you might end up with something like herb-infused grits cakes with shaved Parmesan when all you were hoping for was a pair of eggs over easy with whole hog sausage, a fresh biscuit, and *grits*. For the most part, Charlotte's "Southernness" is a caricature, a pleasant but not very interesting parody of the real thing. And that, I gather, is precisely the point of the New South.

But then you get out to the speedway, and all at once the entire legend of NASCAR courses through your veins, the whole half-century of wild-eyed Southern boys soaked in their own testosterone; hot rods with noisy, souped-up V-8s; moonshiners and whiskey-runners who (as the story goes) invented the sport in the Carolina hollows right after World War 2. You look out at the thousands of fans milling around their infield campsites, and you know, as certainly as you know your own name, that none of them started their day with a bowl of yogurt or granola. You wander through the RV villages and the campfire aromas slam into your olfactories like a race car into the wall. Wham! — charcoal, bacon, roasting animal flesh. Bam! — cheap perfume, ripe T-shirts, tobacco, beer. Downtown, it's sushi bars; out here, it's Budweiser for breakfast.

You can't be in Charlotte as I was, spending half my time with university professors and the other half with NASCAR fans, and not sense the chasm in American culture that separates city from country, professionals and clerks from factory workers and mill hands, the politically correct from the rednecks and good ol' boys, the New South from the Old. No wonder Charlotte race fans reacted so negatively to the renaming of their speedway. The track — one of the few meaningful links that remain between the modern city and its own legacy — is about the only thing left in Charlotte that would make one think of it as a Southern city. My trip to The Winston revealed that America's cultural tensions are found no less in NASCAR than anywhere else; how these tensions play out is only one of a number of story lines that emerged in Charlotte and that now thread their way throughout this book. The Charlotte expedition didn't give me any answers, but it brought some important questions into sharper focus, and at that very early stage in the project, sharper questions were plenty good enough.

1

Car Culture and the American Dream

In the rarefied university circles where I have spent my adult life, cheek-to-jowl with Spiro Agnew's "effete intellectual snobs" and "nattering nabobs of negativism," confessing that you are a stock-car racing fan is on a par with suggesting that maybe—just maybe—the South had a point. Many of my intellectual acquaintances are reflexively hostile to athletic contests of every sort, but even people who will gladly burn off a Sunday afternoon watching the New Orleans Saints lose yet another football game are stupefied that an apparently sane man would rather spend his Sunday afternoon glued to the weekend Winston Cup event. Steve Rushin, a writer for *Sports Illustrated*, pretty much says it all. "Race fans fall into one of two categories: tattooed, shirtless, sewer-mouthed drunks; and their husbands."[1] Bid-a-boom! Great gag, and anyone is certainly entitled to ask (as I am asked all the time), Just what is the thrill in watching a bunch of white guys drive around in a circle? And why write a book about it?

The thrill I will try to explain later. As for the book, *Fixin' to Git* is essentially a retirement fantasy brought to premature fruition by a one-term sabbatical and a near-desperate need to get my head out of the routines of academic research and teaching. I am a sociologist (at Tulane while this book was being written and at the University of Central Florida now), and this is my seventeenth book. I published my first book, on political alienation, in 1976, with the fifteen that followed covering a variety of ponderous sociological topics. Like most academic monographs, these books have typically sold a few thousand copies (okay, a few hundred copies in more cases than I'd care to admit), and over the twenty-five years I have been writing them, I have often been asked (by my mother, my wife, my children, and assorted others) why I don't write books that people want to read. Ouch! But it's a fair question. This book is my first crack at an answer.

To begin, I am a lifelong racing fan, and writing this book has provided the perfect excuse to indulge myself in what would otherwise be forbidden pleasures. Telling your dean that you intend to spend your sabbatical following the NASCAR Winston Cup Series around the country is certain to raise eyebrows, but no dean would think twice about a research monograph on stock-car racing as an emergent element in the popular culture. (Don't worry. That's only what I told her, not the book I've written.) Rebecca Adams—a sociologist at the University of North Carolina at Greensboro, past president of the Southern Sociological Society, and in her spare time a confirmed Deadhead—got to listen to a lot of great music, interacted with and interviewed some strange and wonderful people, and (one infers) had a blast researching and writing her book *Deadheads: Community, Spirituality, and Friendship.* I figure that if the Deadheads deserve a tribal sociologist, then why not racing fans?

Some of my earliest childhood memories are of Saturday nights at the racetracks. When I was a boy growing up in Logansport, Indiana, my father and his friends raced stock cars at the little quarter-mile dirt tracks one finds, even today, throughout the small towns of north central Indiana—Monticello, Winamac, Bass Lake, Warsaw, Anderson, Kokomo, to name a few.[2] Several old black-and-white photographs in our family album are of my father and his race cars circa 1950 or 1951. I don't remember much about those early years, but I do remember going to the races: the sounds of those great old Ford flathead V-8s firing up; the smell of oil, gasoline, and exhaust fumes; the clods of dirt that would fly into the stands as twenty or thirty reckless young men in souped-up jalopies slid full throttle through the wet clay turns. I also remember that my old man was a "balls out, belly to the ground" driver (the phrase is from Stroker Ace, *Stand On It,* a cult classic of racing literature), always charging hard, always running up front, always in contention, if not always first

My father and his race car, circa 1951. "Big Jim" Wright—also known as "Tex" when he was a young man, "Alamo" during the heyday of CB radios, and "the Cowboy" for the last twenty years of his life—drove stock cars on the Indiana dirt tracks in the early 1950s. He died on 15 March 1999.

to cross the finish line. I don't know that all this is true; it's just what I remember.

That's not all I remember. As a working-class hick who hailed from the ass end of nowhere, I remember thinking it was very, very cool that my old man raced stock cars at the local speedways, tuned engines by ear, and often fabricated car parts in his own shop. I remember taking a set of his micrometers (he was a lathe operator at the time) to grade school for show-and-tell, astonishing everyone with the fact that these instruments could measure the thickness of a hair. Again, very, very cool. I also remember turnip greens and ham hocks and hominy grits, the guy from the finance company coming to repossess my mother's washing machine, and the seemingly endless string of old beat-up used cars that served as our family sedans. It took several years of higher learning to realize just how déclassé all this was, and several more years of maturation after that not to care. (I say this here just in case my fondness for—indeed, identification with—the white trash and rednecks is not entirely evident.)

My father taking a victory lap, circa 1951. In the Wright family photo album, this photograph is captioned in my mother's hand, "Seven Races in One Day." Back in those days, on Saturday you could start racing at mid-day at one track, then haul your race car thirty or forty miles and finish the day at another track.

In 1953, a few months before I turned six, Dad found himself at the bottom of a pile-up with a broken neck that put him into a coma for nearly a month. The wreck I do remember, the extended hospital stay less so. I also remember the few races Dad drove in after he had recovered from the wreck, my mother's tearful anger about them, my own fears, and the loud, bitter arguments that broke out driving home from the tracks, race car in tow. My dad was never one to do what other people thought he ought to, but for whatever reason, he drove in only three races after his wreck, then quit. He spent another year or two working as a pit guy for other drivers, but he would just as soon have not been at the track as have been there without being in the middle of the action. So, by 1954 or so, his career as a dirt-track driver was over.

Dad's career-ending wreck taught me an important lesson about automobile racing: *you can die out there.* Many drivers have: Fireball Roberts, Grant Adcox, Bill Vukovich, Neil Bonnett, Jimmy Clark, Tiny Lund, J. D. McDuffie, Joe Weatherly, Richie Evans, and, most recently, Adam Petty,

Kenny Irwin, and Dale Earnhardt (all of whom were very much alive and racing when the first draft of this book was written). The sheer physical danger of trying to drive a hot rod as fast as it will go, fender-to-fender and bumper-to-bumper with a few dozen other testosterone-crazed wild men, even when experienced vicariously, is what makes automobile racing so addictive. And any fan who says otherwise is lying.

The three most recent Winston Cup deaths, particularly that of Dale Earnhardt at the 2001 Daytona 500, have spawned widespread concerns about driver safety and about NASCAR's role in assuring it. While no sensible fan would oppose reasonable safety measures, the furor over Earnhardt's death has, I think, obscured three essential points. First, there is no way to drive a race car 180 or 190 miles per hour on a track with forty-two other competitors and be 100 percent safe—physical peril is an *inherent* aspect of the sport. Second, given my first point, Winston Cup racing is already remarkably safe. A nineteen-car wreck at the 2001 Daytona 500—far more spectacular than the one that killed Earnhardt—took out eight or nine race cars, all of them mangled nearly beyond recognition in what the *Charlotte Observer* described as a "savage maelstrom of sheet metal," yet everyone involved walked away with only minor injuries. A similar pileup on the interstate at a third the speed would have resulted in multiple fatalities. Third, as I have already said, the inherent hazards are what make automobile racing so appealing to so many. You could, I suppose, engineer all the dangers out of the Winston Cup, just as you could legislate all the strip joints and nudie bars off Bourbon Street, but what would you have when you were through? Who would still be interested?

I was thirteen in 1960, and in those days drag racing was all the rage.[3] The Bunker Hill Drag Strip was about twenty-five miles from Logansport, and a lot of us hung out at the strip some Saturday nights during the racing season. (In the winters, we'd hang out at Chogas' Pool Hall instead.) The more daring of my high-school pals would "borrow" the family car to, oh, "go to the drive-in," then get to the track, pop off the hubcaps, paint a number on the left rear window with white shoe polish, and enter the car in the "run what you brung" class, where victory earned you nothing but bragging rights. A few of my buddies built serious drag-racing cars, and hanging around in the pits with them was always a gas (and not a bad way to attract the attention of females, who, then as now, made up an unexpectedly large share of the fan base). But drag racing—

a straight ten-second shot down a flat quarter-mile track—was never all that appealing to me. One furious straight-line blast of acceleration seemed tame in comparison to the sustained mayhem of a thirty-lap feature race at the dirt track.

Then there was that annual Memorial Day extravaganza of speed, backyard barbecues, and galvanized tubs of iced Fall City beer that was the Indianapolis 500, known then and today as the "Greatest Spectacle in Racing." The Indy 500 was not televised in those days, so if you were not among the lucky few who went to the track (it is about 90 miles from Logansport, so a lot of people from town did go), you listened to the race on the radio. Today Indy 500 racers are in Indianapolis for only ten days, but back then they stayed for an entire month of practicing, testing, qualifying, and racing. By race day, practically every Hoosier boy could recite the thirty-three drivers and cars in the starting grid—eleven rows, three abreast—in order of starting position. You'd know the qualifying speed of the pole sitter, the spread in qualifying times from first to thirty-third, the previous Indy records of all the drivers, and endless other dots of race trivia. In Indiana in those days, May *was* Indy, and that was that.

Speeds then were much, much slower than they are today. I remember heated speculation in the 1950s and 1960s about whether anyone would ever turn a 150-mph lap at the Brickyard. (The 150-mph lap was thought to be an insurmountable barrier, much like the four-minute mile.) Today's Indy racers qualify at speeds as high as 230 mph and the 500-mile race is over in a few hours, but back then it was an all-day affair, often lasting until 5:00 or 6:00 in the afternoon. I'd spend the whole day with family and friends in the backyard on Melbourne Avenue, listening to Chris Economaki and the other Motor Racing Network announcers describe the action on the track. On Memorial Day weekend in Indiana, everyone was a race fan.

The fifties and sixties were simpler times, in racing no less than in society. Local guys, mere backyard mechanics, would build Indy-style roadsters and haul them down to the track early in May, hoping to qualify them for the race. Way back, a local driver or two had even made the race, although by the 1960s Indy was strictly for professional drivers and teams. One of Dad's racing buddies, George Tichener, had tried to qualify a car at Indy three different times and had actually made the field once, only to be bumped by a faster car later in the day. Our next-door neighbor on Melbourne Avenue, a man named Hank Easley, had also driven a car at Indy in an unsuccessful qualifying effort sometime in the mid-1950s. Hank's opinions about each year's drivers, cars, engines, and such were thereafter held in high esteem. Hank had a real kick-ass street rod that he was always working on in his garage: a 1932 Ford three-window coupe with a Mercury flathead V-8, lots of chromed engine parts, and great big racing slicks for rear wheels. I have no idea what became of this hot rod; I never did see the thing out of his garage, and I couldn't say if it even ran. But Hank was always working on it, I'll give him that.

Between dirt-track racing, drag racing, and the annual Indy 500, I was a semiserious racing fan throughout high school. Like most kids at the time, I understood basic automobile mechanics, could tear down and rebuild a carburetor if the need presented itself, and did most of the work on my own cars myself. I left Logansport for Purdue in 1965 and Purdue for graduate work at Wisconsin in 1969. Those years were times of great turmoil in society at large, as well as in the mind of a working-class kid from the sticks of Indiana who was trying to craft an intellectual persona appropriate to the era. I studied philosophy, then sociology, affiliated myself with various left-wing groups and causes, hooked up with a woman who spoke seven languages and actually liked classical music, and began systematically discarding my small-town Hoosier self. I found that showing an interest in chamber music and improvisational jazz turned more of the right heads than listening to Roy Orbison or Patsy Cline, that carting around the latest issue of the *Nation* or the *Village Voice* created an impression that carrying that month's *Motor Trend* did not. So my enthusiasm for motorsports went into the personality trash can along with every other hicksterism — of which, I must say, there were quite a number — that I could identify in myself, including, even, how I pronounced certain words.

This period of — forgive me, sweet Jesus! — existential inauthenticity persisted for years. But I was a lucky young professor who managed to publish a lot and to rise quickly through the ranks, so, with some successes as a bona fide intellectual under my belt, it was possible to renew certain youthful passions. One memorable turning point was hearing Bob Dylan's album *Nashville Skyline*, the first cut from which was a maudlin, off-key duet with — Johnny Cash!

I spent the first fifteen years of my career at the University of Massachusetts, Amherst. About thirty miles south of Amherst is Riverside Park, an amusement park that featured one of the world's greatest roller coasters and a top-of-the-line half-mile paved oval racetrack where NASCAR "modifieds" compete every weekend. (I learned recently that the Riverside track no longer exists.) Although modifieds are not stock cars, they are very cool, very noisy racing machines that are lickety-split fast on a half-mile paved track. I can't remember why (or when) I went to the Riverside races for the first time, but the experience fanned a spark in me that I had thought had long before been extinguished. Going to the races at Riverside became my favorite weekend entertainment. Sadly, neither my then-wife nor my friends took much of a shine to such a "low-life" amusement as auto racing, so my visits were limited to perhaps two a year.

In 1988, with a new wife and a new-and-improved outlook on life, I left Massachusetts for Louisiana, where I stayed until my move to Orlando, Florida, in 2001. For a Southern state, Louisiana has little in the way of interesting racing venues; the nearest track of any significance is in Mobile, about two hours away, and there are a few quarter-mile dirt tracks around, but that's about it. Shortly after I moved to the South, however, my brother-in-law Ed, who lived in Florida, offered me a spare ticket to the Pepsi 400, the Fourth of July Winston Cup race at Daytona.[4] Ed and I have been to almost every Pepsi 400 since. I call it my annual pilgrimage, to emphasize the religious nature of the experience. Being at nearly every Pepsi 400 in the last decade has allowed me to witness A. J. Foyt's next-to-last race in a stock car, Richard Petty's Daytona finale, Jimmy Spencer's and John Andretti's first NASCAR victories, and a whole bunch of nose-to-tail racing action featuring the heaviest of NASCAR's heavy hitters—the fifty or so drivers who compete in the Winston Cup.

Much like every other racing enthusiast, I suppose, my first Winston Cup race was a Class A head rush. I wondered all day long why I had wasted the first forty years of my life having never attended such a grand spectacle. More than two hundred thousand people go to the Daytona International Speedway for the Pepsi 400. Before the race, fans are treated to country-music performances, awards ceremonies, introductions of the drivers, parades, governor's greetings, and reverential benedictions. Then, just as the National Anthem singer gets to "the land of the free and the home of the brave," the Blue Angels scream past—four very bad F-16 fighter jets in tight formation, close enough to touch if your arms were just a little longer, all fast and powerful and noisy and, well, so damned *American*—and for a fleeting instant you remember the legions of servicemen and -women whose sacrifices have kept this land free (this is the Fourth of July weekend, remember). And then, the command to "start your engines" booms over the loudspeaker, and forty-three 750-horsepower V-8 engines come to life, and all of a sudden it's more speed, more noise, more power, and goose bumps break out on your legs and forearms and your heart pounds and a great big grin breaks out from ear to ear and, hot damn, they're racin' again at Daytona![5] Like the Grand Canyon and oral sex, that first sensation of a Winston Cup event cannot be adequately described—it is something that can only be experienced.

And there's another important lesson I've learned about racing: when the engines fire and the racing's about to begin, if you don't get tingly all over, then racing is not the sport for you. You can teach yourself to like classical music or to enjoy bridge, but racing is something you either like or you don't, and there's nothing anyone can say that will make you change your mind.

I (sort of) decided to write *Fixin' to Git* toward the end of the 1998 Winston Cup season. Although many hard-core fans travel to nearly every one of the annual Winston Cup races, my aspirations were much lower: I would be happy if I were to get to most of the legendary tracks and to a reasonable sampling of venues. When the 1999 season was over, I had attended Winston Cup events at Daytona, Indianapolis, Darlington, Charlotte, Richmond, Atlanta, and Talladega. And, yes, I had a ball.

Self-indulgence, however, was not my only reason for writing this book. As a sociologist, my business is to observe and comment on the human condition, and the surging popularity of NASCAR strikes me as a significant social phenomenon, something that begs to be adequately understood. I wanted to learn why stock-car racing had gotten so popular and what that said about our society and ourselves.

The intellectuals tell us that American culture is obsessed and infused with sports. "Sport is an element of American life so pervasive that virtually every individual is touched by it."[6] Well. Of the twenty most heavily attended sporting events in the United States in 1998, eighteen were automobile races: the Indianapolis 500 and *seventeen* Winston Cup events. Is there no significance in this? Winston Cup stock-car racing is widely considered to be "America's fastest-growing sport." According to Richard

Huff, author of *The Insider's Guide to Stock Car Racing*, attendance at NASCAR events has increased in each of the past fourteen years with no leveling off in sight.[7] To the contrary, every track on the circuit seems to be adding seats as fast as it can, with the few available tickets now distributed by lottery at some of the more popular venues. Even minor-league stock-car races are now covered live on TNN, ESPN2, and Speedvision. In 1996, nearly six million people went to the tracks to watch a Winston Cup race live, and an estimated 149 million tuned in for one of the thirty-one televised Winston Cup events that year, numbers that are certain to have increased since. And all this, mind you, for a sport in which there are no home teams to spark fan interest.

The General Social Survey, fielded periodically by the National Opinion Research Center at the University of Chicago, is considered to be an authoritative source of data on American society. In 1993 the survey asked whether respondents had attended "an amateur or professional sporting event" in the past twelve months. The majority (55 percent) had. And of those who had attended any such event, 29 percent had been to an "auto, stock car, or motorcycle race." That translates into 15 percent of the adult population of the United States going to the races in a typical year. Another survey, the University of North Carolina's 1998 Southern Focus Poll, asked a sample group whether they had "*ever* been to a NASCAR stock-car race." Twenty-two percent of Southerners and 24 percent of non-Southerners had been to one (a surprisingly small and counterintuitive regional difference to which I return later). About half of each group had been to a NASCAR race in the past year, roughly the same result as that of the General Social Survey. And when asked, "Do you ever watch NASCAR on TV?" 45 percent of both Southerners and Yankees responded yes.[8] (At the risk of historical inaccuracy, I will use "Yankee" as a generic term to refer to *all* non-Southerners.)

Perhaps nothing illustrates the contemporary popularity of NASCAR quite so well as the national reaction to Dale Earnhardt's death, which was a headline story in papers all across the nation and even made the cover of *Time*. Newspapers normally indifferent to racing news ran front-page Earnhardt stories for weeks; the major networks aired tearful retrospectives on the man and his career; overeager NASCAR enthusiasts e-mailed death threats to Sterling Marlin, another driver involved in the crash, and to Bill Simpson, the designer and manufacturer of NASCAR's seat belts

Dale Earnhardt's death in a wreck on the last lap of the 2001
Daytona 500 was a singular event in the popular culture, as
moving to many as the death of Princess Diana. Fans found a
number of ways to memorialize their fallen hero at subsequent
races. These four photos (this page and following) were taken at
the 2001 Pepsi 400 at Daytona, the first race to be contested at the
track after Earnhardt's passing. In what many fans and commentators described as "closure," the race was won by Earnhardt's son.

A pre-race ritual is bouncing inflated beach balls around
the stands. At the Pepsi 400, all the balls that bounced
our way had been adorned with felt-tipped messages
eulogizing Earnhardt, who drove car Number 3.

T-shirts are a favorite medium of expression for NASCAR fans, and there were literally thousands of T-shirt tributes to the Intimidator (Earnhardt's nickname). Another shirt (not pictured) read: "I reserve the right to be intimidated forever."

Since Earnhardt's passing, fans have taken to penning sentimental tributes on the sides of the Earnhardt souvenir trailers. Among the messages on the Team Realtree trailer (one of Earnhardt's associate sponsors): "You are forever in our lives," "Forever in our hearts and sorely missed," "We have lost what heaven has gained," "the Heartbeat of NASCAR," and a dozen variations of "We miss you."

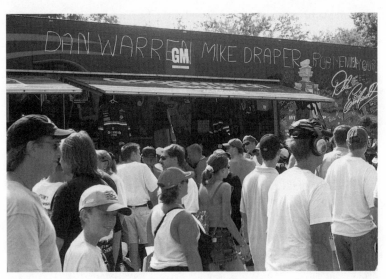

Note the crowd at another Earnhardt souvenir trailer. Five months after his death, Earnhardt memorabilia were still selling like hotcakes.

and other safety equipment. In St. Petersburg, Florida, which is hardly a NASCAR hotbed, an impromptu on-the-beach memorial service drew 2,000 people with less than an hour's notice; in Charlotte, the mood was somber, as if a president had been assassinated. According to *Sports Illustrated*, "When Dale Earnhardt died, people went straight to their computers to tell *SI* how they felt," a more than mildly ironic phenomenon as the magazine's typically pitiful racing coverage is a bone of contention for many fans. Within the flood of *SI*'s e-mail were some two dozen poems of tribute.[9] (Are you surprised to learn that there are amateur poets among the NASCAR fan base?)

The only event in recent memory that had an equivalent effect on popular culture was the death of Princess Di (who, it seems appropriate to add, also perished in a high-speed automobile crash). And just as the lovely Diana was memorialized by Elton John's remake of "A Candle in the Wind," so too was Earnhardt celebrated by country star Travis Tritt, who worked his friend's name into the lyrics of "Put Some Drive in Your Country," and by Kentucky-Derby-jockey-turned-country-performer Shane Sellers, whose redneck reminiscence entitled — get this! — "Matthew, Mark, Luke, and Earnhardt" topped out at number two on the country charts within weeks of Earnhardt's death.

Car Culture and the American Dream 29

"Long considered a sport enjoyed only by southern rednecks, stock car racing has become a fan favorite to people nationwide."[10] The sport's mythic origins lie in the moonshine hollows of North Carolina where young men wanted big, fast cars—big to hold a lot of 'shine, fast to elude the local gendarmery—and, as soon as they got them, wondered straight away whose car was fastest, whose owner ballsiest, and voila, stock-car racing was born. (This, of course, is a good yarn as much as an accurate history, which I'll turn to later.)

So, how is it that a redneck amusement became America's fastest-growing sport, apparently enjoyed equally by Yankees and Southerners alike? As we will see, stock-car racing culture is suffused with the lore and legacy of the Old South, and a sensitive, politically correct Yankee should by all accounts be—what is the right word here?—*disturbed* by the display of Confederate flags at major Winston Cup events. And yet, every year since 1989, Winston Cup drivers have headed west to Sears Point in the heart of the Sonoma Valley to entertain the sport's wine-and-cheese contingent with a 350-kilometer road race. Who'd even guess there *was* a wine-and-cheese contingent among stock-car racing fans? The fast-growing popularity of a white-trash bubba sport like stock-car racing in what intellectuals describe as an increasingly urban, citified, sophisticated, "postindustrial" society is remarkable. The incisive observer of the contemporary scene is compelled to ask, What the hell is going on here?

There's more. Since the end of the Civil War (or, as they prefer to call it down deep in the heart of the vanquished nation, The Late Unpleasantness), there has been a hope and even an expectation (mostly among Yankees) that the South would eventually come to resemble the rest of the country, with periodic announcements by learned people that this had, in fact, already occurred.[11] Now, in general, the *homogenization* of American culture is something intellectuals detest. (These are the people who are really upset that you can buy a Big Mac within eyesight of the Eiffel Tower.) Far better, they say, to encourage cultural diversity, which to the politically correct is the highest possible human goal. But when it comes to things like Southern culture, gun culture, or (I'd guess) stock-car racing culture, encouraging diversity goes out the window and the more homogenizing going on, the better. So let me simply point out that the wild popularity of stock-car racing—among Yankees and Southerners alike—reveals *a nation becoming more like the South,* not the South becoming more like the rest of the nation. Stock-car racing thus joins country-western music and good old-time religion (as in Bible-thumping, snake-handling Southern fundamentalism) as once-regional (or largely regional) cultural phenomena that have literally swept across the nation in the last decade. These trends run strongly against the grain of intellectual expectation and, again, beg for some sort of explanation.

It is perhaps not overly flatulent to refer, therefore, to the popularity of stock-car racing in an "urban postindustrial society" as the NASCAR Paradox or to seek an intellectually satisfying resolution of it. Just how did something like NASCAR get to be so popular in a society like this?

Part of the answer, certainly, is that the nation is not nearly as urban, citified, sophisticated, or postindustrial as the intellectuals have depicted. Although the Census reminds us every ten years that we have become "more urban" than we used to be, most of the big American cities have been losing population for decades. Between 1970 and 1990, for example, the U.S. population increased from 203 million to 249 million, an increase of 23 percent. In that same period, the percentage of people living in the ten largest U.S. cities declined from 11 percent to 9 percent. Persons living in the hundred largest cities likewise fell from 24.5 percent to 20.8 percent. Thus, while the nation continued to grow more "urban" in terms of actual numbers, the *proportion* of us living in the largest cities continued to decline. According to the 1990 Census, about 80 percent of us did *not* live in one of the hundred biggest cities. (Preliminary counts from the 2000 Census suggest that these trends continue.)

The predominant trend of the twentieth century was not urbanization but suburbanization, the movement of population out of the inner cities and into the developing hinterlands, a diaspora whose consequences surely rival the massive postwar migration of African Americans from South to North. When the Census folks say we have become "more urban," what they mean is that more people live in what the Census defines as "metropolitan areas"; these areas include not just the cities themselves but also the surrounding suburbs, nearby small towns, and even a great deal of open countryside. If one treats the suburbs as de facto small towns (there are good reasons to do so) and adds the suburban fraction of the metropolitan population to the small town and rural (nonmetropolitan) segment, the resulting number represents a substantial majority of the U.S. population—all together, just about two-thirds.[12] Given this, the depiction of an urban, citified society is at best misleading.

In defining metropolitan areas, the Census looks for areas that have "a large population nucleus, together with adjacent communities that have a high degree of economic and social integration with that nucleus." So just what is it that ties the cities, the suburbs, the surrounding small towns, and the open countryside in a given area into an "integrated" economic and social unit? The short, simple answer is highways. The highways, especially the interstates, allow people to live where they want and work where they can, without too much concern for getting from one of these places to the other. Highways *create* metropolitan areas.

But highways are useless, of course, if you don't have a car, so it is really cars that enable the development of suburbs and metropolitan areas. Cars! If NASCAR is about anything, it is about cars. I mean, what other organization manages to get both "car" and "automobile" into its name? Cars get us to and from work, out to the malls, and on the road for our summer vacation. We drive them for business, for pleasure—and for sport. I'd even venture to guess that more American kids lose their virginity in cars than anywhere else. Cars represent the second-largest investment of the average American household. In fact, it would be no exaggeration to refer to the twentieth century as the "Century of the Car."

Of all the wonderful, transformative inventions of the twentieth century—and there've been a lot of them: the telephone, radio and television, satellites, computers, airplanes—none has more profoundly altered the American landscape than the car. The entire physical and social ecology of the country is made possible by cars. I've heard it said that, in an average U.S. city, one tenth of the acreage is devoted to cars or car-related infrastructure—highways, roads, streets, and parking lots. Seems right to me. From Henry Ford's Model T right up to today, cars have fueled the American industrial revolution and the American economy. A carless America cannot be imagined. We are truly a car culture, a "nation on wheels," more so than any other nation.

The primordial essence of stock-car racing is accessible to every person who has buckled up behind the wheel of the family sedan and, facing a twenty-five-minute commute, tried to make it in twenty. The experience must be well-nigh universal, regardless of race, gender, region, or social class. Shaving a few minutes off the drive to work or a few hours off the drive to California; getting there quicker than the next guy; making that one last pass before you change lanes for your exit—now, that's America! And that's racing.

Many commentators have written about America's love affair with cars. But "love affair" hardly captures our hot, lustful, passionate fixation, an obsession really, with these mechanical Chariots of Fire. Cars embody, express, and even enable all the great American values: freedom ("the faster I go, the freer I feel"), mobility, independence, self-sufficiency, status, leisure, control, speed, mastery, sensuality, affluence, power. Is this not what cars are all about? What America is all about?

A Martian anthropologist might look at America's 42,700 miles of interstate; or at our 3.9 *million* miles of highways, streets, and roads; or at the hundreds of thousands of acres of parking lots and garages, and conclude that the whole shebang is one immense concrete altar built to appease and glorify the Car God.[13] And if that metaphor doesn't make you gag, try this: the hundreds of race tracks that dot the American countryside—from local dirt tracks to the vast, majestic NASCAR venues—are shrines honoring that same Car God, sacred places where one's devotion and faith can be shared with other Believers, and thus affirmed. It's where the American car culture goes to worship.

But NASCAR is not just about cars. Hell, the Indy Racing League is about cars. The Sports Car Club of America is about cars. Formula One is about cars. NASCAR is about *American* cars—great big two-ton American sedans with great big 358-cubic-inch American V-8 engines, lousy gas mileage, muscular good looks, and horsepower to spare. It's about Fords and Chevrolets and Pontiacs and Dodges, about cars built by American workers and driven by good old American boys with honest-to-God American names—names like Dale (Jarrett and Earnhardt), Ricky (Rudd and Craven), Jeff (Burton and Gordon), Bobby (Labonte and Hamilton), Jimmy (Spencer and Hensley), Mike (Skinner and Wallace), Steve (Park and Grissom), Dave (Marcis and Green), Kenny (Irwin and Wallace), Bill (Elliott), Rick (Mast), Joe (Nemechek), Rusty (Wallace), Jerry (Nadeau), Ted (Musgrave), and John (Andretti). Not a Mika or an Emerson or a Gianfranco or a Roberto in the batch! No Euro-weenie drivers or cars here, by God, and no Japanese junk either—no BMWs, no Toyotas, no Hondas, no Fiats, no Ferraris. No sir, these are big, loud, powerful, fume-belching, gas-guzzling American sedans — the sort of car a big, loud, fume-belching American can identify with.

From the first NASCAR-sanctioned stock-car race in 1949 (at Charlotte, you'll recall) through the end of the 1999 Winston Cup season, there were 1,889 NASCAR championship stock-car races. Buffalo's Al Keller won one of these races — at Linden, New Jersey, in June 1954 — driving a British-made Jaguar, and that is the *only* time a non-American car has won a NASCAR championship event.[14] The drivers are almost all Americans, too. The *Stock Car Racing Encyclopedia* lists somewhat more than 3,000 different drivers who have started at least one NASCAR championship race. I counted a mere fifty-four non-Americans in the list: thirty-two Canadians, six Brits, six Aussies, two each from France, Germany, and Peru, and one each from Mexico, South Africa, Italy, and Belgium.[15] Nearly all these foreign drivers had ten or fewer lifetime starts. The most active foreigner was Canadian Trevor Boys, who had 102 starts from 1982 to 1994. Also notable is Canadian Earl Ross, with twenty-six starts between 1973 and 1978 and one victory, in 1974 at Martinsville — the only NASCAR championship race ever won by a non-American. Ross won in a Chevy, just in case you were wondering.[16]

Although Winston Cup cars are identifiably American, the experts are quick to point out that the resemblance of a high-performance stock car to the family sedan is mostly superficial. Or as Harry Hogge (played by Robert Duvall in *Days of Thunder*) put it, "Hey, there's nothin' stock about a stock car." In terms of performance and components, this is certainly true: a Winston Cup car shares with its production namesake a similar silhouette, but that's about it. Still, the resemblance is not *entirely* superficial. Unlike Indy or Formula One cars, stock cars have motors up front where they're supposed to be, a driver in a driver's seat on the left-hand side, windshields that wrap around from door to door, roofs on top, fenders over the wheels, and a trunk in the back, where you could put the groceries if you had to. They come with Ford, Chevy, Pontiac, and Dodge logos and body silhouettes. They look like real cars in ways that many other race cars don't. And there is little doubt that the ability to identify with NASCAR stock cars as cars is part of their appeal. The average fan can imagine hopping into one of these babies and taking her for a spin. You look at an Indy car sitting there and you just know there's a five-hundred-page technical manual that you'd need to plow through before you could even start the engine.

If America can be described as a car culture — and just how else would you describe her? — then NASCAR racing is a festival of cars, a celebration of America, a metaphor for the American Dream. Patriotic sentimentality hangs thick in the air over every NASCAR event. At the 1999 Pepsi 400 at Daytona, the chaplain delivering the pre-race prayer was moved to thank God for "the United States of America, the greatest country on earth," "the greatest anthem in the world," "the world's best drivers in the world's fastest cars," and "the greatest sports fans in the country." (At a USAR race I attended in 1998, sponsored by Hooters Restaurants and Jackaroo Steak Sauce, the reverend intoned, ". . . and God bless Hooters" — the only prayer in my experience that got a roar of approval from the crowd.) In the televised pre-race chatter at the 1999 Charlotte 600, run later the same day as the Indianapolis 500, constant reference was made to "these all-American cars, all-American drivers," just to drive home to the dim-witted the difference between the Charlotte 600 and that *other* race up there in Indiana — the palpable implication being that those *other* drivers in that *other* race, well, some of them were *foreigners,* and probably Communists, too.[17] The American flags streaming from the infield RVs (even at the Southern venues, there are way more American flags in evidence than Confederate flags), the singing of the National Anthem and the Blue Angels flyover, the benediction, the cars, the competition, the postrace fireworks, and just about everything else you encounter in a day at the track drips with traditional Americana.

Like old-time religion and country-western music, unrepentant patriotism has surged since the Vietnam nadir, during which (at least in my circles) public expression of unconditional loyalty to one's country was held in great suspicion. People aren't ashamed of being Americans anymore — fact is, most never were. Most Americans are proud of their national heritage and sincerely believe they are blessed to live in "the greatest country on earth." Of America's several armed adventures since the Vietnam era (Grenada, Libya, El Salvador and Nicaragua, Panama, Iraq, Somalia, Croatia, Kosovo, and Afghanistan), only Kosovo generated any sort of audible mass doubt about the righteousness of the American cause. So, as a uniquely American sport with all-American cars and all-

American drivers, NASCAR has been well-positioned to profit from this resurgent patriotism, and it certainly has.

Family, community, and spiritual values have also enjoyed a renaissance in the past couple of decades, and while it would be a stretch to claim that NASCAR somehow stimulated the resurgence, it has at least ridden the wave with consummate skill. Practically everything written about NASCAR these days extols its fan-friendly, family-oriented image: "NASCAR is a great sport for the family: Drivers bring their families to races. Many of the drivers participate very actively in the Christian ministry the tour has built up over the years. These drivers take their role model status very seriously and seem very proud to be in the public eye."[18]

NASCAR itself promotes the concept of the "NASCAR Family," which, according to financial writer Robert Hagstrom, "encompasses two different units: the traditional family unit of drivers and crews with their wives and children, and the larger NASCAR family," the latter meaning practically everyone connected to the sport, even the sponsors and fans.[19] It is, if not a family, at least an extended clan that is explicit about its values: fair play, courage, and sportsmanship on the track; piety, reciprocity, patriotism, mutual support, and encouragement off the track. These values, displayed publicly and unabashedly by everyone connected to the sport, resonate deeply with the American population and unquestionably add to NASCAR's appeal.

Family, community, and spirituality are every bit as evident at a NASCAR race as Confederate flags and hot race cars, and they're equally on display. A NASCAR season is grueling—thirty-three or thirty-four races, or nearly one per weekend, from the Daytona 500 in mid-February until the last race at Atlanta in mid-November. If they are going to have any sort of family life at all, the drivers and teams must bring their families with them as they travel around the country, and many now do. NASCAR cordons off special sections in the infield of each track where the team RVs are parked—little instant communities of NASCAR wives and children that, inexplicably, the media seem to leave alone. There is something strangely appealing about the thought of a bunch of kids frolicking in the infield while their fathers are out on the track dueling for supremacy, fender-to-fender, at 190 mph. One common and engaging media image is the wife of the day's winner rushing to Victory Lane to embrace her conquering hero. It certainly helps that the wives are well-spoken and often drop-dead gorgeous, the children well-mannered and well-scrubbed. NASCAR: American Gothic on wheels.

Cynicism comes easily in our time, so in fairness it has to be said that in the ten years or so that I have followed the Winston Cup, I have yet to hear of a single driver who was caught cheating on his wife (to be sure, one does hear rumors from time to time that a NASCAR marriage may be in trouble, and some Winston Cup drivers are on their second or even third wives), of a single case of spouse abuse, a single unwed mother among the drivers' children, or a single delinquent NASCAR kid being hauled off to the pokey for drugs. It is possible that these things go on and are successfully covered up, although when you consider the attention our scandal-mongering media now lavish on the sport, this seems unlikely. So perhaps the NASCAR Family is less an orchestrated marketing strategy than some critics seem to believe.

Not to say there are not or have never been Winston Cup bad boys whose hell-raising and carousing embarrassed the sport. As the tale is sometimes told, back in the good old days all the top NASCAR drivers were hard-drinking, fast-driving, foul-mouthed womanizers — virtual outlaws, one and all. And, while this has never been entirely true — not in 1949 or 1959 and certainly not today — a few top drivers have undeniably lived, and died, on the edge. Among recent competitors in this category is Tim Richmond, a popular and successful young driver of the middle 1980s, suspended in 1988 for failing a drug test and dead of AIDS in 1989 at the age of thirty-four. Or Rob Moroso, the 1990 Winston Cup Rookie of the Year, who died drunk behind the wheel at age twenty-two while driving back from a race at North Wilkesboro (his rookie honors were awarded posthumously). But these days, as cultural historian Mark Howell points out, the top drivers have little or no time to carouse or womanize or otherwise get out of line, so heavy are the demands on them from their fans and sponsors and, of course, from the sport itself.[20]

As in other professional sports, there is a visible Christian fellowship in NASCAR that also connects with larger cultural themes. Motor Racing Outreach holds church services and Sunday-school classes at the track each weekend for the drivers, crews, and families. Entire teams such as Joe Gibbs Racing (Gibbs, the former coach of the Washington Redskins, owns the Tony Stewart and Bobby Labonte Pontiacs) now openly and proudly identify themselves as Christian teams and bow in prayer as a team before

Winston Cup stock cars starting to line up for the start of the 1999 NAPA 500 at Atlanta, the last race of the season. This picture was taken about one hour before the start of the race. Note the thousands of fans milling around in the pits and garage areas even as the teams are attempting to get their cars onto the starting grid. The accessibility of the teams, cars, and competitors to the average fan is, at least in part, what makes NASCAR such a wildly popular sport.

every race. Jeff Gordon, NASCAR's hottest star, and his former crew chief Ray Evernham, along with others, always make a point of thanking God for the day's successes. Gordon to TV announcer Glenn Jarrett: "Boy, the Man Upstairs sure was with us today!" Just why the Deity would take an interest in stock-car racing, or in the outcome of any other sporting contest, escapes me, but evidently He does.

NASCAR carefully cultivates its image as a fan-friendly sport (to be clear, this image is completely deserved). Fans are welcomed into the pits before every race (you do need a special pit pass for the purpose). You can walk around the infield, the pits, and the garage areas, even strike up a conversation with your favorite driver. This is like the NBA or NFL inviting fans into the locker room. Joe Gibbs makes a telling observation: "If you were at an NFL game and got within 20 yards of Troy Aikman, you'd get arrested. These guys [NASCAR fans] can walk right up and talk to Dale Earnhardt or Bobby Labonte."[21]

The average Winston Cup driver spends fifty to seventy-five days a year, and top drivers more than a hundred days a year, promoting their sponsors' products, meeting fans, shaking hands, posing for photographs, and signing autographs (for which there is never a fee—NASCAR policy). Someone recently claimed that Richard Petty has signed more autographs than any other living person. As the sport's all-time number one star and with a career spanning forty years, this could well be true. Petty once told *Stock Car Racing,* "The people who come to see me race pay money to get in. If they didn't come, there'd be no racing and hence there would be no Richard Petty. The very least I can do in return is be nice . . . and spend time with them."[22] Odd thing, when you hear Petty say something like that, you know he means it.

When I hear that racing is a "family sport," I think of the surprisingly numerous families with multiple ties to big-time stock-car racing, ties that often span generations. Sibling rivalries among currently (or recently) active Winston Cup drivers include the Labonte brothers (Terry and Bobby), the Waltrips (Darrell and Michael), Jeff and Ward Burton, the Bodine boys (Geoff, Brett, and Todd), the Green brothers (David and Jeff), and the Wallace clan (Rusty, Kenny, and Mike). Seven-time Winston Cup champion Dale Earnhardt was the son of driver Ralph Earnhardt and the father of 1998 and 1999 Busch Grand National Champion Dale Earnhardt Jr. Dale Jarrett, the 1999 Winston Cup champion, is the

Richard Petty (a.k.a. the King). Petty holds many of NASCAR's all-time records, among them most victories (200), most starts (1,184), most poles (126), most victories in a single season (27), most wins in a row (10), and most Winston Cup championships (7, in a tie with Dale Earnhardt). More than any other single driver, King Richard made NASCAR the fan-friendly phenomenon it has become. Photo credit: International Speedway Corporation Archives.

son of two-time champion Ned Jarrett, the brother of NASCAR announcer and former driver Glenn Jarrett, and the father of Jason Jarrett, a young driver making some waves in the sport's lower echelons. Eight-time winner Sterling Marlin is the son of driver Coo Coo Marlin. Other currently active drivers with children coming up through the ranks include Bobby Hamilton, Terry Labonte, Jimmy Spencer, Mike Skinner, and Geoff Bodine, as well as others I am certain to have overlooked.

Brother-brother and father-son combos have been a part of the sport from the beginning. In NASCAR's inaugural 1949 season, the Flock brothers (Bob, Fonty, and Tim) were among the competitors. Then there were brothers Bobby and Donnie Allison, who raced against each other for more than twenty years. Bobby's son Davey had nineteen victories in a nine-year career, which was cut short by a helicopter crash at Talladega in 1993. Davey's brother Cliff was killed in a racing mishap but never drove in the Winston Cup. Famed Indy and Formula One star Mario Andretti had one victory in fourteen Winston Cup starts; his nephew John Andretti now drives the Richard Petty Pontiac. Nineteen-time winner and NASCAR broadcaster Buddy Baker is the son of two-time Winston Cup champion Buck Baker. Chuck Bown (seventy-three Winston Cup starts) is the brother of Jim Bown (twenty-three starts) and the son of Dick Bown (twenty-one starts). Canadian Trevor Boys, mentioned earlier as the all-time most active foreign driver in the circuit, was the son of Buddie Boys, who ran in three Winston Cup events. And, as you can tell if you are following closely, that only gets me through the Bs.

But the all-time First Family of stock-car racing has to be the Petty family. The patriarch Lee, who died in 2000 at the age of eighty-six, ran in six of the eight events in NASCAR's inaugural stock-car season and won fifty-four races and three Winston Cup championships in his sixteen-year career. His son Richard, "one of three figures known in the South as the King—the others are Jesus and Elvis,"[23] started driving in the NASCAR championship series in 1958 and subsequently won 200 races (the all-time record by a margin of ninety-five) and seven Winston Cup championships before he retired in 1992. Richard's brother Maurice drove in twenty-six NASCAR championship races but is remembered mainly as Richard's crew chief through the decades of Team Petty domination. Richard's son Kyle has racked up eight wins since his Winston Cup debut in 1979. With his earring, goatee, ponytail, and affection for Harley motorcycles, Kyle is as close to a hippie as you will find in the Winston Cup. Kyle's son Adam, the fourth generation of Petty stock-car racers, was an established presence in the Busch Series by 1999 and made his Winston Cup debut in the April 2000 race at the Texas Motor Speedway, only to die tragically a month later in a wreck at Loudon, New Hampshire. (Later in the 2000 season, Hoosier Kenny Irwin was also killed in a crash at the New Hampshire track.) When Adam won an ARCA race in October 1998 at the Charlotte Motor Speedway, it was the first time in the history of racing that four generations of drivers from the same family had posted wins at the same track.

NASCAR's carefully nurtured association with Americanism, commu-nity, Christian virtue, and family values, along with its unwavering loy-alty to its fans, certainly explains part of the NASCAR Paradox. Television explains another part. Put bluntly, stock-car racing has profited because it gave the cable TV industry something interesting to put on the air. Huff insists that live television coverage is possibly the single most im-portant factor in NASCAR's stunning success, and who would disagree? Until 1979, the only Winston Cup action you could see on TV was the occasional clip on *The Wide World of Sports,* "stuck," as Benny Parsons put it, "between arm wrestling and cliff diving." Back then, when speeds were slower, races were longer — five or six hours in many cases, way too long to cover live on network TV (or so the thinking went). Too, a stock-car race provides no regular opportunities to cut away for commercial breaks. Then, there was that "regional problem," the sport presumably being "too Southern" to show without embarrassment on national TV. Hell, you might catch some redneck pissing over the side of the fence or whomping up on his woman or picking his teeth with a pocketknife, right there in public, right in front of the cameras, and how would you explain *that* to the network brass?

The first live television coverage of a Winston Cup event was the CBS broadcast of the 1979 Daytona 500. CBS apparently considered this ex-periment successful because the network did live broadcasts of every sub-sequent Daytona 500 until the 2001 race, when the live coverage shifted to Fox. The annual February broadcast is the highest-rated televised motor sports event in the United States, rivaled only by coverage of the India-napolis 500.

But NASCAR's real TV stardom awaited the advent of cable in the middle 1980s. Cable TV had been around for quite a while but mainly as an alternative means of transmitting the same signals that were being transmitted over the conventional networks. The middle '80s witnessed the growth of TV channels that were only viewable via cable, and that gave us the incredible proliferation and specialization of programming that we enjoy today, whole channels devoted entirely to golf, cooking, popular music, history, animals, classical movies, home shopping, religion — and racing.

One of the earliest and now most successful of the specialized cable outlets was ESPN, the first all-sports network. ESPN needed sports programming at reasonable prices and stock-car racing was just the thing. As more and more homes were wired for cable, more fans could watch Winston Cup races live, as they happened, and despite the long association of the sport with Southern white trash, the Winston Cup broadcasts were soon among ESPN's most successful offerings. This brought other bidders to the table: first the Nashville Network, a country-music channel not bothered in the least by the possibility that rednecks might be watching (that was the whole point of TNN); then the Atlanta-based Turner Broadcasting System (when you watch a hundred and fifty thousand people show up in your city for a Winston Cup race, you begin to get the idea that there might just be a television market for this product); then the other regular networks (ABC, NBC, Fox); then still other cable outlets (ESPN2, Speedvision). Today, every Winston Cup event, most Busch and Craftsman Truck races, and even a number of minor league stock-car races are aired live, and all the fan has to worry about is what channel the race is on. Television rights that could once be bought for less than $100,000 soon ran upward of $2,000,000. In 1998, CBS coughed up $20 million for the Daytona 500 and a package of additional races. In 1999, NASCAR announced a six-year, $2.8 *billion* deal for Winston Cup broadcast rights that moved all the events of the 2001 season onto the major networks: Fox, NBC, and their corporate affiliates. On an annual average, this deal is worth more than four times what NASCAR received for television rights in the 1999 season.

Did television *create* a popular base for the Winston Cup or did it simply cash in on a base that was always there? From the first live broadcast in 1979, TV coverage of Winston Cup races has always been more popular than anyone expected it to be, so a strong fan base has always been present. Fact is, there are racetracks all over America with fans in the stands every Saturday night. Anyone who'll go out on a Saturday night to watch local boys (and girls) bang up against one another in old beater-mobiles is certainly a potential Winston Cup fan. It was only the networks' bigotry that prevented them from cashing in decades before they did. That said, TV coverage has widened the base enormously, and it has also increased the number of fans who want to get to the tracks for a live view of these magnificent contests. That has certainly been my experience.

Well, that pretty much completes Lap 1 of the *Fixin' to Git* feature event. Each of the following chapters adds its own piece to the puzzle of the NASCAR Paradox. The sport is not as critics have described it; championship stock-car racing is *not* the moonshine-besotted redneck excrescence it is sometimes made out to be and has always been more than a racist, sexist, white-trash amusement (chapter 2). There is more—much more—to racing than just a bunch of guys driving around in a circle; indeed, a surprisingly important part of the thrill is that the tracks are *not* circles (chapter 3). The NASCAR subculture connects easily and seamlessly to other important subcultural strands in American life—to the regional culture of the South (although this is easy to exaggerate) and of the American heartland, to the outdoors subculture, to hunting, fishing, camping, and guns (chapter 4). In the past two decades, NASCAR has made a conscious effort to reconnect to a national constituency that was present in the formative years and then abandoned; the result has been the transformation of championship stock-car racing from a regional to a national sport, one that is wildly popular everywhere, not just in the Old South (chapter 5). Heavy corporate involvement in Winston Cup racing has also widened the fan base, and, contrary to a common argument, has *increased* the overall level of competition and made for a more interesting, more exciting sport. The many, varied, increasingly important, and spectacularly lucrative links between NASCAR and corporate America have not destroyed, but rather reinvigorated, the sport (chapter 6). The net result of all the above is a sport whose popularity can only grow in the coming decades (chapter 7).

Laced in between each chapter are short travelogues that recount my experiences and observations as I chased the Winston Cup competition around the country during the 1999 season. "Year-in-the-life" books and articles about NASCAR have been done before, always by authors who have special relationships with NASCAR or specific Winston Cup teams.[24] But writers who can count on free tickets to the best seats, reserved parking, pit passes, invitations to the hospitality tents, and unrestricted access to the drivers and teams cannot know NASCAR in the same way average fans do, and it's for us average fans that these vignettes were written.

When the dust finally settled, I and the *Fixin' to Git* research team had traveled to eight of the season's events. I did not keep a running tally of the miles traveled or the dollars spent, but it was well into the thousands in both cases. I continued the research between trips by watching the other races on TV.

The *Fixin' to Git* Road Tour was a family affair. At various times, the *entourage* included my wife and chief research assistant, Chris; my brother, Kelley, his wife, Denise, and her son, Damon; and my brother- and sister-in-law, Ed and Elaine. My father-in-law, Bud, joined me for the race at Talladega and my old friends Steve Nock and Daphne Spain, sociologists at the University of Virginia, accompanied the team to the race at Richmond. Say what you will about the "NASCAR Family," I spent more time with my extended clan in 1999 than in any previous year of my adult existence.

About the title: *fixin'* is a common white-trash solecism that means "preparing," as in "I'm fixin' dinner." If you are fixin' dinner, you're not repairing a broken chuck roast or anything like that but are rather getting dinner ready. *Git* is the usual Southern pronunciation of the word *get*, taken in the sense of "let's git the hell out of here." Thus, "fixin' to git" can be roughly translated as "preparing to leave." You start fixin' to git when the chatting and socializing have come to an end and it is about time to go home.

Now, just before each Winston Cup race, TV commentators scurry up and down Pit Road doing live interviews with the drivers. Usually, it is obvious that the drivers have other things on their minds and respond to reporters' questions by uttering some universal racing platitude — "We jes' wanna hang back 'til the final laps and then get racy" or "We'll be fine today if we can keep outta trouble" or "I jes' wanna keep this Reese's Peanut Butter Cup Ford off the wall and be there at the end." At this point, the drivers are facing four, five, or even six hundred miles of hot competition, and they are understandably anxious to get under way. Some years ago, a driver whose identity I've forgotten politely but abruptly ended one of these interviews with the line, "Well, I'd best be fixin' to git," whereupon he closed his visor, hooked up his radio, fired up his engine, and blasted off on the parade lap. So, it's been *Fixin' to Git* ever since.

Daytona Pilgrimage

I left New Orleans for Daytona the first day of July on a mission to intercept Brother Kelley and his wife, Denise, in the Orlando airport the next morning. My usual companions for the Fourth of July weekend — in-laws Ed and Elaine — had to be in Michigan on family business, and Chris, who'd been to the races at Daytona before, was not anxious to go again (she prefers smaller tracks with closer, easier-to-follow action). So Kelley and Denise would be joining me for the first of four races we'd end up seeing together in the 1999 season.

Riding shotgun was my dog, Xavier, who was enjoying his first road trip since we'd sprung him from doggie prison the previous Christmas. The Dixie Chicks were crooning on the Sebring's six-speaker stereo system before we hit the interstate on-ramp, and I had a rack of country-western and classic rock CDs in the stack awaiting their turn. Man and dog, a bevy of crying cowgirls, a 700-mile road trip in my sporty new car — heaven! I was off in style to the 1999 Pepsi 400 (formerly the Firecracker 400) at Daytona, where the Winston Cup bug had first bit me a decade before.

Xavier and I had been on the road for five or six hours when we neared Tallahassee. I was getting hungry and needing a jolt of caffeine, so we pulled down off the interstate and hunted up a Burger King. In Dixie's suffocating midsummer heat, you can't leave a dog in a parked car for long, even after the sun has set, so a road trip with the little guy means eating in fast-food joints, okay with me because you can count on these places for clean bathrooms, hot coffee, and decent french fries. Burger King it would be. It was near 9:00 P.M. when I ordered a cheeseburger, fries, and coffee, only to be told, "Ain' gah no sma' mee. . . ." Huh? "Ain' gah no *sma' mee*. . . ." After a bit of experimentation with word-ending consonants, it finally dawned on me that the restaurant was out of regular-sized hamburger patties ("small meat") and that only the unwieldy Whopper was available, which you absolutely cannot eat with one hand and drive with the other. Wasn't this Burger King? How does a Burger *King* run out of burgers? Burger *Pauper*, if you ask me.

Kelley and Denise had swapped some days in their Orlando time-share for a luxury condo right on Daytona Beach, about eight miles east of the track. Near the speedway, everything reeks of NASCAR, but out on the beach, you'd hardly know it was a race weekend. While we did run into a few race fans at the IHOP across the road and a few more in the little grocery store where we picked up our weekend essentials (beer mainly, a bottle of sunscreen, and, in a rare attack of dietary virtue, some fresh fruit), the folks in the condos near us were in Daytona only to sun themselves, cruise the beach, and seek relief from the relentless heat in the cool waters of the Atlantic. Odd, I thought: the same sun shines everywhere, but there's only one place each weekend where you can see the Winston Cup bad boys in action. How can you be in Daytona on a race weekend and not be into the racing scene? It's like being at the Vatican and blowing off the Sistine Chapel.

We spent Friday afternoon researching logistics, doing some shopping at the souvenir trailers, and taking in Happy Hour — not a three-for-one drink special at the local watering hole but the last hour of Winston Cup practice the day or evening before the race. Each Winston Cup team has its own souvenir trailer (some teams have more than one) where fans buy hats, T-shirts, miniature race cars, leather jackets, key chains, radios, and a dazzling variety of other race memorabilia. These trailers are towed from race to race, parked somewhere near the track, and always draw thick, enthusiastic crowds. You can judge the relative popularity of the drivers by the size of their trailer throngs, swarms of fans often five or six deep, each clutching a roll of twenties, all jockeying to buy race mementos. Most fans hit several trailers, and many will walk away with hundreds

Crowd scene at the souvenir trailers. This happens to be the Pepsi 400 in Daytona (July 2001), but a similar photograph could be taken at any Winston Cup event. For the most popular drivers, annual sales of racing memorabilia far outstrip race winnings. Watching avid fans shop for hats, T-shirts, jackets, model race cars, and other racing mementos at the souvenir trailers is not unlike watching sharks feed on a large, bloody carcass. A couple of T-shirts and a pair of gimme hats represent roughly a $100 investment; many fans will drop that much, and more, at each of the three or four trailers they visit.

of dollars worth of goods in tow. I picked up a tie-dyed T-shirt at the Bill Elliott souvenir trailer, a T-shirt that served as my race-day colors for the rest of the season. It was the first tie-dyed item I'd seen for sale since my last trip to Berkeley. Elliott is a perennial fan favorite, but he is nearing fifty and his most competitive racing is probably behind him—just the kind of driver an aging baby boomer like me can identify with.

Our research also uncovered a perfect parking spot that would get us back to the condo after Saturday's race in less than fifteen minutes, as opposed to the two- and three-hour postrace delays that I had come to accept as part of a Daytona race weekend.

Bristol and Richmond were the first of the Winston Cup venues to feature night races, but Daytona had installed lights the previous year, guessing (correctly) that there would be a large prime-time television market for stock-car racing at NASCAR's most famous track. In earlier years, the Pepsi 400 had started at 11:00 A.M. Under the lights, the green flag wouldn't fall until 8:00 in the evening, so on race day the fans made good use of a full day of partying they didn't use to have. Local bars and eateries responded with gala outdoor celebrations featuring food, beer, live and recorded music, ticket raffles, trivia contests, and a gratifying number of small bikinis stretched taut over thin, well-tanned, nubile young GRITS, many with demure tattoos in just the right places. Has *Playboy* ever featured the "Women of NASCAR"? They surely could. Granted, to borrow a line from the old Cowboy, some female race fans look like they've been rode hard and put away wet, but many others are knockouts.

We found a congenial place maybe five blocks from the track, where we sat for a spell, drank a few beers, and enjoyed the merriment. A dee jay offered a Chad Little John Deere racing T-shirt to anyone sporting undies with a racing theme. I was hoping for some checkered-flag bikini briefs or maybe even a well-endowed female fan in a NASCAR see-through bra. (Who knows? There probably is such a thing.) But the prize went to Brother Kelley—he was wearing a pair of Daytona International Speedway boxer shorts that he'd picked up the day before at the souvenir trailers.

When Ed and I had first started going to the races, we'd haul in a couple of coolers of beer, sodas, sandwiches, fruit, and ice, plus a bag full of chips, crackers, and race gear. A wad of twenties turns out to be far less trouble, although getting from our seats to the concession stands and back is no simple matter. And despite all efforts to minimize the load, by the time you get your race bag packed with scanner and headphones, camera, binoculars, cigars, tickets, a program, note pads, and a rain slicker just in case, you're carting a hefty bag of supplies.

Our season tickets to the Pepsi 400, which we still renew, are excellent: three seats on the top row of the Segrave grandstand, right at the exit from Pit Road. They are hundred-dollar tickets (face value, not the scalping price), and while they aren't exactly the skyboxes in the Winston Tower, they're damned close to being the best seats in the house. We scaled the imposing face of the Segrave grandstand until we reached our seats on the forty-fifth and final row. From the top of the grandstand, the speedway stretches out in a magnificent 180-degree panorama. Although it was my eighth trip to the track, the sheer scale of the place still took my breath away. The venue accommodates something near a quarter-million people

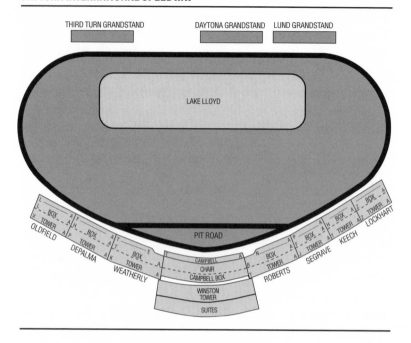

if you include the tens of thousands in the mile-long infield. We got to the track about 5:00 P.M., when there were only little clusters of people here and there, but by the time the Blue Angels thundered through, every seat was filled. The corners at Daytona are banked thirty-one degrees—only Talladega and Bristol are steeper. The angle is so steep and the track so wide that from bottom to top the turns tower *five stories* above the plane of the infield.

The conviviality so evident outside the track continued inside. Country recording star John Michael Montgomery entertained the crowd for an hour or so before the race—not exactly the Dixie Chicks or LeAnn Rimes, but pleasant. Pro wrestler Goldberg (no first name, just Goldberg, like Cher or Madonna) also made an appearance at Daytona USA, the track's museum and theme park. During the parade lap, I noticed that Goldberg's likeness (and, I presume, sponsorship dollars) graced one of the race cars, and I've since learned that Goldberg also sponsors an entry in the national Monster Truck competition. I also noticed a fan in a T-shirt proclaiming "America: God, Guns, Guts!" and another T-shirt that announced "The 1999 Winston Cup: 34 Races, 43 Drivers, 12,093 Miles of Competition, 1 Champion." As befits a family sport, there were islands of young couples with kids in a sea of rednecks, good old boys (and girls), and loudmouthed drunks, more of the latter than I remembered from previous years. But I'll say this about NASCAR fans: once the racing begins, even the drunks shut up and pay attention.

The summer race at Daytona marks the season's halfway point, and some of the season's key racing stories had already emerged:

North Carolinian Dale Jarrett had two wins and fourteen Top Ten finishes in the season's first sixteen races and was leading the points race. The owner of the Jarrett car, Robert Yates, was a legendary engine builder who started fielding his own teams in the late 1980s. Would Jarrett and Yates be able to hold on and nail down the first Winston Cup championship for either of them?

Hoosier Tony Stewart was well ahead in the Rookie-of-the-Year competition and had already built an impressive fan following. Even at midseason, he was being described as a win looking for a place to happen. Still, it is rare for any rookie to win a race in his inaugural season—the last Winston Cup driver to do so had been Davey Allison in 1987. Would Stewart chalk up a win, at Daytona or elsewhere, to end the long rookie drought?

Joe Nemechek had qualified on the pole for the Saturday race. "The pole" is the inside of the front row—the starting position awarded to the fastest qualifier. Nemechek's qualifying speed was just under 195 mph, but every car in the field had qualified at 190 mph or faster. Front Row Joe had earned his nickname by qualifying well over the years, but he'd been racing in the Winston Cup since 1993 and was still looking for his first victory. Would 1999 be the breakthrough year for this star-crossed Floridian who had recently lost his brother in a racing mishap?

Virginian Ricky Rudd would start the Pepsi 400 next to Nemechek on the outside of the front row. Rudd had won at least one race every year for the previous sixteen, a remarkable streak. With the second fastest qualifying time, Daytona looked like his best chance so far in his campaign to extend the streak to seventeen.

At midseason, Jeff Gordon led all competitors with four victories but had been plagued by a continuing string of poor finishes in the races he didn't win. Would this handsome, pious young man find a way to race back into the points lead and to his fourth Winston Cup championship? At race time, the best you could do with the parking lot bookies was even money on Gordon for the win. Lots of people just detest this guy, but nobody wants to bet against him.

Prior to Gordon's arrival on the Winston Cup scene, the central figure in the sport had been "the Intimidator," the late Dale Earnhardt. A seven-time Winston Cup champion (the only other driver to have won seven championships was Richard Petty), Earnhardt had already notched one victory in 1999, and, with more wins at the Daytona track than any other competitor in history, he also went off at even money for the win. (You could get Tony Stewart and Bobby Labonte, then second in the points race, at 2:1 and Jarrett at 3:1.) Although Earnhardt was competitive to the very end—he finished second in the Winston Cup standings in 2000, which was to be his last full season, and he was running third in the 2001 Daytona 500 when he crashed and died—he was by no means the dominant driver he had once been. A question much on the minds of race fans in the 1999 season was whether he would find a way to beat back the Young Turks and score a record-breaking eighth Winston Cup championship.

The race itself (total purse: $2.5 million) was a corker, one of the best in years. Seventeen lead changes among nine drivers meant spirited racing at the front of the pack all night long. Pole-sitter Nemechek led for the first four laps then began to fade and never again contended for the lead; he ended the night in the sixteenth position, his first Winston Cup victory still in the future. Rudd inherited the lead that Nemechek ceded and managed to hold it for ten laps, but neither was this his night. He ended up in thirteenth.

Other drivers who took their turn leading on the green-flag laps included Rusty Wallace, Dale Earnhardt, Dale Jarrett, Bobby Labonte, and Mike Skinner. Wallace led the most laps and looked for most of the race as though he might finally break his Daytona jinx (the one-time Winston Cup champion had never finished better than fifth in all his years racing at Daytona). At the restart following the second of the night's three caution periods, Wallace was running second to Jarrett and looked like he had a solid run at the leader. He pulled up high on the track, thinking, he said, that Earnhardt (running seventh at the time) "would go with me," creating a high-speed drafting train that could blow by the leader. Instead, the Intimidator "hung me out to dry," stayed low, and, with the help of other competitors, shuffled Wallace back to eleventh (his finishing position), neither the first nor the last Winston Cup driver to suffer by misjudging Earnhardt's intentions.[1]

As is frequently the case in restrictor-plate racing, the first two-thirds of the race featured close racing and frequent lead changes but produced no dominant car. By Lap 130 or so, it seemed that the race would come down to pit strategy. Everyone needed one final fuel stop. Who would maximize track position with a straight gas-and-go? And how would they fare against teams who took longer in the pits but also put on new tires? The leaders pitted on Lap 144: Jarrett and Wallace took just a splash of fuel and no tires; other leaders took a full can of gas and no tires; Earnhardt was pushing badly in the turns, so he took on a load of fuel and new right-side tires. The line-up at the restart was Jarrett, Wallace, Skinner, Labonte, and Stewart in the top five, with Earnhardt in seventh. With new tires, Earnhardt quickly moved up to second and looked ready to take the lead and the win, when the night's third and final caution flag came out on Lap 157, three laps from the finish. With no passing allowed under the yellow, he wound up in second. (Most fans would be thrilled if their favorite driver did as well, but to Earnhardt fans — the most boisterous fan contingent NASCAR has ever known — a second-place showing was like kissing your sister.) Jarrett was leading the race at the final caution but was nearly out of gas, the near-victim of an inadequate splash at the last pit stop; had it not been for the yellow flag, he would have had to pit and cede the victory to Earnhardt. Under caution he was able to nurse his car around the bottom of the track and take the win. He ran out of gas on the victory lap. Stewart finished sixth, a respectable showing that solidified his hold on the Rookie-of-the-Year competition. I had ten bucks on Gordon, who hung around in the top ten most of the night but got shuffled back in the pack at the last restart and finished twenty-first, a poor showing that put him further behind in the points race. Bill Elliott, another of my favorites, finished twenty-third.

Much of the pre-race buzz had focused on Rudd's sponsorship problems and on the health of Richard Petty. Earlier in the week, Tide had announced it was dropping its long-term sponsorship of the Rudd Performance Motorsports entry for the 2000 season. Rudd's creditable Daytona showing did not make the button-down minds at Tide rethink their decision. More's the pity. On the way back to the car, I listened to an attractive young female fan in Ricky Rudd regalia telling her male companion that it didn't matter how clean Tide got the damned clothes, she'd never buy a box of the stuff again. I do believe she meant it. NASCAR fans are famous for their loyalty to sponsors, and that sword is sharp on both edges.

Fans rejoiced audibly when Richard Petty climbed up to his observation seat in the number 43 pit. The King had been hospitalized earlier in the week with bleeding ulcers. Born on 2 July 1937, Petty had spent his sixty-second birthday—Friday, the day before the race—at home. Petty had spent his youth working on his father's race team and his entire adult lifetime as a racer and car owner; he said later that 1999 marked his first birthday in the past fifty that he had not spent at the Daytona speedway. (He did, however, make it to the track early Saturday morning to honcho the Team Petty entry.)

Also on Friday, in a move that deserved more national media attention than it received, NASCAR announced that it was forming a diversity management council to find ways to increase minority participation in the sport. "We can't create a race team for anybody," NASCAR President Bill France Jr. said, "but we can provide access to mentors and people who know the sport."

Diversity, the skeleton in the NASCAR Family closet, is one of those issues that smacks you upside the head no matter which way you turn. NASCAR's critics, some of whom we'll meet in the next chapter, seize on the abundance of Confederate battle flags at Winston Cup events as the perfect opportunity for carping and generalized harrumphing at the organization and its fans. And the realities of contemporary political discourse are such that there is only one right answer to the Stars and Bars question. When the complications, compromises, complexities, uncertainties, frailties, and plain dumb thinking of the mid-nineteenth century are cleaved with the meat-ax of present-day ideological ardor, self-righteous indignation, and political correctitude, things like the Confederate flag can only be excoriated as odious, bigoted, hate-mongering, and racist. And no amount of "heritage, not hate" puling will change the verdict. Contemporary political discourse will not forgive the Confederate flag by acknowledging it as a symbol of regional heritage or historical fact; the flag's only possible intent, according to this discourse, is to express hatred of black people.

Let me hasten to add: I've met plenty of NASCAR fans who were—

how shall we say?—unambiguous in their opinions about—what is our phrase?—America's ethnic mosaic. But most fans whose campsites or RVS display the Stars and Bars also fly the Stars and Stripes, often a NASCAR flag, and usually a driver's banner or two as well. In the large majority of these cases (or so I've come to believe) the semaphore is both obvious and benign: I'm an American and proud of it, I'm from the South and not ashamed of it, I love stock-car racing, and I hope Dale Jarrett wins the race. If a NASCAR fan wanted to convey a message of race hatred, he wouldn't be subtle about it. I've seen NASCAR guys walking through the crowds in T-shirts that said FUCK YOU, YOU FUCKING FUCK! and gals with T-shirts that proclaimed BAD ATTITUDE, GOOD FUCK. The complete absence of explicit race-mongering or public expression or display of racial slurs at NASCAR events is surely not the result of the fans' sense of propriety.

After the race and a day on the magnificent white sands of Daytona Beach, we set out on the second leg of the July itinerary, an eleven-hundred-mile run up to Logansport for a gathering of the clan. Long road-runs provide time and reason to occupy the mind with thoughts of other things, and I fought off a thousand miles of white-line fever by chewing on the notion of the NASCAR Family. By that time, I had first drafts of a couple chapters, and it was already clear that the NASCAR Family would be a recurring theme. What *was* this thing? Its significance? Its proper place in the NASCAR story? And, while I was in Indiana the weekend after Daytona, the NASCAR Family revealed itself to me.

The reunion was a festive affair, the first time my extended family of aunts, uncles, and thirty-some-odd first cousins (plus spouses and children) had found itself in one place since gathering to bury my mother four years before. We dispensed quickly with the mandatory condolences, then set about a long afternoon of beer, barbecue, covered dishes, and short canoe trips down the Eel River, a clean, pretty river that runs past my brother's house. The day was redolent with nostalgia, and everyone was in a talkative mood. Since Kelley, Denise, and I had just been to the Pepsi 400 and the August running of the Brickyard 400 at Indianapolis was less than a month away, the collective conversation turned almost at once to racing.

Cousin Bob, the oldest of the boys, was there: I was reminded that Bob's oldest son A. J. is named after Indy legend A. J. Foyt. Bob's younger brother Ron was also there: Ron turns wrenches at a speed shop out-side Milwaukee and had just read Shaun Assael's NASCAR book, *Wide Open*. (We'd both found it disappointing — too cranky for our tastes.) Our born-again cousins, Penny and Chuck, were there from South Carolina: they live about a half hour from the Darlington Speedway, so I prom-ised to look them up in September, when I planned to be in their neck of the woods for the Southern 500. Toni and Dave were there: They own a block of seats for the Brickyard 400 and go every year. My sister Nancy was there: She and her husband Neil go with seventy of their friends in a chartered bus to the Indy 500 each May. Cousins Ed and Gary and their garrulous wives and children were there: they live in Indy and get to the races whenever they can.

I've known only a few of my cousins closely as adults, and stock-car racing had never been a topic of conversation at any previous gathering, yet on the Saturday after Daytona under the big white tent by the Eel River, it was practically all we talked about. The NASCAR Family, I saw with crystal clarity, was *my* family: men, women, children — race fans, one and all.

2

Deconstructing NASCAR

Deconstructionism: A term tied very closely to postmodernism, deconstruction-ism is a challenge to the attempt to establish any ultimate or secure meaning in a text. Basing itself in language analysis, it seeks to "deconstruct" the ideological biases (gender, racial, economic, political, cultural) and traditional assumptions that infect all histories, as well as philosophical and religious "truths." Decon-structionism is based on the premise that much of human history, in trying to understand, and then define, reality has led to various forms of domination—of nature, of people of color, of the poor, of homosexuals, etc.—*Internet Glossary, www.pbs.org/faithandreason.gengloss/*

Q: What do you get when you cross a postmodern literary deconstructionist with an Italian mafioso?
A: An offer you can't even understand.

The "chattering classes" (George Will's term for the intellectual elite who "chatter" for a living—professors, columnists, media commentators) have not had much to say about stock-car racing and for that I suppose we should be grateful. To get some sense of the literary attention devoted to various sports, I logged on to Amazon.com, then entered the following keywords and got these results:

Keyword	Number of Titles
Baseball	6,396
Fishing	4,595
Football	4,581
Basketball	3,123
Golf	2,877
Hockey	1,556
Soccer	1,551
Boxing	472
Rugby	306
Bowling	264
Billiards	122

We can leave it to others to debate whether or not baseball remains the true national pastime, but as these results attest, baseball is by a wide margin the favorite pastime of our literati. Twice as many books have been written about baseball as about basketball, sometimes said to be the new national pastime (especially in cities). Sure, the majority of Amazon.com's baseball books are children's books, how-to (hit, pitch, run, throw), self-improvement manuals, pulp celebrity effusions, player biographies, P.R. pieces, and related fluff. Still, the sport has produced serious works of literature, commentary, and even history, written by such intellectual eminences as Roger Angell, Dashiell Hammett, Roger Kahn, Ring Lardner, Ernest Lawrence Thayer, George Will, Bernard Malamud, and Robert Kemp Adair. A serious author who intended to write a book about baseball, in other words, would not be thought to have taken leave of his senses.

So, too, with fishing, second by a narrow margin over football on the list I generated. Angling apparently shares with baseball enough Zen-like characteristics to appeal to those of a literary bent. Both sports feature long stretches of inactivity when the mind is free to wander. Izaak Walton's *The Compleat Angler: Or the Contemplative Man's Recreation, Being a Discourse of Fish and Fishing Not Unworthy the Perusal of Most Anglers* is the earliest and most famous book to illustrate fishing's literary possibilities, and ever since Izaak, more than a few authors have dipped their line into this fertile pool. Fly-fishing (961 hits) has been a particular favorite, perhaps because fish so rarely interrupt the fly fisherman's contemplative mood.

Other sports with a thousand or more hits included football, basketball, golf, hockey, and even soccer, the latter with more than 1,500 entries. As with baseball, by far the largest share of these are insubstantial literary efforts, but many are works by writers of stature: Dan Jenkins, George Plimpton, Truman Capote, John Updike, Ernest Hemingway. Hemingway has been quoted to the effect that "there are only three sports. Bullfighting, mountain climbing, and car racing. All the rest are just games."[1] But if he ever wrote anything substantial about racing, I've not been able to find it.

How does racing fare in these literary sweepstakes? The keyword "racing" produced 3,554 hits, which I thought was a respectable showing until I realized that most of these titles discussed fast horses, dogs, and boats. So I narrowed the search to "automobile racing" and got 1,171 hits, a poorer showing than hockey or soccer but at least well ahead of rugby and bowling. Further research revealed, however, that most books about "automobile racing," on my list at least, dealt with drag racing, Formula One, Indy cars, and the Grand Prix, so as a last pass through the Amazon.com holdings, I searched specifically for books about "stock car racing" and came up with a mere 110 hits. Conclusion: There are more books dealing with bowling or billiards than with America's fastest-growing sport.

From this thin stream of literary production must be subtracted books about "*sports* car racing" that wormed their way through the search engine's sieve, as well as picture books and official driver biographies, NASCAR-sponsored publications, and books written for prepubescent boys. Most of the remaining titles are behind-the-scenes books by NASCAR insiders. As for serious works of analysis, criticism, or literature—well, with the exceptions of Mark Howell's *From Moonshine to Madison Avenue*, Robert Hagstrom's *The NASCAR Way*, Peter Golenbock's *American Zoom*, and (depending on your sense of the serious) the cult classic *Stand on It* by the pseudonymous Stroker Ace, there aren't any.

The Hollywood corpus is equally unimpressive: here you get the Tom Cruise movie *Days of Thunder* (about which more later), Richard Pryor's *Greased Lightning* (Pryor plays Wendell Scott, the first African American to compete at NASCAR's championship level), a substantial handful of B-grade drive-in movies with titles like *Moonshine Highway* and *Thunder Road,* and that's about it. In contrast, think of the scores of movies with boxing or football or baseball themes, some of them outstanding cinematic productions.

Then there's the periodical literature of stock-car racing, which falls mainly into two categories: fluff pieces that appear in the sport's fanzines written by knowledgeable but sometimes overly enthusiastic insiders; and snotty, vitriolic essays for mainstream media written by woefully uninformed outsiders who can barely disguise their contempt for the sport and everything connected to it. Two fine examples of the latter — ripe for deconstruction — are here before me: Steve Rushin's essay on the 1999 Daytona 500, "A Fun Ride, I Reckon," which appeared in *Sports Illustrated;* and Steve Lopez's piece in *Time,* "Babes, Bordeaux, and Billy Bobs: How I Learned to Love NASCAR and Not to Hate Superstar Jeff Gordon."[2]

In reading these and a number of similar pieces, I learned there's a formula for writing about NASCAR in mainstream outlets. Start by confessing a near-total ignorance of the sport. Rushin: "I don't know what a 'rear spoiler' is. I haven't a clue what a 'pole-sitter' does. And while I gather, from medical journals, that prolonged polesitting can cause rear spoilage, I know very little else about auto racing." Lopez: "Just so you know up front, they picked the wrong guy to write this story. Did not take auto shop in high school, never bought a can of STP, never watched a car race."[3] One wonders: Are the writing stables so bereft of talent that self-confessed ignoramuses have to be sent to cover Winston Cup events? What if *Time*'s cover story that week, which was about violence in the schools, had begun: "Just so you know up front, although I attended school for sixteen years, I really don't know much about education and nothing at all about how the schools have changed since I was a kid. Also, while I think I have a pretty good idea of which end of the barrel a bullet comes out of, I don't really know doodley-squat about violence either." Would you continue reading? Would *Time*'s editors allow such a thing to see the light of print?

But prideful ignorance is not enough. You must also poke fun at the social, regional, and ethnic backgrounds of stock-car fans and personalities. Rushin: "I could have listened all weekend to the delightfully undecipherable Buddy Baker, and did. The CBS color analyst comes from the deep end of the Deep South. He sounds like Strom Thurmond shot full of novocaine while eating Saltines during larynx surgery." Lopez, writing about the spring race at Talladega: "It has not come to the attention of Eastern Alabama that the Civil War ended. The track infield has so many Confederate flags flying that it looks like a Klan picnic." A further Lopez observation on the Talladega infield: "Guys with pickups . . . stand an Ellie May or a Daisy up in the back and drive slowly through the cheering throngs. When the girl collects enough Mardi Gras beads from slobbering Bubbas, she answers their obscene chant with a lift of her shirt. Fights break out. Sirens wail. It's like spring break, except nobody came from college."

Strom Thurmond on novocaine? Billy Bobs? Klan picnic? Slobbering bubbas? Does anyone but me detect a hint of ethnic or class derogation here? A condescending stereotype? Imagine a story about basketball players and fans that began . . . oh, never mind. Seems that the only remaining ethnic group in America you can safely savage with stereotypes is the white South or groups associated with the white South, such as gun nuts and stock-car racing fans.

A third obligatory element in the genre: You must feel genuine contempt for stock-car racing as a sport. Rushin: "By the time Jeff Gordon pole-sat on Sunday, got the green, traded paint, . . . I had watched 1,050 miles of racing in 24 hours. That is like driving from Gas City, Ind., to Sulphur, La., and about as pointless." Lopez: "What's the big deal with racing? Essentially, forty extremely mobile billboards circle a track for three hours, driven by men in jumpsuits that make bowling apparel look sharp."

Now, really. What's the big deal with golf? Essentially, a bunch of middle-aged men in funny-looking clothes chase a white ball around a meadow with a stick. (Have golf writers ever had the courage to say in so many words just how ridiculous golf garb is? Is there some unwritten rule about this?) What's the big deal with basketball? Essentially, ten improbably tall men run up and down a hardwood court trying to toss a ball into a bottomless basket. What's the big deal with boxing? Essentially, two grown men of approximately equal weight stand toe to toe and try to knock each other senseless. If watching 1,050 miles of racing in twenty-four hours is pointless, how about six or eight consecutive hours of televised football? Just how brain-dead does some poor schlub have to be to do something like that?

More generally, what is the point, the big deal, with baseball, hockey, soccer, bowling, what have you? None of these things have any point, which is why they are called "sports" or "games." Is not the point of sports, in a sense, to be pointless? And if the pointlessness of stock-car racing offends you in a way that the pointlessness of, say, bowling does not, then the solution to your problem is obvious: Go to the bowling alley and stay away from the track.

Finally, almost everything written about stock-car racing for the mainstream media clucks with knowing disdain about the corporate domination of the Winston Cup, which in the opinion of *Sports Illustrated* "is the most commercially saturated sport in the U.S."[4] Granted, corporate influence in Winston Cup racing is real enough, but this hardly puts stock-car racing in a league of its own. These days, you can take in a baseball game at Bank One Ballpark, Cinergy Field, or Coors Field; a basketball game at Fleet Financial Services Center, United Airlines Center, Compaq Center, or America West Arena; a hockey match at the Corel Center or the Canadian Airlines Dome; or a football game at Alltel Stadium, PSINet Stadium, the RCA Dome, Qualcomm Stadium, or 3Com Park. Lopez whines that "the right side of [Jeff] Gordon's Chevy is plastered with more than 40 logos,"[5] yet the same issue of *Time* was plastered with, according to my count, forty-three full- or half-page ads placed by major corporations (let's think of them as *Time's* corporate sponsors). A recent issue of *Sports Illustrated* was no better. It had advertisements from thirty-eight major corporations including Doral, Camel, and Winston cigarettes, Miller beer, and Jack Daniel's whiskey. Stock-car racing is by no means, then, the only undertaking that profits from the wishes of major corporations to get their names and insignia out before the public.

It seems appropriate to let the "delightfully undecipherable" Buddy Baker have the last word on corporate influences in big-time stock-car racing. Baker, the first man to turn a 200-mph lap in a stock car, used to provide color commentary for Winston Cup broadcasts. Just before the start of one race, he drawled, "Ya know, when you fire up them engines, you just divorced your corporate image and becum the race driver you wuz when you wuz eighteen years old."

Both Rushin and Lopez show some restraint in not invoking the all-time number one stereotype about stock-car racing, the well-nigh universal belief among both fans and detractors that the sport arose as an amusement of, by, and for redneck whiskey haulers in the American southeast. I've already sketched the basic elements of this stereotype, but you can find detailed elaborations in virtually anything written about NASCAR, stock-car racing, or the Winston Cup.

Racing historian Peter Golenbock writes in his "Brief History of Stock Car Racing" that "when the sport of stock car racing first began to organize itself in the late '40s, the leading drivers were mostly bootleggers, men who ran whiskey from illegal stills to hundreds of markets across the Southeast."[6] Illegal whiskey production was an old and well-established tradition by the 1940s, and not just in the South: we'll do well to remember, as we wend our way along, that the Whiskey Rebellion was all about the rights of country folk to make whiskey without government interference or taxation and that it took place in western Pennsylvania, near present-day Pittsburgh, in 1794. The moonshine tradition received a substantial boost when Prohibition became law in 1920. Prohibition of alcohol (like today's prohibition of drugs) did nothing to slake the American appetite for whiskey; it just created a lucrative illegal market to satisfy the thirst. Much of this illegal market, you will recall, was dominated by organized crime and operated on an immense international scale, but there was a fair amount of mom-and-pop moonshining that went on in the backwoods hollows of the southern Appalachians (and everywhere else in rural America), and not all the whiskey thereby produced was for local consumption. No, quite a bit was produced as a cash crop to be marketed in the cities. In more than a few cases, it was very probably the only cash crop available, or at least the most profitable.

Since it was a little hard to operate a commercial-sized, illegal still in the middle of a city, most untaxed moonshine was produced out in the countryside, away from the gaze of the despised federal "revenooers." How, then, to get the product to market? Here is Paul Hemphill's answer: "Once the whiskey had been distilled and bottled, . . . the moonshiners needed a way to deliver it to cities . . . where great hordes of their brethren had moved in search of jobs. . . . They needed to look no further than the nearest wild hare of a boy whose souped-up car, the first one he had ever owned, was his love, his life, his passion, his passport out of there. . . . Those cars they had built were the family jewels, the proof of their manhood, the pride of their life, and it seemed inevitable that soon they would race them."[7]

So there you have it: Wild boys with souped-up cars rigged to haul whiskey to the cities, a natural curiosity about whose liquor-running hot rod was the hottest, a convenient vacant field, and—poof!—Winston Cup racing.

Just for the record, here is NASCAR writer Richard Huff's rendition: "The foundation of today's stock car racing was laid in the late 40s by bootleggers in the South. During prohibition, moonshine runners used souped-up family sedans to outrun police who were trying to shut down their illegal liquor operations. . . . Moonshiners bragged to each other about their liquor running exploits and the prowess of their hot rods. Eventually, an argument would ensue leading to a race."[8]

And here is cultural historian Mark Howell's: "The rural, southern nature of Winston Cup stock car racing is responsible for America's initial conception of drivers and their place within the [domain] of professional sport. Some of the earliest stock car racers, according to folklore of the rural South, were men who hauled moonshine through the mountains of North Carolina during the 1930s and 1940s. They faced arrest and imprisonment if caught; this provided them with the inspiration to make their automobiles the fastest and strongest available. . . . Folklore of the South represents these men as noble renegades who were willing to pay the price for their illegal activities when—and if ever—caught."[9]

We can begin our deconstruction of the NASCAR moonshine myth by getting our facts straight. First, the dates. Illegal whiskey production went on all over rural America from the first days of the republic. The Whiskey Rebellion of 1794 was only the best known of a series of confrontations between the new federal government and its citizens over untaxed whiskey; Shay's Rebellion, for instance, which took place in western Massachusetts in 1786, was another. Automobiles, on the other hand, were invented around the turn of the twentieth century (the actual inventor and date are in dispute), and no sooner did they exist than people got the idea of racing them—against horses, in some cases, but soon enough against other automobiles—whether or not moonshine was involved. It is also safe to assume that cars would have been used to transport illegal whiskey as soon as there were cars available to whiskey producers. Cars, the use of cars to haul hooch, and the racing of cars against one another were all firmly established in their own rights in the first decade of the new century—they were not thought up or "invented" by backwoods moonshiners shortly before or after the Second World War.

Prohibition took effect in 1920 and was repealed in 1933, so the years between would likely have been the heyday for moonshine producers everywhere. Demand for moonshine survived Prohibition, of course, in part because people had developed a taste for the vile poison and in part because, being untaxed, it was quite a bit cheaper than store-bought whiskey. That many counties in and out of the South remained nominally "dry" after Prohibition would have also stimulated demand. So, beyond all doubt, some demand for moonshine persisted into the 1950s. (And even to the present day. A pal of mine who was gracious enough to read and comment on earlier drafts of this book wrote me to say, "I can afford to drink any whiskey I want but from time to time I still drive into the mountains to buy a pint jar of 'squeeze' because it reminds me so much of my past." His words demonstrate, among other things, a cultural as well as an economic motive in the demand for moonshine.)

Moonshining was widespread throughout rural America, not just in the Appalachian South. Rickety backwoods stills would have been found not only in the Carolinas but also in the Dakotas, not only in Georgia and Alabama but also in Indiana and Ohio, not only in Virginia and West Virginia but also in rural Pennsylvania and upstate New York. One final point: the interests of the local sheriffs in moonshiners and whiskey haulers were not so much that those boys were illegally selling untaxed whiskey and needed to be stopped; rather, if they could catch a hauler in the act, they could sell the car at auction and keep a share of the proceeds.

Now, let's indulge ourselves in a little hypothetical deconstructive thinking, the reality equivalent of a front-end alignment check. Let's suppose you are a backwoods Carolina dirt farmer with an illegal still you use to produce moonshine to sell in the nearby city. Would you contract with the noisiest, fastest, most conspicuous hot-rodder in the hollow to run your product up to Charlotte at a hundred miles an hour? Or would you be more inclined to load boxes of full whiskey jars into the back of a harmless old pickup truck, throw in a cover of fresh hay or watermelons, and slowly, inconspicuously make your way along the road, doing all that you could to remain unnoticed?

The idea that stock-car racing was somehow invented by moonshine haulers from the Carolina hollows thus faces a number of difficulties: auto racing is as old as autos themselves; moonshining went on all over rural America, not just in Appalachia; sensible moonshiners would have found less conspicuous means to get their product to market. This is not to deny—not by any means—that the liquor-runners and moonshiners gave early postwar stock-car racing much of its tone, its panache, especially in the South. But as a literal history of stock-car racing in America, the moonshine accounts obviously leave much to be desired. Howell is correct to refer to these accounts as part of "the *folklore* of the rural South."[10]

I can't say where NASCAR's moonshine legends originated and I'm not sure anybody can, but they were seared forever into the literary zeitgeist by Tom Wolfe's 1965 *Esquire* profile of the legendary Junior Johnson, entitled (more or less) "The Last American Hero is Junior Johnson. Yes! . . . The South has risen again. . . ." This now-famous essay marked the beginning of national attention to the sport of stock-car racing and transformed Johnson into a folk hero.

Some facts: Junior Johnson raced from 1953 to 1966 in the NASCAR Grand National Series, the immediate forerunner of today's Winston Cup.[11] His accomplishments as a driver included fifty wins in 313 starts, good enough to hold eleventh place on the all-time win list. He continued in the sport after 1966 as a team owner whose cars registered 139 wins in 1,071 starts. He retired abruptly at the end of the 1995 season, and at that time he was second among all owners in victories and third in all-time earnings. He never won a Grand National Championship mainly because he pioneered a wide-open, hard-charging driving style that blew up motors as often as it won races. Still, he won plenty of races, and his reputation as one of NASCAR's living legends is thoroughly deserved.

Wolfe's essay depicts Johnson as larger than life, a mythic creature, a Dixie bigfoot "who had sprung from the deep woods of the Southern Appalachians, the shambling semiliterate son of a bootlegger who had gone on to become a legend."[12] All his legendary driving skills were honed while hauling whiskey for his father, in particular the "bootlegger's turn," a driving trick that spins a car 180 degrees and sends it back down the road in the opposite direction from which it came, which he is said to have invented and perfected along with drafting and, in some of the more exuberant accounts, the very sport of stock-car racing itself.[13] The son-of-a-bootlegger theme is no literary contrivance. There is ample evidence that Junior spent much of his youth hauling moonshine for his father and did a year's stint at the federal penitentiary in Chillicothe, Ohio, because of it. (Biographies almost always include a copy of Johnson's Chillicothe mug shot.) Still, Tom Wolfe is not a historian but a writer, and the sort of writer who wouldn't let his story suffer for lack of an occasional embellishment. Always remember, too, that a favorite sport of good old backwoods boys is pullin' the other fella's leg. A careful reading of Wolfe's essay shows it to be less about Junior Johnson than about the *legend* of Junior Johnson—which are not the same thing.

Still, we can count Junior Johnson as a confirmed whiskey hauler and, if not the ultimate source of the moonshine myth, certainly a mother lode of mythographic material. It is a little inconvenient that NASCAR stock-car racing began in 1949, whereas Junior's Grand National career did not begin until 1953, but who's going to let a little detail like that stand in the way of a good story? (Another driver frequently mentioned in the moonshine stories, Wendell Scott—described by Howell as "a moonshine hauler from Virginia"—did not start driving in the Grand National Championship series until 1961.)[14]

How many of the other early NASCAR drivers were also involved in the illicit whiskey business? All of them? Half of them? One in fifty? I took the top fifty drivers from NASCAR's inaugural 1949 stock-car season and cross-referenced each name against the text and index of every moonshine account in my NASCAR library. Among the fifty, I found only nine or ten who had been specifically identified as moonshiners, bootleggers, or whiskey haulers: the Flock brothers, Red Byron, Bob Smith, Curtis Turner, Roy Hall, Otis and Pee Wee Martin, and possibly one or two others. The four moonshiners who figure most prominently in Hemphill's "Haulin' Whiskey, Haulin' Ass"—Lloyd Seay, Clay Earles, Raymond Parks, and Buddy Sherman—were racers but never drove in NASCAR. (Seay was dead by the time NASCAR was founded). A few other confirmed moonshiners, such as Junior Johnson, Wendell Scott, and Joe Weatherly, did not compete in the inaugural season but came along some years later, after NASCAR was reasonably well established. Granted, absence of evidence is not evidence of absence, and memories are fallible. Still, it seems possible, and perhaps even likely, that the entire mythology of NASCAR's moonshine origins has been crafted from the biographies of—oh, let's be generous—fewer than two-dozen men.

Now, nine or ten moonshiners among fifty contestants is certainly more than one would expect from chance, so my point is not to deny that moonshiners had a presence in the origins of NASCAR stock-car racing. Although they were probably not in the numerical majority, moonshiners like Red Byron and Curtis Turner are among the true legends of NASCAR's early days and no doubt had a profound effect on the organization's reputation, an effect that was, however, entirely disproportional to their numbers. (Julius Erving, after all, was only one of several hundred hoopsters who played in the early years of the American Basketball Association, but his basketball artistry and persona are defining elements in the public perception of that now-defunct league.) Then, too, there may well have been more moonshiners among the car owners than among the drivers. Raymond Parks and Hubert Westmoreland are two of the early owners who never drove in NASCAR but were involved in the whiskey trade. Also, many of the early drivers—Buck Baker, Fireball Roberts, and no doubt others—were hard-drinking wild men, even if they did not haul illegal whiskey for a living. All that granted, we are still left with a substantial majority of early drivers who, so far as my research reveals, were not haulers, moonshiners, or otherwise involved in the commerce in illicit whiskey.

Let's take a brief look at some of the drivers in the 1949 field who apparently were not involved in moonshine. One of them was Gober Sosebee (total career: seventy-one starts and two victories from 1949 to 1959), who took pains late in life to disavow *any* connection with illegal whiskey and who dismissed many of the moonshine stories about him and others as hearsay. Another 1949 competitor was Lee Petty, whose father, Judson, was described by grandson Richard as "a quiet, God-fearing Quaker gentleman." To my knowledge, no one has ever suggested that the Pettys were involved in the whiskey business.[15] Still another racer from the 1949 season, Herb Thomas, was once described by legendary engine builder and car owner Smokey Yunick as "a dumb farmer . . . , practically a sharecropper starving to death," hardly the kind of guy you'd find running whiskey.[16] Nor does the biographical material available on

Atlanta's Sara Christian competed in NASCAR's first Strictly Stock season in 1949 and was thus NASCAR's first woman driver. Note the masking tape on the front cowl of the car, which was there to prevent stones and clods of dirt from chipping the paint. Sara's race car, you see, was also the family sedan. (In NASCAR's early years, it was common for the cars to be "street legal" and to be driven to and from the tracks.) Photo credit: International Speedway Corporation Archives.

Thomas suggest he was involved in the whiskey business in any way. Curtis Turner, definitely a hell-raiser, is described in some sources as a backwoods moonshiner but elsewhere as a successful businessman and millionaire sawmill owner (he was evidently all of the above).

Elsewhere in the 1949 field we have Ray Erickson from Chicago, Bill Rexford and Jack White from upstate New York, Jim Roper from Kansas, Dick Linder from Pittsburgh, and a fair number of other drivers—altogether, seventeen of the top fifty—who did not hail from the moonshine hollows of the Appalachians nor from anywhere else in the South and who have never been linked, so far as I know, to the traffic (nice word here!) in illegal whiskey. Mention might also be made of 1949 competitor Sara Christian of Atlanta, the first woman to compete in NASCAR and not likely a moonshine hauler either, although I have been told that her husband was. (Christian ran in six of the eight events in NASCAR's inaugural season and finished thirteenth overall in the points standings that year. She started one race in the 1950 season, and that was the end of her NASCAR career.)

NASCAR's founding genius and first president, William H. G. ("Big Bill") France, with his wife, Annie, as portrayed in a bronze statue outside the Daytona International Speedway. According to the *Orlando Sentinel*, the statue is intended to convey "the modest roots of NASCAR's founding couple." The elder France ceded NASCAR's reins to his son in 1972 and died in 1992 at the age of eighty-two.

The National Association of Stock Car Automobile Racing was founded by William H. G. ("Big Bill") France on 12 December 1947 at the Ebony Bar atop the Streamline Hotel in Daytona Beach. (I was one month and six days old on that date, so NASCAR and I are practically crib buddies.) At the time, stock-car racing was going on all over the country and had been for many years. In postwar America it was not just rednecks and moonshine-runners from the Appalachian uplands who wanted to know whose car was fastest; it was also farm boys from Wisconsin, factory workers in Ohio, mill hands out of Pennsylvania, coal miners in downstate Illinois, even brash young ice-delivery men from Logansport, Indiana. Here, there, and everywhere, those hot young men—many of them real heroes just back from the war, with gonads pulsing, new jobs, and pockets full of cash—were buying cars (newly available again after a five-year hiatus), souping them up, and heading off to the tracks to renew their blood battle for supremacy against more familiar foes. There was no Southern monopoly—much less a Southern moonshiner's monopoly—

on stock-car racing in the sport's formative years, a point to which we return shortly.

The idea of bringing discipline, order, and stability to the sport, or at least making a profit from it, was clearly on the minds of many all over the country (not just in the Southeast), as is evident from the formation of several rival sanctioning organizations at about the same time: the National Stock Car Racing Association, National Championship Stock Car Circuit, Stock Car Auto Racing Society (with the unfortunate acronym SCARS), National Auto Racing League, National Auto Racing Club, American Stock Car Racing Association, United Stock Car Racing Association, United States Auto Club, and, according to the *Official NASCAR Handbook*, "literally dozens of others." For a variety of reasons, not least Big Bill's unflinching dictatorial hand, NASCAR eventually emerged as the most successful of these competing organizations. If one of the midwestern groups had been a little more aggressive, well — who knows? — today stock-car racing might be associated in the popular mind with corn farming, not corn liquor.

Assembled in that Daytona bar were a group of businessmen, mechanics, owners, track promoters, and drivers who, according to Mark Howell, sought honest organization, equality, guaranteed purses, safety, and fairness for the sport. By no means a ragtag bunch of drunks and whiskey-runners, these were serious men embarked on a serious venture to bring order to an emerging sport.

The first president of the organization was Big Bill himself, but the first national commissioner was E. G. "Cannonball" Baker from Indiana; the first vice president was Bill Tuthill from New England; other Yankees were also present. NASCAR was founded on the belief that the keys to long-term growth and fan popularity would be fair rules consistently applied; large, honest, guaranteed purses to attract the best drivers; and a points competition to determine a single national champion. And so it has been.

The first NASCAR stock-car race was a 200-lapper at a three-quarter-mile dirt track in Charlotte on 19 June 1949. (NASCAR sponsored a modified series in 1948, but a stock-car season originally planned for that year had to be canceled to give Detroit enough time to get its new models out.) There were eight races in the 1949 season, all of them "strictly stock," meaning that the cars had to be raced just as they came off the showroom floor. No car built before 1946 was allowed to compete. Until France hit on the idea of racing cars right off the showroom floor, NASCAR was little more than another sanctioning body for dirt-track modified races — races like those my father and his friends ran in back in the forties and fifties. France's true stroke of genius was not in founding NASCAR but in recognizing that the public would pay top dollar to see people race the same new cars they could buy themselves, and that remains an important element in NASCAR's appeal.

NASCAR's first stock-car race was won by Glenn Dunnaway in a 1947 Ford. However, a postrace inspection revealed that the rear springs of the winning Ford had been modified — stiffened with wedges to hold the car tighter in the corners, a well-known bootlegger's trick. The immediate presumption was that the winning car was used as a whiskey hauler. Since the modified suspension violated the strictly stock provision, Dunnaway's car was disqualified and the victory was awarded instead to the second place finisher from Kansas, Jim Roper.[17] It is clear from this incident alone that NASCAR was eager to repudiate any residual association with the moonshine business at its first opportunity.

There's a final wrinkle worth telling. The owner of Dunnaway's car was Hubert Westmoreland, unquestionably a moonshiner, who was perturbed by the disqualification and sued NASCAR for the prize money. According to Golenbock, the NASCAR attorney kept repeating the term "boot-legger" over and over during the trial and as a result Westmoreland's suit was unsuccessful. Golenbock comments that "the era during which most of the cars were owned by bootleggers had [thus] come to an end."[18] If this account is correct, then it was NASCAR's *inaugural event* that drove the whiskey element out of the sport of stock-car racing. The idea that NASCAR was created by or was at least a tolerant, much less congenial, home for a gang of wild-eyed whiskey-runners is nonsense.

Regional Fables

Before we get too far into this discussion, we have to decide what's a Southern state and what's not. In such matters I defer to John Shelton Reed, the nation's leading expert on all things Southern. Following Reed's argument in "The South: What Is It? *Where* Is It?" I define "the South" as the Confederate South plus the "border states" of Missouri and Ken-

tucky.[19] Although one case or another can be made for including Okla-
homa, West Virgina, and even Maryland, I have chosen not to do so.
Specifically, then, the South here comprises Texas, Arkansas, Missouri,
Louisiana, Mississippi, Alabama, Georgia, Florida, Tennessee, Kentucky,
Virginia, North Carolina, and South Carolina.

In the face of the frequent claims that stock-car racing is, or was, a
sport enjoyed mainly by Southern rednecks and dominated by Southern
drivers, one must again consider facts. NASCAR's first race was won by
non-Southerner Jim Roper (albeit on a technicality). Three of the eight
races in the inaugural season were contested on Union soil (two in Pennsylvania and one in New York). Seventeen of the top fifty drivers in that
first season hailed from non-Southern states: New York (seven drivers),
New Jersey (five), Pennsylvania (three), Kansas (one), and Illinois (one).
So, in NASCAR's first year the Yankee presence amounted to one-third of
the drivers and three-eighths of the races.

The second year saw even more Northern exposure for the sport (indeed, it was a high-water mark, but more on that later). In 1950 there were
nineteen Grand National Championship races, ten of them in Northern
states: four were in New York, three in Ohio, two in Pennsylvania, and one
in Indiana. Twenty-four of the top fifty drivers, six of the top ten drivers,
and the national champion himself—Bill Rexford of New York—hailed
from the North.

By 1951, the NASCAR season had grown to forty-one races, of which
twenty were held in non-Southern states: five each in Ohio and California, three in Pennsylvania, two each in New York and Michigan, and
one each in New Jersey, Connecticut, and Arizona. (Note the early Western expansion.) In that 1951 season, there were NASCAR venues in more
non-Southern states (eight) than in Southern states (six: North Carolina,
Florida, Alabama, Virginia, Georgia, and South Carolina). In the same
year, twenty-five of the top fifty drivers were Yankees, including drivers
from New York, Ohio, New Jersey, Iowa, Pennsylvania, Michigan, and
California. Note, too, that wherever NASCAR went to race, local drivers
were there, ready to rise to the challenge.

The common misperception that stock-car racing has always been a
Southern sport, at least until very recently, is a slow car that we'll lap
a couple more times before we're done. For now, it is sufficient simply
to note that there was a significant Yankee involvement at the begin-

ning, an involvement that NASCAR essentially abandoned in the sixties. Since the onset in 1972 of the so-called modern era of NASCAR, however, the *National* Association of Stock Car Automobile Racing has managed to become a truly national racing organization that has events, fans, and drivers all over the country.[20] The oft-heard argument that it was only the young, handsome, talented, successful, California-born, and Indiana-raised Jeff Gordon that allowed the sport to "overcome" its Southern roots reveals a sorry innocence of the sport's real history (e.g., Steve Lopez in *Time:* "NASCAR didn't go national until a Yankee became its star").[21]

Still, while researching the venues and drivers in NASCAR's first three seasons, I came across the first instance of a pattern that was to dominate the sport for two decades, a pattern that partly explains the misperception that stock-car racing is a Southern sport. Although twenty of the forty-one races in 1951 were held outside the South and twenty-five of the top fifty drivers were non-Southerners, the only non-Southerner to crack the top ten was Dick Rathmann of California. (Or maybe it was Jim Rathmann—who can say? For God knows what reason, the Rathmann brothers swapped identities in the 1940s, and people still get them confused.) So, while there were plenty of Yankee drivers in competition in those early years and plenty of races outside the South, most of the checkered flags and championship points went to Southerners.

Aha, you say: superior driving skills honed in the whiskey-hauling business. But the answer is more prosaic, a simple matter of who competed in the most races. The 1951 NASCAR champion, Herb Thomas of North Carolina, competed in thirty-five of the forty-one events; the runner-up, Georgia's Fonty Flock, competed in thirty-four. All the top five drivers ran in twenty-seven or more events; the drivers who placed from twelfth to fiftieth all competed in fewer than twenty. The average number of starts for the top ten drivers was 21.4 and for the remaining forty of the top fifty, 8.4. This, as we shall see, was the common pattern until the onset of NASCAR's modern era.

It is not surprising that drivers competing in the most races amassed the most points and therefore ended up on top. More surprising by far is that good old boys from Georgia and the Carolinas had the wherewithal to haul their race cars and teams to California, Arizona, Michigan, New York, Connecticut, and elsewhere in order to compete in so many events, while the drivers from the Northern and Western states tended to compete in only a few nearby races. The fact was that the winning drivers were *not* good old Southern boys in bib overalls with manure between their toes but relatively well-funded, well-paid, professional drivers whose car owners could afford to send them around the country to beat up on local competition. Which is what they did until the modern era, when increased corporate involvement in Winston Cup racing gave nearly every team the means to race a full schedule—and that, more than any other single factor, leveled the playing field and put real competitiveness back into the sport.

The Culture of the Proles

Having dispensed with moonshine myths and regional fables, what say we tackle the matter of social class? And who better to get us started than Tom Wolfe?

> After the war there was a great deal of stout-burgher talk about people who lived in hovels and bought big-yacht cars to park out front. . . . But there was a great deal of unconscious resentment buried in the talk. It was resentment against (a) the fact that the good old boy had his money at all and (b) the fact that the car symbolized freedom, a slightly wild, careening emancipation from the old social order. Stock car racing got started at about this time, right after the war, and it was immediately regarded as some kind of manifestation of the animal irresponsibility of the lower orders. . . . Stock car racing was something that was welling up out of the lower orders. From somewhere these country boys and urban proles were getting the money and starting this sport.[22]

"The animal irresponsibility of the lower orders"—now there's a concept to sink your teeth into. Say what you will about Wolfe's historiography, the man can turn a phrase.

So far as I've been able to determine, Wolfe was the first to describe stock-car racing as a "prole sport" but certainly not the last. The most fatuous elaboration on the theme I have yet found comes from a recent textbook in the sociology of sport, written by James Bryant and Mary McElroy.

The working class tends to be attracted to sedentary sporting experiences such as auto racing, demolition derbies, and motocross racing. These sports combine the machines, the necessary tools, and the equipment associated with every day life. They also offer an alternative to the repetitive nature of many blue collar jobs. The speed, excitement, and daring associated with auto racing, for example, provide a pleasant weekend alternative to assembly-line responsibilities in the automobile plant. These proletariat or prole sports *incorporate speed, daring, physical strength, violence, and risk.* They portray a strong macho image with an individually oriented focus as opposed to a team concept. Prole sports are in direct contrast to the sports of the wealthy, representing entirely different values and attitudes. Most prole sports are not related to school or local community experiences or driven by an economic market of professional instructors and elaborate equipment.[23]

As a cultured prole in a properly deconstructive frame of mind might say, "What a crock!"

We'll leave it to another chapter to decide whether stock-car racing in fact appeals more to "the lower orders" than to the middle class. For now, let's just try to figure out what is being said here and whether there's any good reason to believe it.

Auto racing is described by Bryant and McElroy as a "sedentary" sporting experience, but in what way is racing more sedentary than any other sport that people mainly watch for enjoyment, whether live or on TV? There are a few "sports," I suppose, that more people play than watch — walking, jogging, maybe bowling and fishing, too — but most Americans engage in sports primarily as spectators, that is, while sitting on their butts. And since this is true of nearly everyone, it is certainly not a useful criterion for defining "prole sports."

There are at least some nonsedentary participatory sports (bowling, for example) with definite working-class overtones (granted, some middle-class people also bowl, but, as my agent, Laura Dail, says, "They do it with irony") and some sedentary participatory "sports" (chess or bridge, for example) with definite middle-class overtones (granted, some working-class people play a mean game of chess). I'll even grant that middle-class people are probably more apt than factory workers to jog, walk for their health, go to the gym, play tennis, or get in an occasional round of golf. But then you have to grant me that factory workers wouldn't normally have the same need for cardiovascular exercise that college professors have.

Just why would working-class people be attracted to motorsports? Bryant and McElroy assert that prole sports appeal to workers because they are "associated" with the machines, tools, and equipment of everyday life. But automobiles are machines of everyday living for persons in all social strata, not just the working class. And what is there about bowling or roller derby or professional wrestling or other allegedly "prole" sports that workers could "associate" with everyday living? What is the everyday equivalent of rolling a sixteen-pound ball down a wooden lane?

Yes, these sports "offer an alternative to the repetitive nature of many blue collar jobs." As a moment's reflection makes obvious, however, the same could be said of *any* leisure-time pursuit, including a hot game of chess, a day on the lake with a fishing pole, a Sunday afternoon of televised football, or a long evening curled up with a book. And, as a matter of personal experience, I can assure you that "the speed, excitement, and daring associated with auto racing" also provide a most pleasant weekend alternative to the everyday drudgery of teaching sociology, working on research papers, or plowing through the third volume of *Das Kapital*. It is not just factory workers who look for boredom-relieving diversions on the weekends.

Is it that "prole sports incorporate speed, daring, physical strength, violence, and risk"? Here the problem is that practically *all* sports incorporate elements of speed, daring, strength, violence, and risk; otherwise, they wouldn't be sports. Even low-risk sports like golf, tennis, and bowling reward strength; "finesse" sports like baseball, soccer, and basketball reward speed; sports like football, boxing, and hockey incorporate speed, daring, strength, violence, and risk. Are motorsports any different from these other sports?

To say that motorsports appeal to workers because they "portray a strong macho image with an individually oriented focus as opposed to a team concept" won't do either, because almost all sports have strong overtones of competition, opposition, struggle, rivalry, domination, and related "macho" themes. And many sports—golf, tennis, boxing—are "individually oriented."

Do prole sports such as auto racing express "entirely different values and attitudes" than the sporting pursuits of the wealthy? No. All sports represent and express common values of fairness, competition, hard work, sportsmanship, and the like. And just what are these "sports of the wealthy" whose values contrast so sharply with those of stock-car racing? Polo? Thoroughbred horse racing? Sports-car racing? Formula One?

Fact is, Winston Cup stock-car racing is itself a sport of the wealthy. It takes something on the order of $10 million to put a competitive Winston Cup car into the field *for one season.* Seven-time champion Dale Earnhardt earned more than $41 million in race winnings and many times that figure in endorsements, licensing deals, and sales of memorabilia before his death in 2001. Jeff Gordon won more than $9 million in the 1998 season alone. Many back-of-the-pack Winston Cup regulars have career earnings well into the millions, and even that old moonshine-hauler Junior Johnson won more than $22 million as an owner before his retirement in 1995. (Oh yes, that legendary Junior Johnson, by gum, he was one hard-charging multimillionaire!) Neither the drivers nor the owners of Winston Cup stock cars are dirt-poor hayseeds or even "middle class." They are wealthy people, often millionaires many times over, and their sport is as much a serious business venture as a leisure-time amusement.

Finally, the prole sports (our authors allege) are "not related to school or local community experiences or driven by an economic market of professional instructors and elaborate equipment." Certainly, none of this describes automobile racing. The everyday analogue of stock-car racing is driving your car, a common "community" experience. And the sport has both elaborate equipment and professional instructors; take, for instance, the Richard Petty Driving Experience (dial 1-800-BE-PETTY — no joke), where, after an hour or two of instruction, a paying customer gets to pilot a stock car around a NASCAR track at near-racing speeds. And there are a number of other such organizations to which you can pay serious money to learn the sport's finer points.

I have no doubt that stock-car racing originally welled up out of "the lower orders." I don't think insurance agents in Wausau or high school teachers in Toledo or bank tellers in Charlotte would have had that same overwhelming urge to find out whose car was the fastest or whose *cojones* were the biggest. Working-class people were also overrepresented among the spectators in the beginning, and to a significant extent, they still are

A show car advertising the "Richard Petty Driving Experience." Note the toll-free number on the hood.

today. But any sport that has become as popular as Winston Cup racing must have appeal across the whole social spectrum.

Gender and Race

NASCAR's critics have accused stock-car racing of being a sexist and racist sport. The first of these can be dispensed with quickly, but the second requires more extended consideration.

I have already mentioned 1949 competitor Sara Christian. With even a single female driver, NASCAR outshines practically every other professional sport in its inclusion of women at the highest level of competition. But a few other women have also driven in the NASCAR championship series: Christine Beckers, Ann Bunselmeyer, Ann Chester, Janet Guthrie, Clare Lawicki, Ethel Mobley, Patty Moise, Mopsie Pagan, Goldie Parsons, Ann Slaasted, Louise Smith, and no doubt others. (In the commentary preceding the June 2001 race at Michigan, where Shawna Robinson became the first woman to start a Winston Cup race since 1989, it was said that "fourteen or fifteen women" have driven in NASCAR's top stock-car series, so I have evidently overlooked at least a couple.) Most of these drivers had short and largely unsuccessful NASCAR careers, but Janet

Guthrie, the first woman to drive in the Indianapolis 500 and the only woman to date to drive in the Daytona 500, had thirty-three starts and five top-ten finishes from 1976 to 1980. Given the evident appeal of the sport to women (see below), there is clearly room in the Winston Cup for a female driver with female-oriented sponsors and maybe even a female pit crew. Already, companies like L'Eggs and Underalls pantyhose and Lovable intimate apparel have sponsored race teams.

Proficiency at high-speed driving, as with proficiency at any other skilled undertaking, requires an early start and years of hard work. Increasing the presence of women in racing (and, for that matter, of blacks and other minorities) won't happen until more young girls (and young minorities) are encouraged to start racing Go-Karts and quarter-midgets at an early age. When as many young girls as young boys fantasize about driving hot rods as fast as they will go and are encouraged in this fantasy by their parents and peers, then a decade or so thereafter, there'll be as many female stock-car drivers as there are male.

On the fan side of the Winston Cup equation, a major female presence is unmistakable. As early as 1990, David Thigpen mused in a *Time* article that women comprised almost half the attendees at Winston Cup events, and while this is a little high (the female percentage is closer to a third), no one who has ever attended a Winston Cup race would doubt for an instant that the sport enjoys a following among women. So, with a long (if thin) history of women drivers and lots of women in the stands, the argument that NASCAR somehow excludes women is unpersuasive.

The allegation that African Americans and other minorities have been systematically excluded from stock-car racing is harder to refute. In fact, the lack of minority participation (whether as competitors or as fans) is an embarrassment that grows more serious every year and one that NASCAR has at last begun to address. Naming their diversity management council in the middle of the 1999 season is only the most visible of a number of steps the organization has taken to increase minority participation in the sport.

So far as I know, only two African Americans have ever driven at the NASCAR championship level: Wendell Scott (495 starts, one win, and 147 top ten finishes in a career spanning 1961 to 1973) and Willy T. Ribbs (three starts and no top tens in 1986). And while there are some blacks and Hispanics involved at other levels of the sport, they are very few.

Wendell Scott (1921–1990) was the first African American driver to compete in NASCAR's top championship series and the only black man ever to have won a Winston Cup race. He is pictured here at the wheel of his winning Chevy in Jacksonville, Florida, in December 1963. Photo credit: International Speedway Corporation Archives.

Bryant Gumbel used these and other observations to raise the specter of racism in NASCAR in a 1999 edition of his HBO program *Real Sports*. He got Willy T. Ribbs to talk angrily about his experiences in trying to break into the Winston Cup, and he had Richard Petty on tape making reference to "colored people," right there on the air. You'd have thought the King showed up for his interview in a white sheet. And — my sakes! — all those Confederate flags. This certainly *seems* to have racism written all over it.

Steve Lopez also played the race card in his *Time* story in which he likened a Winston Cup race to a "Klan picnic." Lopez was disturbed by his inability to find black people at Talladega, by the racist comments of a couple of fans, and, again, by all the Confederate flags. But he did eventually locate two black guys in the motor-home section of the infield, one of whom commented, "Tell them black people love racing, too."

There is little doubt that NASCAR would welcome black drivers and teams into the Winston Cup, as well as more black fans into the stands, if only to counter these charges. NASCAR's efforts to diversify have borne some fruit. One example is the Busch Grand National racing team owned by former NBA superstar Julius Erving (Dr. J) and former pro footballer Joe Washington. Another was the 1999 announcement by Olympic gold medalist Jackie Joyner-Kersee and her husband Bob Kersee that they would field a Winston Cup team in the 2000 campaign; Joyner-Kersee Racing debuted at the 1999 Pepsi 400 at the Michigan International Speedway with Craftsman Truck driver Tom Hubert at the wheel, but alas, the car failed to qualify. *Sports Illustrated* has noted that while black-owned teams "have been getting open-door treatment from NASCAR as it seeks to diversify, corporate America hasn't responded with the funding" that these new teams will need to race competitively in the Winston Cup.

However much progress is being made by NASCAR as an organization, you can still hear some pretty scurrilous racist garbage spewing from the mouths of stock-car fans, no doubt about that. At the 1999 Brickyard 400 in Indianapolis, one of the concession booths was being operated as a benefit for the local chapter of the NAACP, and the drunken ass just behind me in line used this as his cue to comment loud and long on the food, the service, the length of the line, race relations in America, the souls of black folk, and (I gathered) the end of civilization as he knew it. I'm sure you could hear worse at Darlington or Talladega — or Pocono. But in fairness I have to report that I went directly from the Brickyard 400 to the annual convention of the American Sociological Association in Chicago where I also overhead some nasty things being said about black people, much of it disguised in a fog of academic jargon that only an insider could decode. NASCAR and its fans are not alone in their need to get right on the race issue.

In July 1999, at the Jiffy Lube 300 in Loudon, New Hampshire, two white employees of Winston Cup drivers Derrike Cope and Terry Labonte put on white sheets, imitating Klansmen, then taunted another employee who was black. Was this tasteless incident sloughed off as the sort of harmless prank one expects in a racist sport? No. Both men were fired. NASCAR's official spokesman, Kevin Triplett, commented, "It just needs to be understood that there is a line that cannot be crossed." Cope, who hails from the state of Washington, said "behavior like this simply cannot be tolerated in today's society." Texan Labonte was equally forceful: "These actions are deplorable and will not be tolerated." NASCAR's official response to this incident is an indication of just how far the sport has come, but that it happened at all shows that there's still a ways to go.[24]

Kelley, Denise, and I got to the Daytona race track about three hours before the Pepsi 400 started. We couldn't help but notice the Confederate flags flying over the infield RVs and that kicked up a conversation about blacks, the white South, and NASCAR. On a lark, I asked Kelley how many Confederate flags he thought there were out there in that immense Daytona infield, and without hesitation he responded, "A hundred?" It seemed like a reasonable guess. Then he took one pair of binoculars, I took another, and starting at opposite ends of the infield, we endeavored to count them. He got thirty-five, I counted thirty-eight — either way, there were fewer than forty. (I wonder: Did Steve Lopez count flags at Talladega or did he just look and guess?) Then Kelley looked around the stands and added, "Yep, probably about as many Confederate flags here as black people." Somehow, that ratio didn't sound like much progress to me. Well, not *enough* progress, in any case.

Whether the coming years will witness more progress is hard to say. An African American driver or team would almost certainly bring more black people into the stands, but so far none of the minority "start-up" teams looks ready to make the jump to the Winston Cup. What the sport needs are some well-heeled black businessmen to step up with the mega-millions necessary to field a competitive Winston Cup entry. On the fan side of the equation, my informal impression (not based on anything systematic) is that the number of African American spectators is already increasing. As one illustration, for the first time ever in my Winston Cup experiences, the guy in the seat next to mine at the 2001 Pepsi 400 at Daytona was a black man, and there were several dozen other African Americans seated in our section of the grandstand. I was also very encouraged by the surprising near-total absence of Confederate flags at the October 2001 race at Charlotte, the first race I attended after the terrorist attack on America. The emphasis at Charlotte (and pretty much everywhere else, I've been told) was on the things that unite us as a nation and a people. The things that once divided us (and their symbols) were suddenly rendered passé, even hateful and unpatriotic.

Several readers of earlier drafts of this book have asked me what fans themselves have to say about these issues. Frankly, race is not something NASCAR fans talk about, at least not in any conversation I ever overheard.

Maybe there is a racist element in the subculture so deep that it can remain tacit—unspoken but understood. The occasional drunken ass notwithstanding, however, most of the NASCAR people I ran into on the *Fixin' to Git* Road Tour were the nicest folks you'd ever want to meet—open, friendly, generous to a fault. It is hard for me to imagine that they collectively harbor a deep racist streak.

Days of Blunder

The movie *Days of Thunder,* starring Tom Cruise, Robert Duvall, Nicole Kidman, and Randy Quaid, is the highest-grossing sports movie of all time.[25] Cruise (who also cowrote the story) plays Cole Trickle, a young upstart driver from California trying to break into the Winston Cup. And break in he does, thanks to the support of car owner Tim Deland (Randy Quaid) and the gruff but lovable car builder and crew chief Harry Hogge (Robert Duvall). Few stock-car fans and even fewer movie buffs recognize that the story is (very) loosely based on the real-life partnership involving driver Tim Richmond (the one who died of AIDS), team owner Rick Hendrick, and crew chief Harry Hyde (who died in 1996).

The movie was filmed with the cooperation of NASCAR and the Winston Cup drivers (several of whom had cameo roles), apparently because they were assured by the producers that every effort would be made to provide an accurate and realistic depiction of the sport. But Hollywood is, well, Hollywood, not *60 Minutes.*

The opening footage shows pan-over shots of infields at various Winston Cup venues. The first identifiable flag in this footage, strangely, is Canadian, but then the predictable procession of Confederate flags begins. Confederate flags recur in infield shots throughout the movie. When Deland is talking to Hogge about his new driver, Cole Trickle, it comes to light that poor Cole is from California. Hogge sneers incredulously, "He's a Yankee?" (as though that alone would disqualify a man from driving in the Winston Cup). Trickle's credentials include open-wheel sprint cars "out West" and also some driving in the ASA (American Speed Association, another of the stock-car minor leagues). This generates more snorts from Hogge, even though sprint and ASA experience can be found on the resumes of many Winston Cup stars. And when old Harry finally gets around to building a Cup car for Deland and Trickle, he builds the thing in a drafty old ramshackle barn on his farm outside of Charlotte. Actual car fabrication operations are ultra-modern, ultra-sleek, super-sophisticated, high-tech speed factories with engine builders, chassis specialists, body fabricators, wind tunnel and aerodynamics engineers — this list goes on. In these ways and a dozen others, *Days of Thunder* tells its audience that stock-car racing is a cracker sport. Harry Hogge is the quintessential good old boy, Cole the mouthy, upstart Yankee. A key plot theme — that all Cole's talent will count for naught if he doesn't defer to Hogge's wisdom and experience — is predictable from their first encounter.

With these *themata,* one would not expect the film to forego an allusion to moonshine. Cole wins his first Winston Cup race at Darlington and that leads to a drunken party in the team transporter on the way back to Charlotte.[26] As the scene opens, Harry and the rest of the crew are swigging moonshine from mason jars (the jars are apparently meant as an "authentic" touch). Cole starts with a beer but switches to a jar of 'shine soon thereafter. In a joke set up by the crew, the transporter is pulled over by bogus state troopers for "illegal transport of untaxed whiskey." Hogge: "This ain't transportation, it's consumption." Drivers Dale Earnhardt and Rusty Wallace expressed public outrage at this element of the movie's depiction.

But the most egregious misrepresentation is the reckless folly of the drivers, who are forever ramming into one another, rubbing fenders, and causing wrecks just to win a race. Every racing sequence in the movie portrays some variation on this theme. At one point, upstart Russ Wheeler snarls in a pre-race interview, "He comes near me, I'll put him in the wall." In the real world of Winston Cup racing, a comment like that would get a driver suspended. In the movie, a NASCAR official (played by Fred Thompson, now a U.S. Senator from Tennessee) eventually reprimands Trickle and his chief rival Rowdy Burns for their careless on-track behavior, but not until they have nearly killed each other. NASCAR would never tolerate even a tenth of the shenanigans that are depicted in the movie as standard driver behavior. As the late Alan Kulwicki said of the movie's racing sequences, "They portrayed us like we're running bumper cars."[27]

No one expects technical accuracy from the movies. But NASCAR has not been well served by its print interpreters either, many of whom have proven incapable of overcoming "the ideological biases and traditional assumptions that infect all histories and all truths." So, some deconstruction of the principal NASCAR myths was necessary just to get us off on the right foot. But the wreckage has now been cleared from the track, the lights on the pace car are off, and we'll get the green light to go next time around.

Back Home Again in Indiana

My route to the Brickyard 400 in Indianapolis was circuitous. I flew into O'Hare, rented a car, then drove from Chicago to Ft. Wayne to Logansport to Indianapolis and back to Chicago, an irregular 500-mile triangle of an itinerary that traced, more or less precisely, the perimeter of my youth. Within that triangle were my brother and sister, their spouses, and most of my aunts, uncles, and cousins, the graves of my parents and grandparents, every school I had attended and every woman I had fallen in love with up to the time of my twenty-first birthday. Indiana. Known to Hoosiers as the Heartland, the Crossroads of America, and God's Country. Home to the Indianapolis Motor Speedway, the most legendary venue in all of motor sports.

The Brickyard opened in 1911 and open-wheeled roadsters have been racing there ever since in the annual Indianapolis 500, "the greatest spectacle in racing." I've been to the Indy 500 twice, once in 1965 and again in 1998. Like Daytona, the track is 2.5 miles around; unlike Daytona, it is a perfectly symmetrical squared oval with two identical, completely flat, .625-mile-long straightaways and four identical corners, each banked a mere nine degrees. By Winston Cup standards, it is a flat track with tight, narrow corners. It also tends to be a one-line track—there's only one fast line or racing "groove" around the track and the cars usually go through the corners in single file. For one whose previous NASCAR experience was

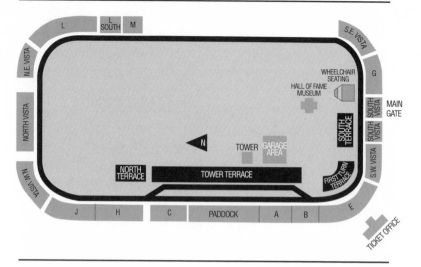

A schematic drawing of the Indianapolis Motor Speedway. Our seats were in the Southeast Vista right at Turn Two. Note the various grandstands and the museum on the inside of the track. These structures obscure the view of fans seated in all the grandstands. From our seats in Turn Two, we could see most of the short chute between Turns One and Two, Turn Two itself, and the entire backstretch. 16th Street forms the southern boundary of the track; our Park @ Indy campsite was across 16th Street from the main gate.

limited to the high-banked tri-ovals at Charlotte and Daytona, where two-, three-, and even four-wide racing is common, the flat, one-groove racing at Indy seemed weird, the track ill-suited for the big muscular stock cars of the Winston Cup.

For its first eight decades, the Indianapolis Motor Speedway hosted just the one annual race. The surging popularity of the Winston Cup, however, compelled Indy's owners to open a second racing date, and the inaugural Brickyard 400 was held in 1994. (In 2000 the Speedway began hosting an annual Formula One race as well.) The 1994 race drew the largest crowd and paid out the highest purse of any race in NASCAR's history up to that time. The speedway accommodates more than 300,000 people and is, therefore, the largest venue in all of sports and probably in all of history. In 1999 the Brickyard 400, with a purse of $6.2 million, was the Winston Cup's second most lucrative event, the Daytona 500, at

$7.3 million, having been first. Last place at the Brickyard paid more than $90,000.

For the past few years, more people have come to Indy for the Winston Cup race in August than for the 500 in May, a fact that makes racing purists cringe. Compared to Indy cars, which scoot around the track at speeds around 220 mph, the Winston Cup cars seem slow and cumbersome, plodding mules on a course built for thoroughbreds. Indy Racing League (IRL) fans sometimes refer to Winston Cup cars as "glorified taxi cabs." But then NASCAR has those "all-American drivers, all-American cars," and a fan base that, by at least some measures, now extends to half the adult population. Given the size of the crowds and purses, Winston Cup racing at Indy is clearly here to stay.

The Indiana leg of the *Fixin' to Git* Road Tour began with my brother-in-law Neil's fiftieth birthday party in Ft. Wayne, where I met a young woman named Leslie who worked for the American Motor Sports Club. AMSC was a membership organization (now no longer in business) that arranged travel, hotel, and ticket packages for race fans, mainly Winston Cup fans. Leslie and I exchanged business cards and about two weeks later I received a member's packet: a copy of the *AMSC Magazine* with features on Ned Jarrett and the 1999 Daytona 500, various promotional materials, a card identifying me as an Inaugural Member, and an AMSC "gimme" hat (from the phrase, "Gimme one of them hats!"—also known as "baseball caps," even when they have nothing to do with baseball). I never used the organization to book a race weekend, so I couldn't say whether their services were a bargain or not, but I thought their mere existence was a significant statement about the popularity of racing.

By the time I had gotten to Ft. Wayne, I had written enough of this book to feel comfortable talking to NASCAR strangers about the project. Word spread quickly through the party that I was writing a NASCAR book, and just like the family reunion a month before, once word got around stock-car racing was just about all I talked about the rest of the evening. Every person at that party seemed to be a race fan of some description— Formula One, Indy cars, CART, or NASCAR, and, frequently enough, all the above.

Leslie and nearly everyone else, even my sister, just assumed that NASCAR or perhaps Winston had sponsored the project and were surprised that this was not so. (There's not much about Winston Cup racing that isn't sponsored by something, I guess.) I assured them all that I was trying to write a book from the perspective of an average fan and felt virtuous telling people that the whole Road Tour was being funded out-of-pocket. If, on the other hand, AMSC wanted to pick up the tab for the rest of the season, I'd be pleased to acknowledge their sponsorship. But, apparently, a complimentary club membership was as far as they were willing to go.

Corporate sponsors, promotions, and season ticket holders make tickets to the August race difficult to acquire. Brother Kelley's connection had fallen through and we were sans tickets five days before the race. But my cousin Toni and her group had four tickets to spare, so the entourage for Indy was me, Kelley, Denise, and Denise's son Damon, a Mark Martin fan and Jeff Gordon hater. The price? Face value, $65 a ticket. I was surprised that tickets were that cheap, but when you are multiplying by 300,000, I guess you can afford to give fans a break. (I'll save you the trouble: It adds up to nearly $20 million in race-day ticket revenue alone.)

We headed to Indianapolis early Friday, the day before the race. With the immense capacity of the stands, race-day traffic jams at Indy are intense, so our plan was to arrive a day early and camp out for the night —with luck, somewhere within walking distance of the track. I hadn't camped out in years (unless you include nights in Motel 6) and never at a Winston Cup race, but tens of thousands of fans do so every weekend. So, while I was a bit dubious at first, I was also happy for the opportunity to add to my fund of racing experiences. Kelley remembered a little parking lot-cum-campground right across the street from the south entrance to the track. Maybe if we got there early on Friday, a spot would still be available.

The Friday morning traffic on I-465 was thick as we neared the speedway, and I despaired of finding an open campsite anywhere in a ten-mile radius. But Park@Indy, 3805 West 16th Street, had one campsite left. For $125, we would have a place to park two vehicles and pitch a tent. And if that seems like highway robbery, the only motel rooms still available were not only at least that much *per room* (we'd have needed two of them) but also miles from the track; furthermore, race-day parking near the track would be $25 per vehicle. So, the camping fee was actually a bargain. Park@Indy had an all-night attendant, clean bathrooms and showers, and even a little concession stand and convenience store. On Saturday morning, they gave out free coffee and donuts. And the location was superb. We could walk from the campsite to our seats in Turn Two in ten minutes.

While making arrangements, we were alerted by an attendant that a stripper and her boyfriend were camped in the slot next to ours and that the night before, she'd put on "quite a show." That perky bit of news caused some misgivings since our group included a twelve-year-old boy, but with no room reservations in hand and a growing line of cars behind us being told that the campground was full, we didn't have much choice. To Damon's delight, we took what was available and resolved to make the best of it. And wouldn't you just know? We were up until the wee hours of the morning and saw neither hide nor hair of the alleged stripper.

We had our campsite set up by eleven in the morning on Friday, and by noon we were at the track to take in Happy Hour and the fourth and final event of the 1999 International Race of Champions (IROC) competition. Tickets were $35 each and there were tens of thousands of fans in the stands. IROC races, like The Winston, are basically All-Star events except that in IROC champion drivers from several racing leagues (Winston Cup, Busch, Indy Racing League, CART) compete head to head in identically prepared race cars. Ostensibly, the point of IROC is to determine the "best" driver regardless of the kind of car he races, but because IROC cars are basically stock cars and all the IROC races are contested on Winston Cup tracks, the stock-car drivers dominate the competition. (The most successful of the non-Cup drivers over the years has been CART driver Al Unser Jr.)

The forty-lap (100-mile) IROC race at Indy was of great interest because the outcome would determine the season's IROC champion. Dale Earnhardt had won all three of the previous IROC races and needed only an eighth-place finish (out of twelve entrants) or better to clinch the championship. Mark Martin, Damon's favorite driver, had already won a record four IROC titles and could steal the championship if he won the race *and* Earnhardt finished ninth or worse. Earnhardt ran well early but slid steadily backward—to fourth, then sixth, then seventh. Martin took the lead on the ninth lap and never relinquished it, winning by a comfortable margin. But the Intimidator squeaked by in eighth place, winning the championship by a single point and with it the champion's purse of $225,000. Green flag to checkered, it turned out to be more exciting than the Cup race the next day.

Earnhardt had created some pre-race hoopla by showing up at Indy without his trademark mustache. He'd been snorkeling in the Bahamas with some NASCAR pals the previous weekend and his lip-bush had prevented the mask from sealing around his face. "I don't think it'll affect any of my racing skills," he said dryly. Still, he nearly lost the IROC championship to Martin and had a mediocre qualifying effort (he started eighteenth in the main event), so, despite his creditable tenth-place showing on Saturday, his mustache was back the next weekend.

Between the IROC competition and Happy Hour, it was near 5:00 when we repaired to the campsite to fix dinner (beer, chips, and bratwurst on the charcoal grill—natch) and enjoy an evening of camaraderie with our neighbors. There were fifty or sixty RVs parked at our end of the lot, almost all of them with huge rooftop air conditioners that kept blowing out circuit breakers. The junction box was mounted on a pole right behind our campsite, so by nightfall we knew almost everybody.

We met Ron from Owensboro, Kentucky—nice guy, soft-spoken, a serious race fan. For a small town (population: 54,000), Owensboro has produced more than its share of Winston Cup drivers—Jeremy Mayfield, the Green brothers, Michael Waltrip—a fact in which Ron took pride. He and his big Tioga RV went to five or six races each year, more when he could, anywhere from Ft. Worth to Daytona to Pocono to Michigan. That weekend, Ron was rooting for Jeremy Mayfield. The rumor in Owensboro was that the Mayfield marriage was in trouble; Ron thought that a big win at Indy might help patch things up.

Between our campsite and Ron's were six guys from Iowa who'd pooled their funds and bought a used RV for $3,000 just to make the Indy trip. Two of these guys raced modifieds at the Iowa short tracks and were big Kenny Schrader fans because they'd raced against Kenny a time or two. (Schrader is known as the kind of driver who'll go anywhere and race anything, even modifieds on back-country short tracks.) The Iowa campsite was decorated with a huge Miller Lite WELCOME, RACE FANS! banner, so I assumed that at least one or two of them were Rusty Wallace fans, Miller Lite being Rusty's sponsor.

Setting aside the enthusiasms of our immediate neighbors and the predictable sprinkling of Dale Jarrett, Bobby Labonte, and Dale Earnhardt sentiment, however, most of the fans in our neck of the campground were rooting for the Indiana Gang—the four (now three) Hoosier drivers who regularly compete in the Winston Cup. The alpha male of the group is Jeff Gordon, who had grown up in the tiny little town of Pittsboro, Indiana (population: 815), about twenty miles up Highway 136 from the speedway. As a favorite son, Jeff Gordon had more fans at Indy than anywhere else I visited in the 1999 season (even so, Gordon's introduction the next day was greeted by a surprisingly healthy chorus of boos). Gordon had qualified on the pole, and with two previous victories in the Brickyard 400, he was the odds-on favorite to win the race. Rookie Tony Stewart, of Columbus, Indiana, had come up racing sprint cars on the Indiana short tracks and had already begun to build an enthusiastic following everywhere, certainly among Hoosier race fans. Nineteen ninety-eight Rookie-of-the-Year Kenny Irwin and John Andretti, winner of the April 1999 race at Martinsville, were both Indianapolis natives and also enjoyed larger-than-average fan support at their home track. Andretti would start Saturday's race in tenth position, Stewart in eleventh, Irwin in fifteenth, and with Gordon on the pole, Hoosier fans were bubbling with pride, enthusiasm, and anticipation.

Our Iowa neighbors hosted a beer-and-barbecue party that lasted well into the morning. There were perhaps twenty young guys and gals sitting around the campfire drinking beer, telling raucous stories, and in more than a few cases, looking to pair up for a night of kissy-face and possibly more. I can't say whether these lads were any good at driving race cars, but when it came to partying, they were champions. Between the revelry next door, the god-awful hum of the streetlights, traffic on West 16th street, and the steady coming and going of airplanes at the nearby airport, there was little sleep to be had. The sun came up at 5:30, maybe three hours after the party had ended, and we rose with it, two or three hours of fitful sleep all we had to show for the night. We put on a pot of campfire coffee, gobbled up the leftover bratwurst, showered, dressed, and made our way to the track about 10:00 for the 1:00 start.

Our seats for the Brickyard 400 were about halfway up the grandstand near the apex of Turn Two, nearly the same location as our seats for The Winston at Charlotte. (My seat at the 1998 Indianapolis 500 was at nearly the same spot but at the opposite end of the track in Turn Four.)

There are no *good* seats at Indianapolis and these were decent seats at best. High-banked tracks like Daytona or Talladega not only let the cars run faster but also bring the cars up into the field of vision—you can easily see the racing in all the Daytona corners from nearly every seat because of that five-story rise at the corners that I mentioned earlier. In contrast, flat tracks like Indy keep the cars down low, often below the average fan's line of sight. At Indianapolis, the problem is compounded by large permanent structures on the *inside* of the track: four large infield grandstands (terraces) and the Hall-of-Fame Museum. No matter where you sit at the speedway, these structures block your view of at least some part of the track.

From our vantage point in Turn Two, we were unable to see *any* of the racing on the front stretch, and all the pit action was also hidden from view. The cars came into our field of vision as they were exiting Turn One. We had a good view of the short chute between the first and second turns, an exceptional view of Turn Two itself, and a clear view of the backstretch. Just at the entrance to the third turn, however, the cars disappeared behind a gigantic television screen. So we were able to see just about half the track, which, I am told, is somewhat better than average at Indy. Only the most expensive seats, high in the grandstand overlooking the start-finish line, offer an unobstructed view of the entire track. Let's face it: as a place to watch a race, Indy stinks.

The poor view, lack of sleep, and a relatively noncompetitive race made the Brickyard 400 the least interesting Winston Cup race I had ever been to. Jarrett had the strongest car and was fifteen or twenty car-lengths in front for most of the race. The other drivers, it seemed, spent the day motoring around in single file. Boring! Jarrett led 116 of the total of 160 laps, 81 of the last 82, and the final 43. I spent more of my day people-watching than following the action on the track. After the race, Denise, whose first race had been a month earlier in Daytona, asked in all apparent seriousness, "Does that Dale Jarrett fellow win *all* the races?" Later in the season she and I would watch Dale Earnhardt win at Talladega and Bobby Labonte finish the season with a win at Atlanta.

The Sunday editions of the Indiana papers headlined the performances of the Indiana Gang, three of whom had finished well: Gordon (third), Stewart (seventh), and Irwin (thirteenth). Andretti had had wheel problems, which you would not expect in a Petty Enterprises entry, and

1999 Brickyard 400 winner and eventual 1999 Winston Cup champion Dale Jarrett (right) chatting with Darrell Waltrip, who retired after the 2000 season with eighty-four career victories. Waltrip signed on as a color commentator with Fox Sports for the 2001 Winston Cup season. Photo credit: International Speedway Corporation Archives.

had finished thirty-seventh. But even the strong Hoosier showing was an insufficient antidote to my race-day ennui.

Most of the interesting NASCAR news of the week occurred away from the track. Confirming the season's worst-kept secret, Darrell Waltrip announced that he would retire after the 2000 season. Waltrip is tied for third, with Bobby Allison, for all-time Winston Cup victories (eighty-four) and was the Cup's winningest active driver after Richard Petty retired. He won at least one race in fifteen consecutive seasons (1975–1989) and won the Winston Cup championship three times (1981, 1982, and 1985). He is regarded as the first of the "new wave," media-savvy drivers, and his career essentially defined the Winston Cup's modern era. But Waltrip's last win had come in 1992 and on a fluke, and he had spent most of the 1998, 1999, and 2000 seasons racing on his Former Champion's provisionals, often unable to make the field on speed alone. (Former champions are awarded "provisionals" that allow them into virtually any Winston Cup race regardless of their qualifying speed.) Waltrip's 1999 run at the Brickyard was emblematic of his previous several seasons: he blew an engine early in the race and finished forty-second (next to last). With his winning personality, easy smile, charming manner, and quick lip, old Dee-Dubya was, and is, a true NASCAR legend. (About midway through 2000, Waltrip was hired by Fox Sports as a color commentator on that network's NASCAR coverage that began with the 2001 season.)

Possible Winston Cup expansion was also in the news. The Kansas Speedway Corporation, a wholly owned subsidiary of the France family's International Speedway Corporation, announced that it would soon begin selling seat licenses for the new track in Kansas City. (The facility hosted its first Winston Cup date in September 2001.) NASCAR (and the Indy Racing League) also expressed interest during the week in the new speedway being built in Chicago (the second new Winston Cup venue of 2001).

There was also some small progress on the diversity front. Doc Watson, a former ARCA driver, announced that he was partnering with Minnesota Vikings coach Dennis Green to form a new stock-car racing team with Californian Freddie Lewis at the wheel. Watson, Green, and Lewis are African Americans. The plan called for a full ARCA schedule in 2000, to be followed by a move into the Busch or Winston Cup Series sometime thereafter. In a related item, Hispanic Racing Team owners Rudy Rodriguez and Mike Vazquez announced a deal with Winston Cup owner Larry Hedrick to field a Busch Grand National team in 2000.

Indy was my first Winston Cup race north of the Mason-Dixon line, and I was hoping to see more fan diversity than I had seen at Charlotte or Daytona. I did not. There are black people at every race working the concession stands, on the custodial staff, and scalping tickets, but even at Indianapolis, there weren't many black fans in the stands, certainly not more than a percent or two. Sure, there were some encouraging signs. At Friday's IROC race, the National Anthem had been sung by four talented black men (the Voice of the Indianapolis Fire Department), several concession stands were being run to benefit the Indianapolis chapter of the NAACP, and not one Confederate flag was visible (by binoculars) anywhere in the infield. Still—only a thin scattering of black fans.

Being parked in a crowded campground right next to the track and needing to be in Chicago later that evening had me fretting all day about the traffic jam that would almost certainly thwart my get-away. But the good folks at Park@Indy let me use a road otherwise reserved for bigwigs and emergency vehicles, and so, with the blessings of the Indianapolis, Marion County, and Indiana State police, I pulled onto the restricted access road at about 4:30 and in less than twenty minutes I had looped around onto I-65 northbound for the Windy City, where I would attend the annual convention of the American Sociological Association and a Sunday meeting of the ASA Publications Committee.

The committee had recently been embroiled in a bitter but ultimately pointless controversy over the editorship of the *American Sociological Review* (ASR), our premier journal. I spent Sunday on my duff, trying to pay attention to the business of the committee but wishing I were back at the races. *What did I think of the incoming president's remarks on the ASR controversy?* What did I think of Jeff Gordon's chances to mount a late-season charge and capture a third straight Winston Cup championship? *Should the committee approve the proposal from the Community and Urban Sociology Section to establish its own journal?* Where will NASCAR find the race dates to fuel its coming expansion? *When in December will it be convenient to meet again?* How long before Darlington, the next race I was scheduled to attend?

Mixing the business of academia with the pleasure of stock-car racing was, I saw, a bad idea, and I resolved not to do so again. I passed the time trying mightily to persuade myself that the business of the publications committee mattered (to me? my family? my profession? the world?) in a way that stock-car racing did not, that the ASR brouhaha was somehow ontologically more meaningful or important than any question you could formulate about racing. But, for the life of me, I was not convinced. I was surprised by my own conclusion that the minutiae of my profession seemed as nothing in comparison to the weekly life-and-death blood duel that is the Winston Cup.

3

Racin' Basics

Many of the people I've talked to about my NASCAR love affair tell me they "just don't get it."[1] They have no problem understanding the thrill of being at a happening with a couple hundred thousand other people. But the racing itself? What's *that* all about? Just a bunch of guys driving around in a circle — right?

Wrong.

Skeptics misperceive automobile racing as an activity of relentless sameness. A few dozen cars go round and round, lap after lap, with only the possibility of on-track carnage to relieve the tedium. So our theme here is *variability* — in track geometry and conditions, in the cars themselves and how they are prepared ("set up") for the race, and in how the drivers and teams respond to these variable forces and conditions.

There is a superficial monotony in all sports that slackens only after you learn to appreciate the finer points of the contest. If, for example, you don't know *something* about the give-and-go or the zone defense or what it means to set a pick, basketball is an hour or two of incomprehensible silliness. If you have no appreciation *at all* for the subtle variations that golfers confront every hole, a round of championship golf makes no more sense than a brisk round of Putt-Putt. And let's not even mention hockey. So, if you too "just don't get it," this chapter's for you.

Alert: If you are a serious race fan, much of what follows will be elementary. But if you're new to the sport, or a protofan, or if you just want to know why your husband spends all Sunday afternoon glued to the weekend Winston Cup event when he could be watching football, then an introduction to racin' basics is just what you need.

Geometry and Physics . . .

. . . and if that seems a bit heady, please bear with me: our path is short and the important lessons are all intuitive.

Let's start by asking what it would be like to drive around in a *circle*. Not to be pedantic, but a circle is an ellipse with a constant radius — perfectly round, in other words, and just what we'd expect from a good circle. A perfectly circular track, then, has no straightaways and no corners either — it's just one long constant-radius turn.

Let's also assume that the track has a constant "pitch" or "banking," the degree to which the track is tilted away from the horizontal. Most of the corners in Winston Cup racing are banked with a tilt that varies from 6 to 36 degrees, with slight banking also on most of the straightaways. For reasons that are obvious when you think about it, the steeper the banking, the faster a car can go through the turn.

A circular track with constant pitch would be said to have a *constant geometry* — every spot on the track would be identical to every other spot. And that constant geometry would in turn compel all the physical forces acting on the cars (gravity, momentum, friction) to operate through fixed "vectors" — just a fancy way of saying that the laws of motion would push on the car with constant forces exerted in constant directions. Drivers could only respond by applying constant compensating forces through the steering wheel and gas pedal. They'd still need to decelerate and accelerate to get into and out of the pits and maybe to avoid running into other race cars, but nothing about the track itself would require any sort of variable response from the driver. No, you would only have to cock the steering wheel just enough to maintain the proper turning radius, get the car going as fast as it could go without ramming into the retaining wall (we'll call that the maximum steerable speed), set the cruise control, and kick back. Compared to real racing, driving around in a circle would, indeed, be boring.

You can try this for yourself by finding a large, empty parking lot that is free of obstructions. After-hours at the local mall works well. Turn the steering wheel to any comfortable angle then accelerate up to some comfortable speed. Hold the steering angle firm and the speed constant. You are now driving around in a circle. Having fun? After four or five loops, probably not.

Now, let's tweak the track geometry—let's grab that perfect circle and stretch it into an oval (an ellipse with a variable radius). What we've created are straightaways and turns. The straightaways provide an opportunity to accelerate the cars and the corners impose a need to decelerate them. Getting around the oval track as quickly as possible involves far more than finding and holding your maximum steerable speed. You must accelerate down the straightaways as hard as the horsepower and distance allow. (This, basically, is drag racing. Drag racers compete on perfectly straight, completely flat quarter-mile tracks. Whoever can accelerate the hardest and get to the end of the quarter mile first, wins.) But there's a corner at the end of every straightaway that you have to get through in one piece, and that requires deceleration—scrubbing off enough speed so you can steer the car successfully through the corner rather than have it be carried by its own momentum up into the wall. The need to back off in the corners, by just so much, and then get back on the gas again once you are safely through, is what makes stock-car racing different from driving around in a circle.

Again, you can try for yourself. Once you have tired of driving around in circles in the mall parking lot, use a pair of light poles to redefine your "track" so that it has straightaways and turns. Accelerate toward one of the poles, slow down enough to get around it (don't take the curve too tight, now!), then step on the gas again as you accelerate back toward the other pole to start the whole process over. You will notice at once that you can't settle in on any particular speed or steering angle and that getting your car around this oval as fast as you can is incomparably more difficult than finding and holding some maximum steerable speed while you were driving around in your circle.

Automobile racing, you see, is like playing *The Price is Right* against Newton's Laws of Motion. In the game show, contestants must guess the price of various objects, and the winning guess is the one that comes closest to the real price *without going over,* even by a penny. Likewise, track geometry, the laws of motion, and physical conditions determine a maximum speed at which a car of fixed characteristics can be driven through a given corner. The challenge for drivers is to find that maximum speed *without going over,* even by a smidgen. Err on the low side and other cars will be faster—you lose. Err on the high side and you will slam into the wall—again, you lose. The winning driver is the one who gets it "just right," who keeps his car right on the edge *without going over.*

Driving around in a circle provides no opportunity to accelerate (once your maximum steerable speed has been attained), no need to decelerate (except to pit or avoid a wreck), and no particular talent at negotiating corners (a circular track doesn't have corners). A track of variable geometry, in contrast, imposes variable forces; the ability of drivers to compensate smoothly, completely, and fearlessly for these variable forces and keep the car going as fast as the physics allow it to go is driving *skill.* And it is the display of skill in competition against others of essentially equivalent skill that makes all sports, and certainly motorsports, exciting.

Thus, ironically, part of the challenge and therefore the excitement of stock-car racing is that the competitors don't drive around in circles after all.

The racing version of *The Price is Right* can be played at any speed. The issue is not how fast you are going in absolute terms but how close you can come to the maximum speed made possible by the physics and geometry of a given track. On short, flat tracks (for example, Martinsville Speedway in Virginia, the shortest and nearly the flattest of the Winston Cup venues), that maximum speed is not much faster than interstate speeds. The fastest qualifying lap turned at Martinsville in 1999 was by Tony Stewart and was a tick faster than 95 mph. I've driven a car that fast a few times and you probably have too—on the open interstates of the rural South, it often seems like *everybody* is going 95 mph. But when you or I blast down the interstate at what feels like breakneck speed, we are still going slower, and usually much slower, than we could theoretically go. In fact, few people have ever even come *close* to driving their cars as fast as they possibly could—doing so would scare most people witless.

When you or I drive our cars, even when we drive fast, we always leave plenty of room for error. We leave plenty of space between ourselves and the next car, plenty of distance to slow down if we need to, plenty of excess turning ability as we head into the corners. We stay *comfortably* inside the limits of the car, the road conditions, and our driving ability. And there, exactly, is the difference between racing and everyday driving. A race driver who stayed *comfortably* within the limits of the car, the conditions, and his driving skill would not be a competitive driver. To repeat: If he is going any slower than the laws of motion make possible, then other cars will be faster and he'll end up at the back of the pack. If, on the other hand, he tries to go any faster than conditions allow, his day will end with an abrupt, unpleasant meeting with the wall. A race driver is always searching for the limit, the maximum speed possible under given conditions, but never exceeding it, getting the car to the edge, the boundary between control and disaster, but never going over. Racing demands the skill to find that boundary; the mental acuity and physical stamina to stay there, virtually error-free, for four or five hundred miles; and the courage to do so without flinching out on a track with several dozen other drivers all trying to accomplish the same thing. There is much more to it than "drive fast, turn left."

The skeptic responds: "Okay, *okay,* OKAY! You've convinced me that stock-car racing is not 'driving around in a circle.' It's driving around a closed, irregular ellipse that has moderately variable geometry. Just like you said, I went to the mall and, yeah, I agree, it was harder to race around the light poles than to drive around in a circle. But after four or five laps, racing around the light poles got to be routine, too — the same basic thing over and over. Isn't a stock-car race the same basic thing over and over — accelerate, decelerate, turn, repeat — and not for four or five laps but four or five hundred mind-numbing miles? I still don't get it."

Here our skeptical friend fails to appreciate the difference between driving fast, which is something many of us do every chance we get, and driving a car somewhere near its absolute physical limits, which is something practically none of us have done even once. The nearest most of us have ever come to the sensation is when we are driving out somewhere on a back-country road, half paying attention, and suddenly find ourselves at the front end of a turn that we are going too fast to negotiate successfully. It's an experience that quickens the senses. We slam on the brakes, crank the steering wheel hard, and just pray that the car sticks to the turn and comes out the other side in one piece. That fearful sensation of being on the brink of disaster is something racers must confront every corner of every lap.

When you are driving a car near its physical limits, ridiculously small changes in the conditions create preposterously large consequences in how the car handles and how fast it can go. (People have trouble appreciating this point precisely because they have no experience driving a car anywhere near its physical limits.) For example, cars begin a race with a full tank of gas. As the race proceeds, the fuel is burned off, and that changes both the total weight of the car and how that weight is distributed over the four wheels—and, believe it or not, those changes have a noticeable effect on how the car handles. (Did you ever notice how the handling of your car changes as you use up your fuel? No, of course not—you are never close enough to the car's real limits to notice very subtle changes in its handling or performance.) After a pit stop, the tires on a race car are relatively cool. As the laps tick off, the tires heat up, the air pressure rises—the handling is affected. (Would you be able to tell the difference a half-pound of pressure in each tire makes in how your car gets through a tight corner?) What looks to our skeptical friend like the same old thing, lap in and lap out, is in fact a continuous process of adapting to changing conditions, all the while trying to keep the car going as fast as those changing conditions allow.

Even track geometry can change over the course of the day. During a race, bits of tire rubber and other racing debris ("marbles") accumulate at the top of the corners and that can narrow the negotiable "line" through the curves appreciably—racing strategy must be altered to accommodate the change. As the day wanes and shadows lengthen, the track cools—speeds increase. Or, alternatively, as the race proceeds, racing residue (oil, fuel, water, rubber) accumulates and the track gets slicker—speeds decrease. Slight changes in temperature, wind velocity or direction, aerodynamics (rubbing fenders with a competitor), weight distribution (a shock absorber beginning to wear), and a hundred other factors create variations to which crews (during pit stops) and drivers (during the race) must respond. No, it is *not* the "same thing over and over." There can be, and frequently is, a new set of circumstances to contend with on every single lap.

The Tracks

And if there's not something different every lap, then there's certainly something different every weekend. As the Winston Cup racers proceed through the season, they race at different tracks and the tracks too are highly variable, each posing unique challenges.

In 1999, the Winston Cup points season was thirty-four races contested on twenty-one tracks in seventeen states, beginning with the Daytona 500 on February 14 (Valentine's Day) and ending with the NAPA Auto Parts 500 at the Atlanta Motor Speedway on November 21.[2] Winston Cup racing thus joins baseball as the only major American sports whose seasons begin and end in the same calendar year. And it is the only sport whose premier event (the Daytona 500) opens, rather than closes, the season.

Numerous sources provide graphics showing the shape, banking, and other characteristics of the twenty-one Winston Cup tracks. If you leaf through one of these sources, you will see at once that while many of the tracks are symmetrical, most are not and not one is circular. Also, with the exception of the Lowe's Motor Speedway in Charlotte and the Texas Motor Speedway in Ft. Worth (which are identical in length and pitch), the tracks are all unique, each unlike every other.

So what?

That each track is unique means that each weekend, success requires a different combination of skills and different set-ups on the cars, and that adds to the competition and excitement. Highly skilled short-track racers are often less skilled at negotiating big high-banked ovals; a driver equally adept at every venue is a rare bird indeed. That many tracks are asymmetrical means that the optimal mix of driving skills and car set-ups isn't necessarily constant even from one end of a track to the other. Asymmetrical tracks pose special challenges, a point to which we return later.

There are numerous points of difference from track to track, some obvious, some not. First, the tracks vary dramatically in shape. Two (Sears Point and Watkins Glen) are road-racing courses with numerous twists and turns in both directions. Many are "dog-leg" ovals with a bend in what would otherwise be one of the straightaways (this configuration maximizes the seating along the front stretch); several are "tri-ovals" with three major bends rather than two; and the remainder are elongated, more or less symmetrical, ovals (usually "squared" ovals with straightaways that are straight, not parabolic).

Secondly, the venues vary in length. Martinsville is the shortest (.526 miles) and Talladega is the longest (2.66 miles). In general, big tracks have long straightaways and lots of room to accelerate: longer tracks mean higher speeds. But the tracks also vary in how steeply they are banked in the corners. In general, steeper banking allows the cars to go through the turns more quickly, whereas flatter corners require more deceleration: steeper banking also means higher speeds. To illustrate the effect, the tracks at Bristol and Martinsville are about the same length—.533 miles and .526 miles respectively—but the corners at Martinsville are relatively flat (twelve degrees of banking) whereas the corners at Bristol are the most steeply banked of the seventeen tracks (thirty-six degrees). The fastest qualifying lap ever at Bristol, by Rusty Wallace in April 1999, was just over 125 mph—or 30 mph faster than the fastest lap at Martinsville. Banking makes a *big* difference in how fast you can get around the track.

Some points of statistical trivia: It is precisely 33.35 miles around the twenty-one venues combined. The average track is 1.588 miles long, and the average banking is 19.3 degrees. At 1.54 miles, the track at Atlanta comes closest to the average length, and with twenty-four degrees of banking in the turns, it is also within five degrees of the average pitch. So, if you want to experience an "average" Winston Cup race, Atlanta is the place to go. The qualifying record at Atlanta is held by Geoff Bodine, who got around the 1.54-mile oval in 28.074 seconds (197.478 mph) in November 1997. That's quick!

I divide the Winston Cup tracks into four categories: short tracks (less than a mile), superspeedways (a mile or more), road courses (any track that requires both left and right hand turns), and what I call megaspeedways (Daytona and Talladega). Each kind of track poses its own special challenges. Short tracks have limited opportunities to accelerate and usually have tight, narrow corners, so the premium is on braking, cornering, and handling more than on sheer speed. Short-track racing is bumper-to-bumper, side-by-side, with lots of fender-banging, tire-rubbing, and yellow flags. For my money, it is the most exciting stock-car racing of all despite the slower speeds.

Superspeedways have long straightaways and wide (usually high-banked) corners. Braking and handling are less important, and the premium is on aerodynamics, horsepower, and speed. Cup cars usually hit 180 or even 190 mph on the superspeedway straightaways, so if sheer speed is your thing, then these are your tracks. Still, the corners in the superspeedways (unlike the megaspeedways) require deceleration going in and acceleration coming out, and in that respect they are similar to short tracks and road courses.

The road courses require equal facility at left- and right-hand turns; sometimes have long straightaways followed by extremely tight, narrow corners; and usually have hills and other variations. Racing purists consider road tracks to be the only real challenge and think that oval-track racing is boring. On the other hand, many NASCAR fans despise the road courses and would rather these races not even count in the annual points championship. Perhaps the enmity here is the association between road courses and European-style racing—road racing seems vaguely un-American.

The two megaspeedways represent a special category. Both are immense tracks with long straightaways leading into wide, steeply-banked, large-radius corners. The width, pitch, and radius of the corners at Daytona and Talladega mean that the cars can take them wide-open—there's no need to decelerate to get into or through the turns. Thus, racing on megatracks is not unlike racing on a circular track: you find your line, mash on the gas, and go flat-out, wide open, for 500 miles.

Based on what I've said about circular tracks, you might think that the megaspeedway races would be boring, but what these tracks lack in intricacy they make up in competitiveness and sheer, flat-out speed. In 1987, Bill Elliott turned a qualifying lap at the Winston 500 in Talladega of nearly 213 mph, the fastest recorded Winston Cup lap ever. In all, nine drivers qualified for that race at speeds over 210 mph. (The first lap of over 200 mph in a NASCAR stock car was turned in by Buddy Baker in 1970, and fifty-eight separate drivers have posted qualifying laps of 200 mph or more since then. Cale Yarborough did this fifteen times, which is the record.) With technological advances since 1987, today's Winston Cup cars could qualify on these tracks at speeds well above 230 mph.

So, why don't they? As speeds crept ever higher in the 1980s, concerns for the safety of drivers and spectators mounted. Two-ton stock cars running at speeds in the 200-plus mph range pose serious risks to drivers and fans. Tires can shred unexpectedly; minor spin-outs can become major multicar crashes; small lapses in judgment or even attentiveness can turn lethal in, literally, the blink of an eye.[3] (Indy and CART cars run even faster but weigh half as much, so the energy released when they come apart is considerably less. Those cars are also designed to absorb most of the energy when they crash and so are less lethal.) In short, you do not want big, hefty pieces of tire and car flying around the track or into the stands at 220 mph.

To hold speeds down and keep Winston Cup racing relatively safe for all parties, in 1988 NASCAR began requiring "restrictor plates" at Daytona and Talladega. These are thin metal plates that sit between the carburetors and the intake manifolds and severely limit the flow of air and fuel into the engines. The practical effect of the restricted airflow is to cut the horsepower from about 750 hp to about 450 hp. In addition to reducing the maximum speed, this also slows acceleration such that the cars take a full lap and then some to get completely up to speed. Still, even with these plates, the cars manage to run at well over 190 mph on both the megatracks.

With all the cars running at reduced horsepower, wide-open all the way around, the other practical effect of the restrictor plates is to keep the cars bunched up in large packs from start to finish, and that also adds to the megatrack excitement. Compared to other venues, the megatracks reward aerodynamics and the driver's skill at drafting, which is a subtle trick of aerodynamics that allows two cars running nose to tail to go considerably faster than either could go on its own. At a track like Talladega, drafting can be *everything*. Also, as can well be imagined, large packs of cars running nose-to-tail at speeds near 200 mph often result in spectacular, although rarely fatal, multicar crashes.

In addition to shape, length, and pitch, the tracks also vary in composition (concrete vs. asphalt), in track width, in orientation toward the sun, and in a dozen other ways. Yep, even orientation towards the sun can make a difference. A shady track is relatively cool, and cool surfaces give the tires more "bite," so speeds increase. A hot track tends to be slick, the tires don't get as much traction, so speeds decrease. Concrete is harder than asphalt and changes less with temperature; asphalt gets progressively softer and slicker as the temperature rises. Different track compositions wear out the tires at different rates and thus require different racing strategies. Wide tracks offer numerous opportunities to pass and feature two-wide and sometimes even three-wide racing all the way around; narrow tracks are more challenging to negotiate and drivers must pick their passing opportunities wisely. Variation — that's the name of the Winston Cup game.

Racing shares with a few other sports (golf, certainly, and baseball, to some extent) this distinction: the venues themselves are part of the challenge and an inherent part of what makes the sport interesting. Serious golf fans will expound at length on the relative virtues of Pebble Beach or Augusta National or English Turn; the gross and subtle differences from course to course (and on a finer scale, from hole to hole) make golf the game it is. So, too, with baseball, although to a lesser degree: Fenway Park is part of the appeal of baseball to a Red Sox fan, and Wrigley Field likewise to a Cub fan. Stock-car racing is the same in this respect and, of course, unlike the NBA or NHL, whose teams compete week after week on fields and courts of fixed shape, composition, and dimension.

The Cars

Newcomers to the sport of stock-car racing sometimes think that each Winston Cup team has a car they haul around from track to track (and perhaps a second car, a backup, to be used in case the primary car is wrecked). They think the Number 24 Du Pont Chevrolet they see racing at Darlington is the same car they see the following weekend at Richmond. Wrong again. A car built from the ground up to go as fast as possible around a track like Darlington is very different from one built from scratch to race on a short track like Richmond, and both will differ significantly from a car built to run on road courses such as Watkins Glen.

An essential point about Winston Cup racing is that each kind of track requires a different kind of car with different chassis, aerodynamics, suspensions, springs, shock absorbers, brakes, cooling systems, transmissions, and rear-end differentials. And since there are four kinds of tracks, so, too, are there four basic types of Winston Cup stock cars: short-track cars, road-course cars, superspeedway cars, and restrictor-plate cars. Depending on the track, then, "the" Number 24 Du Pont Chevrolet might be any one of four different cars — all with nearly identical bodies and paint jobs, but in other ways radically different.

And not just any one of four: for each primary car there must also be a backup. (Without exception, teams bring two complete cars to every

A Winston Cup show car built by legendary car owner Junie Donleavy and parked outside the Suburban Lodge in Stockbridge, Georgia, where we stayed during our trip to the NAPA 500. "Show cars" are one-time race cars that have become obsolete but can be dolled up to resemble the real thing. The "real" Ford Number 90 was driven at the Atlanta race by Ed Berrier, who finished twenty-fifth. The photo clearly shows the decals that adorn every Winston Cup race car and that make the car eligible for various contingency prizes. If this were a real Winston Cup race car, the Suburban Lodge would have paid something around $5 million to have its logo displayed on the hood and rear quarter panels.

race.) At minimum, then, there have to be eight Number 24 Du Pont Chevrolets. Usually there are more than eight. Most teams will have a few additional cars around the shop to press into service if the need arises;[4] one, two, or several new cars under construction; and any number of "show cars" that, while not used for racing, are towed from shopping malls to sponsors' sales meeting to promotional events in an effort to satisfy sponsor and fan demands for a close-up view of these magnificent racing machines.[5] When Ricky Rudd sold his Winston Cup race team at the end of the 1999 season, his Number 10 Ford proved to be eighteen separate race cars.

There are some parameters that are the same for all Winston Cup cars, regardless of type. All the cars weigh at least 3,400 pounds "race ready" (loaded with oil, water, and fuel, but not including the driver). The wheelbases are fixed at 110 inches. The motors must be "small block" V-8s with a displacement between 350 and 358 cubic inches. The maximum compression ratio is 12:1. There are further restrictions governing the minimum ground clearance, the height and angle of the rear spoiler, and just about everything else. But within these fixed parameters, which are all spelled out in detail in the Winston Cup rule book, there is a great deal of wiggle room in the aerodynamics, the chassis and suspension, the brakes, even the motors to some extent, that can be exploited to create an optimal design for racing at a particular kind of track.

Why do you need different cars for different kinds of tracks? A few examples may prove helpful. In an oval-track race, all turns are to the left. As the car leans into a left-hand corner, inertial forces shift the weight to the right, which causes the car to "push" up the track towards the wall. This effect can be compensated for by tweaking the chassis and suspension to distribute more weight to the left. In a recent interview, Rusty Wallace claimed to have built a race car with 64 percent of the total weight to the left of the central axis. A road-course track has both left- and right-hand turns, so the car's chassis and suspension should be "neutral," the weight evenly distributed to either side of the central axis. More generally, the flatter the track, the more severe the tendency to lean and the greater the need for some offsetting adjustments in the car's suspension.

A short, flat track such as Martinsville features brief furious blasts of acceleration down the short straights, followed by hard braking to get into and through the corners. Short tracks require super-high-performance brakes, and even at that, Winston Cup short-track cars have special air vents in the front cowls with ducts that force air past the brakes and brake rotors to prevent overheating. (Short-track cars also have small pumps that circulate and cool the brake fluid.) These vents are obviously not aerodynamic, but that scarcely matters on a short track with a maximum speed of 100 or 125 mph. On the megaspeedways, the corners can be taken at full throttle and braking is nearly an afterthought. Brake-cooling vents would be pointless on a restrictor-plate car, first, because the brakes are rarely used and therefore do not need any special cooling, and second, because the resulting loss of aerodynamics would slow the car considerably.

The rear-end differential contains the gear at the end of the driveshaft that transmits the rotational torque of the engine to the rear wheels. The rear gear is described by a ratio, such as 6:1 or 3:1, which is the number of times the motor has to turn to rotate the rear wheels once. A high gear ratio (also called a "short gear") optimizes acceleration but limits the top speed and is therefore found in short-track cars for which the top speeds are slow anyway. A short gear keeps the engine revved up as the car runs through the corners, providing quicker acceleration out of the turn and down the straight. A low gear ratio (or "tall gear"), in contrast, limits acceleration but gives a much higher top-end speed and would therefore be found in cars built to run on the superspeedways. A road course with both tight corners and long straightaways would require something in between.

Teams can also trade horsepower for fuel efficiency. The fuel cell (or "bladder") in a Winston Cup car holds exactly twenty-two gallons of high-performance racing fuel, and the cars get between four and five miles per gallon. Just where in that narrow range a car's mileage falls can make a critical difference in the outcome. At four miles per gallon, a race car could go eighty-eight miles before it needed fuel, so completing a 500-mile race would require *five* pit stops (taking into account the full tank with which a car begins, that would be 6 tanks × 88 miles per tank = 528 miles). At five miles per gallon, a car could go 110 miles per tank, so a 500-mile race would therefore require only *four* pit stops for fuel. A car that was a tick slower to begin with might still win the race because it would need one fewer pit stop along the way.

There are also big differences — more variation — between how the cars are set up for qualifying and how they are set up for the race. Qualifying times determine the starting order, faster cars starting toward the front. In qualifying, the car and driver compete only against the clock; the objective is to run a qualifying lap (sometimes two laps) at the highest possible speed. The durability of the engine is of little concern — it only has to last for a few miles. Fuel efficiency doesn't matter, nor does the cooling system, nor do a lot of other things that matter critically in the race itself. On race day, however, the engine must be capable of sustained high speeds for four, five, or six hundred miles. Since, as the saying goes, "to finish first, first you have to finish," durability is essential for the race itself; some horsepower can be sacrificed to increase reliability and mileage. So, again, different engines are used for these two different purposes.

Also, racing conditions often change between qualifying and race day.

Usually, qualifying takes place on Friday and the race is run on Sunday. In the interim, the weather might change: cloudy and cool (therefore fast) during qualification, then hot and sunny (therefore slow) for the race. At most venues, other races take place after the Winston Cup cars qualify but before the Cup race. Each intervening race deposits a residue of tire rubber and motor fluids on the track: as the residue builds, the track gets slicker and therefore slower. On the other hand, a hard rain will wash the residue away, the result being a "green" track with better traction and higher speeds.

When Winston Cup cars are lowered from the transporters, they are initially outfitted with qualifying motors. Once qualifying is complete, those motors are pulled out of the cars and replaced with race motors. (At the same time, transmissions, rear gears, and other components might also be changed.) And since you can blow a qualifying motor on the first day of qualifying and need another for the second day, or blow a race motor during practice sessions and need another for the race, each team must bring at least four complete engines to every race (most bring five). Two complete cars, four or five complete engines, plus a slew of parts, tools, wheels, and equipment — no wonder the teams travel from race to race in immense eighteen-wheelers.

Back in the "good old days," a team would use an engine until it gave out, but being competitive in today's racing environment means having new motors for every race. In the course of a season, a team might go through forty or fifty racing engines, half that many qualifying engines, and perhaps another half-dozen engines in testing sessions. Whether purchased from engine builders such as Robert Yates (considered the premier engine builder in the business) or built from scratch in the team's own in-house facilities, each motor costs between $40,000 and $50,000. An unlucky Winston Cup team can go through a quarter-million dollars worth of engines *in a single weekend.*

Once a car, drive train, and chassis set-up have been chosen, there are endless large and small adjustments that can be and are made during practice sessions and the race to make the car faster or handle better. Often, the car is either "tighter" or "looser" than the driver wants it to be. Simplifying slightly, a "tight" race car is one with a tendency to continue going straight even as the driver attempts to make it turn. Thus, the front wheels refuse to behave; the car "under-steers." In general, the only way to avoid ramming into the wall when the car is tight is to slow down, which, understandably, drivers hate to do. A "loose" car, in contrast, is one that continues to turn ("come around") even as the driver attempts to straighten it. Here, then, it is the rear wheels that refuse to behave; the car "over-steers." If the car is just a little loose, it will "fishtail" as the driver exits the turn; if looser still, the rear end will come all the way around and put the car into a spin ("swapping ends"). In general, a loose car makes the driver stay off the gas until the turn has been fully completed and the car is aimed straight down the track. Whether tight or loose, the car is slower through the corners than one whose set-up is perfect ("neutral").

Winston Cup cars have large jackscrews attached to the suspension components that are used to redistribute the weight. If a car is loose, these screws can be turned to shift weight to the right; if the car is tight, turn the screw the other way and shift weight to the left. Rubber wedges can be inserted into (or removed from) the coil springs, and that will also redistribute the weight and correct the handling. Subtle changes in weight distribution can also be achieved by adjusting the air pressure in the tires. Remarkably, as little as a half-pound of air pressure, one way or the other, can make a noticeable difference.

Nineteen ninety-nine Winston Cup champion Dale Jarrett said in a recent interview, "Racing is about handling. It's a matter of getting your car to handle. You do that by changing the things they allow you to change."[6] Out there at the edge, tiny advantages make all the difference.

As I've said, asymmetrical tracks pose special challenges. On a symmetrical track, the car will tend to perform identically at both ends. If the car is loose, it's loose everywhere and some compensating adjustment can be made. On an asymmetrical track, the car can be perfect at one end and awful at the other. Darlington International Raceway is "too tough to tame" (the track's nickname) because it is an egg-shaped oval. The first and second turns have much larger radii and a different pitch from the third and fourth turns, so the optimal set-up at one end cannot also be optimal at the other. Where do you want to be fast? Where can you afford to be slow? Crews spend the entire race chasing a workable compromise. Watching teams juggle the relevant variables, tinkering here, tweaking there, always looking for the small adjustments that make them quicker or more sure-footed — why, that's half the fun you can have at the races. (The competition on the track is the other half.)

The Teams

Stock-car racing is often misperceived as a sport "with an individually oriented focus as opposed to a team concept" but race teams are real teams, no less than football or basketball teams, and each member makes a contribution to the overall outcome. There are forty-five or fifty race teams who compete every weekend for one of the Winston Cup's forty-three starting positions, and every year there are another fifteen or twenty teams that qualify for at least one event. In 1998, sixty-eight teams competed in at least one of the thirty-three points races; of these, only seventeen competed in all thirty-three.

A basic Winston Cup team consists of forty or so people (some teams have more than that, lots more). The heart and public identity of the team is the driver, but the driver's skill will count for nothing if his team does not put him in a competitive car. Richard Huff says you should think of the driver as the quarterback, but the real quarterback, the guy who calls the shots, is the crew chief. You should really think of the driver as the star running back, the crew chief as the quarterback, the pit crew as the offensive line, and the remainder of the team as the support personnel.

Winston Cup *drivers* must be at least sixteen years old. Ironically, they are not required to have a valid driver's license. Among currently active drivers, the youngest to start as a full-time Winston Cup competitor was Kyle Petty, who broke in when he was only eighteen. The oldest: Dick Trickle, who was forty-eight when he won Rookie-of-the-Year honors in 1989. Usually, drivers are expected to prove their mettle and skill in racing's minor leagues before they are considered for a Winston Cup ride. Most of today's top drivers started competitive racing even before they were teenagers, driving quarter-midgets, go-karts, or sprint cars, then spent their teens and twenties in Busch, ASA, ARCA, or other "second-tier" competitions before moving up to the Winston Cup.

As a result, Winston Cup rookies are usually older than rookies in other sports. The first Rookie of the Year was Shorty Rollins, who was twenty-nine years old when he won the award in 1958. Altogether, there were forty-one Rookies of the Year as of 1998, and the average age of these drivers when the award was bestowed was 30.4 years. The youngest was Ricky Rudd, who won the award in 1977 at age twenty-one. Richard Petty, Rob Moroso, and Jeff Gordon all took Rookie-of-the-Year honors at age twenty-two. Joining Trickle on the other end of the age distribution is Jimmy Hensley, who was forty-seven when he won the award in 1992. While there are some prominent exceptions, successful drivers usually don't break into the circuit until their late twenties or early thirties.

Stock-car racers remain in active competition long after athletes in other sports have retired. According to sports physiologists, age at peak performance in selected sports is lowest for women's tennis players, who peak at about twenty-four to twenty-six, and highest for auto racers, who peak at thirty-five to thirty-six.[7]

Indeed, the fairly large number of middle-aged guys who still compete in the Winston Cup adds to the appeal of the sport to aging baby boomers like me. Harry Gant won four Winston Cup races *in a row,* practically unheard of at any age, when he was fifty-one. Darrell Waltrip wrapped up his illustrious career in 2000 at age fifty-three. Dave Marcis and Dick Trickle are both near sixty and still race. Herschel McGriff raced until he was sixty-six. Richard Petty won his last race (at Daytona on 4 July 1984) two days after his forty-seventh birthday and continued to race competitively until his retirement at age fifty-five. It was my pleasure to witness Petty's last race at Daytona (in July 1992), where he qualified on the outside of the front row (second fastest) and led the first lap. Watching the Number 43 Pontiac come out of Turn Two in the lead on that first lap was the single most thrilling experience I have ever had at the tracks. The fan reaction was indescribable: The King was *not* dead. Long live the King!

Next to the driver, the *crew chief* is the most important and best-known member of the team. The crew chief has overall responsibility for equipment and personnel, makes final decisions about how to set up the car, serves as the team's liaison to NASCAR, devises race strategy, and calls all the shots during the race. Crew chiefs like Ray Evernham, Andy Petrie, Larry McClure, Todd Parrott, Jimmy Makar, Larry McReynolds, and Robin Pemberton are NASCAR stars in their own right and are often as avidly sought by owners, sponsors, and fans as the top drivers. (Larry McReynolds spent the first half of the 2001 season doing color commentary for Fox, a role previously reserved more or less exclusively for retired

Winston Cup cars coming off Turn Two on the first lap of the 1992 Pepsi 400 at Daytona Beach. This was Richard Petty's last appearance at Daytona and that is his Number 43 STP Pontiac in the lead. This precise moment was and remains my single most exciting experience at the Winston Cup tracks.

drivers.) Four or five years ago, crew chief salaries were reported to fall in the range of $150,000 to $300,000 per year and have no doubt risen since.

The *pit crew* services the car during pit stops. A pit crew can be of any size. Usually, there are ten to twelve members but only seven are allowed over the pit wall during a stop: the jack man, who gets the car up in the air so the tires can be changed; the front and rear tire changers, who, uh, change the tires; the gas man and "gas catch man," the two team members who refuel the car; and the two tire carriers (one for the front, one for the back) who carry fresh tires from behind the pit wall to the front and rear tire changers.

In the "good old days," a driver's pit crew would be a bunch of guys from the shop who were available to travel to next weekend's race. Preparation for pit duties was minimal and performance often left much to be desired. In today's competitive environment, where a second gained or lost in the pits can spell the difference between victory and defeat, the seven men who go over the wall are a highly trained, well-choreographed team of professionals who practice daily and work out to stay in shape. Top crews can add twenty-two gallons of fuel, change all four tires, and make various chassis adjustments in as little as fifteen *seconds*. There is also an annual pit crew championship competition that dates to 1967.

Other crewmen stay behind the wall but use long implements to scrub debris off the front of the car, wash the windshield, or offer the driver a cold drink. A race day crew will also include mechanics and wrench-monkeys to work on the car in case it is damaged during the race. Minor repairs are made on pit road, but if something major goes wrong, the cars are taken to the garage area ("behind the wall"), and there is no limit other than economics to the number of persons a team can have on hand for this purpose.

An essential but often unnoticed member of the race-day team is the team *spotter*. When you go to a Winston Cup race, look around the track and locate the highest vantage point (usually, the roof of the control tower at the start-finish line). During the race, look up to this point and you will see forty-three people with binoculars and short-wave radios keeping an eagle's eye on the action. These are the spotters, and their function is to watch everything that is happening on the track and communicate relevant information to the driver. Often the spotters are the first to see a crash and will tell the driver where the wreck is and how to avoid it.

The main grandstand at Daytona. The tall structure in the middle of the photograph is the Winston Tower. Barely visible on the top of it are the team spotters, who watch the action on the track and report important developments directly to the drivers. At the large tracks such as Daytona, teams will also have spotters on the backstretch.

"Crash in Three! Go high, go high!" means that a wreck has occurred in the third turn and that the clear path around the wreck is at the top of the track. Spotters also tell their drivers where other cars are on the track or when a passing car has cleared and it is safe to get back in line. The spotter sees what the driver and crew chief cannot.

The racing crew also includes a *scorer* who keeps track of the driver's position in the race, a *transporter driver* who hauls cars, parts, and equipment from one track to the next, possibly a driver for the team RV, plus an assortment of media-relations personnel, trainers, assistants, and others.

Then there is the *shop crew,* the guys who build and maintain the cars and motors. By no means the drafty barns portrayed in *Days of Thunder,* NASCAR race shops are ultra-modern, supersophisticated automobile factories where custom racing machines are built from the ground up. Most teams build their own engines; that requires a *chief engine builder* plus numerous assistants. *Fabricators* hang sheet metal on the frame and fabricate custom body parts such as the quarter panels, rear deck lids, and rear spoilers. (About the only stock components in today's stock cars are the roofs and front hoods.) The *chassis specialist* is responsible for the internal workings of the car: suspension, brakes, shocks, springs, weight distributions. Many teams also have *gear and transmission specialists* to design, build, and maintain transmissions and differentials. Large teams also have an overall *team manager* who handles logistics and business details; a shop *foreman* (or foremen) to oversee the construction of the cars; a small army of *skilled craftsmen* (mechanics, machinists, welders) to fabricate parts and build cars; engineers, wind tunnel specialists, computer jockeys, parts manager, and purchasing agents; and a full complement of nonracing personnel: public-, media-, and sponsor-relations staff, people to manage and operate the team's auxiliary enterprises, secretaries, receptionists, bookkeepers, accountants, office managers, pilots, cooks and caterers, and custodial personnel. So it is by no means an exaggerated guess that a basic team will consist of forty or so members. Some teams, particularly the multicar teams, are much larger than forty. Hendrick Motor Sports, which fields the Jeff Gordon entry and two others, has 200 people on the payroll.

Everyone on the race team, from the driver to the guy who sweeps up the office, is a salaried employee of the team owner. All revenues also go to the owner: race winnings, sponsors' contributions, proceeds from auxiliary enterprises, licensing and promotion fees—in a word, everything. So when I reported earlier that Jeff Gordon had won more than $9 million in a single season, it would have been more correct to say that he had won that amount for his team owner, Rick Hendrick. Gordon himself is a salaried employee (or was: He is now an equity partner with Hendrick), although no doubt handsomely compensated. Certainly, his contract contains performance bonuses that include a share of any winnings. (According to *The Official* NASCAR *Handbook,* the driver's share of winnings will vary between 10 and 50 percent.) Driver salaries are reputed to start in the middle six figures; salaries for the top drivers are no doubt somewhere in seven figures.

But the salary and share of winnings combined pale in comparison to the most lucrative piece of the Winston Cup action, the marketing, licensing, and endorsement deals that can multiply a driver's income several times over. Dale Earnhardt was not only "the greatest driver in NASCAR history" (a claim that Richard Petty fans might want to dispute) but also the all-time Winston Cup champion in marketing and memorabilia sales. Mark Howell reports that even as early as 1993, Earnhardt was grossing over $40 million per year in souvenir sales. When he won his seventh Winston Cup championship the next year, the souvenir sales for that season surpassed $50 million. In the past few seasons, including 2001, the season of his death, Earnhardt's souvenir and memorabilia sales grossed more than $100 million. There are nearly a thousand different souvenir items bearing Earnhardt's likeness, signature, or endorsement, everything from T-shirts to hats to coolers to Hot Wheels toy cars to pocket knives to shotguns. His marketability has clearly not been diminished by his passing. To the contrary, within a few days of his death in February 2001, there were more than 40,000 Dale Earnhardt items being offered for sale on eBay.

Total compensation to top drivers must therefore amount to several million dollars a year, and even chronic back-in-the-pack drivers must net several hundreds of thousands. So if you've ever wondered why an old veteran like Dave Marcis keeps at it, even though he only qualifies in about half the races he enters, rarely qualifies well, almost never finishes on the lead lap, and hasn't had a top five finish in more than a decade, the answer, or at least part of it, is that being a Winston Cup driver pays much better than a regular job. (I'm sure Marcis also loves the work.)

Other teams members also do well for themselves. Huff provides the following salary ranges. These are 1996 figures and are no doubt higher today. In contemplating these ranges, keep in mind that the average (median) before-tax income for American households in 1996 was $35,172:

Team Member	Salary
Team Manager	$100,000–200,000
Crew Chief	$150,000–300,000
Chief Engine Builder	$100,000–200,000
Shop Foreman	$40,000–60,000
Mechanics, Fabricators, Machinists	$25,000–65,000
Engineers	$40,000–125,000
Gear/Transmission Specialists	$40,000–60,000
Parts Manager	$30,000–45,000

In contrast to other professional sports, Winston Cup drivers, teams, and owners rarely divulge details about contracts or salaries. So far as I know, no driver has ever publicly complained that he should make at least as much as some other driver or demanded to be the best-paid performer in the sport; or publicly asked to be traded to another team (although drivers, crew chiefs, and other personnel do change teams regularly); or has ever "gone public" to express dissatisfaction with his team or compensation. Contract and financial bickering is not unheard of, but such disputes are never made public. NASCAR has a telling promotional slogan: "When our athletes want more money, they race for it." Somebody tell that to Dennis Rodman.

The Race

The longest Winston Cup race is the Charlotte 600 contested over the Memorial Day weekend (four hundred laps around a 1.5-mile track). The shortest is the 350-kilometer (218-mile) road race at Sears Point. The shortest oval-track races are the twice-a-season 500-lap events at Martinsville (263 miles).

All teams start every race with the same basic strategy: Keep the leader in sight (don't fall too far behind, stay on the lead lap), avoid trouble (stay away from wrecks and the wall), work on the car's performance and handling during every pit stop, and get in position to make a run at the leader at the end of the race. The cars, too, are basically identical: same weight, wheel length, displacement, compression, horsepower. Where, then, does the winning driver find an edge?

Answer: wherever he can.

No Winston Cup car can complete a race, even the shortest race, on a single tank of fuel (or a single set of tires), so pit stops are an inherent element of the competition and the overall strategy of a race. Pit stops are made either "under yellow" or "under green." A green flag pit stop is one made while the race is underway. When accidents occur or there is debris on the track or rain has started to fall, however, the yellow flag comes out to signal a "caution period." During these caution periods, all the cars slow down and get into line behind the pace car; no passing is allowed. A "yellow-flag" pit stop is one made during these caution periods.

On most tracks, if the field is under green, by the time a driver gets slowed down, into the pits, serviced, and then back up to speed, the field will have come all the way around, so the pitting driver gets a lap behind (a lap "down" to) the leaders. During caution periods, in contrast, the field is slowed; the driver can get into and out of the pits *before* the field comes around and stay on the lead lap despite having pitted. Now, if everyone pits under green, the lap you lost while you were in the pits can be gained back when the leaders pit—no big deal. And likewise if everyone pits under yellow. But what if you've just made a green-flag stop and as you are coming back onto the track the caution light goes on? Everyone who has yet to pit can now pit under yellow and in most cases they will be able to complete their stops before you've gained back the lap (or laps) you lost.

Since there is no way to know in advance when the caution flags will fly, one strategy is to avoid being the first to pit under green—stay on the track as long as you can and hope for a caution period. However, if the car's handling needs adjustment or the tires need to be replaced, every lap gets you further behind, so the sooner you correct these conditions, the better. Waiting to pit is therefore not always advisable (least of all if you are about to run out of gas).

Races vary in the number of yellow flags you can anticipate. Big, wide tracks with plenty of room for racing will have fewer wrecks and fewer cautions. Here, you can count on one or more green-flag pit stops during the race, and the timing of these stops is critical. In contrast, short, narrow tracks with lots of fender-to-fender action will produce more wrecks and more yellow flags, so pit strategy becomes less important. On a short, flat track like Martinsville, it would be unusual to run through a whole tank of fuel before something caused a yellow flag; on big, wide speedways like Michigan or Talledega, races are sometimes run entirely under green.

Deciding when to pit is one part of racing strategy; deciding just what to do during the pit stop is another. You might think that decisions about fuel and tires, at least, would be routine, but often they are not. Normally, a team will add as much fuel as possible at every stop, but if the race is nearly over, they will only want to add as much as they need to finish — the so-called splash-and-go (take on the "splash" of fuel needed to complete the race, then "go" like a bat out of hell). Adding even a gallon more fuel than necessary takes a little extra time, and that can spell the difference between winning and losing.

Ditto tires. Since new tires are faster than worn tires, a team will normally change all four tires at every stop. But sometimes it is advantageous to change just the right-side tires, thereby getting back on the track quicker and moving up in the field. (Why the right-side tires? In a left-hand turn, the weight of the car bears down on the right-side tires more heavily, so they wear out more quickly.) Jeff Gordon nailed his first Winston Cup victory (in the 1994 Charlotte 600) because in his last pit stop, his crew changed only two tires while the other leaders changed all four. This got Gordon out of the pits in first place, and he managed to hang on for the rest of the race. Since four new tires are faster than two, the other leaders would have eventually caught and passed him, but the race ended first.

Darrell Waltrip's last win, at Darlington in 1992, also resulted from clever pit strategy. It was late in the race and Waltrip was a lap down, when light rain began to fall. The other drivers took advantage of the caution period to pit, but Waltrip stayed out on the track, got his lap back, and took over the lead. A few laps later, the rain began falling more heavily and the race was stopped ("red-flagged"). The rain continued, the race was called, and Waltrip was declared the winner.

Decisions about handling are even more complicated. Getting the car to stick better in the corners may slow it in the straightaways; getting it better coming into the turns may make it worse coming out of them. Even if the objective is clear (for example, to make the car looser), many different corrections can be made to achieve that goal. Do we adjust the sway bar? Fiddle with the air pressure? Take a wedge of rubber out of the springs? Teams tweak ("dial in") the car at every stop, trying to get the handling as close to perfect as possible, so that in the closing laps they can make a run at the leaders.

It is easy to be fast if you don't care about fuel efficiency or tire wear, but then you'll need to pit more often. If caution periods are going to be frequent, saving tires and fuel will be less important. But on long green-flag runs, saving the tires early may make you much faster than the rest of the field later, and a talented driver can turn the difference into a win. Being able to go the distance on your last tank of gas may let you beat faster but less efficient cars that need a splash-and-go in the final laps.

A final element in every team's pit strategy is to avoid mistakes. If the driver speeds down Pit Road, NASCAR will assess a "stop-and-go" penalty: the driver is required to re-enter the pits, come to a complete stop, then get back into the race. Penalties will also be levied for various other infractions: too many men over the wall, failure of the driver to get the car completely inside the pit box during a stop, running over an air hose when exiting the pit box, having an errant tire roll out of the pit box and onto Pit Road, and so on through a long list.

Races are won or lost in the pits. That's an old racing cliché. The pit crew that changes four tires, adds twenty-two gallons of fuel, cleans the windshield, gives the driver a drink of water, and makes a chassis adjustment *one second faster* than the competition will often improve the car's track position more than the driver can do in thirty laps of racing. That's why pit crews practice daily, stay in shape, and videotape and review their performance at every pit stop. At racing speed, one second in the pits translates into the length of a football field on the track.

On-track strategy also makes a difference, of course. On big tracks, drafting is essential and drivers who do it well fare much better than those who don't. Making correct decisions about when, where, and how to pass other cars is also essential, especially as the lead cars come around and begin to lap the field. Errors in the pits can be costly, but errors on the track can be fatal, and even if not fatal, they can put you far behind or even out of the race.

The Championship

Part of Big Bill France's genius was to recognize that fans would want a single national champion crowned at the end of every racing season, and over the years a number of different scoring systems have been used for the purpose. The current system, invented by Bob Latford and instituted in 1975, has suffered nearly constant criticism, mainly because it seems to reward consistently strong finishes more than wins.

The 1999 Winston Cup season featured thirty-four points races (up from thirty-three in 1998). A points race is one that earns drivers, owners, and teams points toward the annual championship. There are always two other races each year—the Bud Shootout at Daytona and The Winston at Charlotte—that are not points races but are more in the nature of All-Star contests; in a couple of recent years, there was also an exhibition race in Japan after the regular season was over. While these are great fun to watch and the competition is as keen as in any other event, the results do not bear on the championship.

A surprising number of fans complain that the championship scoring system is "too complicated," but that is not the problem. You earn points according to where you finish. The winner gets 175 points, the second place finisher gets 170 points, and on down the list. Five points separate each of the top six finishers; four points separate each of the seventh-through eleventh-place finishers; and three points separate all other finishing positions. So, twenty-first place (the last car in the upper half of the field) earns 100 points; last place (forty-third) earns 34. What could be simpler than that?

There is one small complication that involves "bonus points." A driver earns five bonus points for leading *any* lap and five additional points for leading the *most* laps. So it is advantageous to lead a lap if you can—as advantageous as finishing second rather than third and more advantageous than finishing eleventh rather than twelfth. Five points here and there don't seem like much but they add up over the season. At the end of 1996, Jeff Gordon had amassed 170 bonus points — as many points as you get for finishing second in a points race. Terry Labonte, the 1996 champion, earned 130 bonus points during the season, and it was good that he did: his championship points total (4,657) was only thirty-seven points better than Gordon's (4,620).

Bonus points mean that the race winner must earn at least 180 points (a driver must lead at least one lap — the last — to win) and can earn as many as 185 (if he also leads the most laps). The same scoring system is used in every race. Points accumulate from race to race; the Winston Cup champion is the driver who has amassed the most points at season's end.

So, what's the problem?

Several things. First, many fans feel that some races are more important or more challenging than others and should count more heavily in determining the championship. Why should a race at Martinsville (a mere 263 miles on a short track) count for as much as a 600-mile event at Charlotte? And why, for God's sake, should a win on a *road course* count for as much as a victory at Darlington or Daytona or Talladega or some other manly venue?

Second, the scoring system rewards consistent strong finishes as much as victories. The winner will receive at least 180 points, but the second place finisher can also earn 180 points if he happens to lead the most laps. So it is possible to win the race but not move up *even a point* in the championship battle. That doesn't seem right to many fans. With the spread in points from position to position as narrow as it is, and with the possibility of earning bonus points to make up some of the difference, a driver who never wins a race but finishes consistently in the top five or top ten might earn more points than a hard-charging driver (such as Junior Johnson) who won a lot of races but also blew up a lot of motors and often failed to finish. Fans complain, not without some justification, that the points system encourages drivers to be conservative, to finish and finish well, of course, but not to let it all hang out in a blood duel for victory.

This concern is not hypothetical. In 1992, Alan Kulwicki won only two of the twenty-nine races, but he had seventeen top ten finishes and thereby won the Winston Cup championship. Second place in the championship battle went to Bill Elliott, who had won five races; third place, to Davey Allison, who had also won five races. In 1996, Terry Labonte won the Winston Cup championship with only two victories but twenty-four top ten finishes in thirty-one races; the year's second-place finisher, Jeff Gordon, won ten races; Rusty Wallace won five; Dale Jarrett won four. In fact, from the time the current scoring system was implemented in 1975 until the close of the 1999 season, the driver with the most wins had been the Winston Cup champion only ten times. In twelve seasons, at least one driver (and sometimes several) had more victories than the eventual champion, and in the remaining three seasons, at least one other driver had as many wins as the eventual champion. It rankles fans that the year's winningest driver is not always (not even *usually*) the champion.

It is easy enough and mildly entertaining to sit down on a Saturday afternoon with a year's worth of race results in one hand and a calculator in the other, devise variations on the points system, and see what difference it makes. Surprisingly, most plausible variations end up crowning the same champion. For example, you can increase the importance of winning races by widening the point spread between first and second to ten points rather than five. But if you leave everything else the same, this system crowns the same champion in all but two of the past twenty-five seasons. You can tinker with various algorithms for distributing points according to finishing position; you can award five bonus points for finishing on the lead lap as well as for leading a lap or leading the most laps; you can award points for leading laps proportionate to the number of laps led; but no matter what you do, when you recalculate the final standings, you get pretty much the same results. The only system I've found that makes a big difference is simply awarding the championship to the driver with the most victories, but then no driver outside the top five (or so) would have any real incentive to finish a race. So fans, I think, should be happy with the system now in place. Warts and all, under the present system, when the heavy hitters head to Atlanta for the last race of the season, the championship is usually still up for grabs, and there aren't many professional sports of which that can be said.[8]

Sanctioning Bodies

Stock-car racing is the most popular but by no means the only kind of racing there is. Drag racing, Indy-car racing, Formula One racing—all these and more also enjoy large (and growing) followings. Every kind of automobile racing has its own sanctioning organizations that sponsor races, guarantee purses, formulate and enforce rules, sell broadcasting rights, and promote the sport. (And, just so you know, every type of race that features automobiles also features motorcycles, often on the same tracks.)

Drag racing features two cars at a time racing side-by-side down a flat quarter-mile track. There are various classes of drag-racing, which range from Strictly Stock four-cylinder imports to Top Fuel dragsters capable of accelerating to speeds over 300 mph. The two major sanctioning organizations for drag racing are the National Hot Rod Association (NHRA) and the International Hot Rod Association (IHRA).

Formula One or Grand Prix racing (a.k.a. "European-style" racing) involves extremely exotic racing machines competing on road courses around the world. Most internationally famous road races (for example, the Grand Prix of Monaco) are Formula One races. The sanctioning body for Formula One racing is the Fédération Internationale de l'Automobile (FIA). Tom Wolfe's famous Junior Johnson essay has this to say about Formula One: "The sportswriters caught onto Grand Prix racing first because it had 'tone,' a touch of defrocked European nobility about it, what with a few counts racing here and there, although, in fact, it is the least popular form of racing in the United States."[9]

The American analogue to Formula One racing is Indy-car racing, which involves open-wheel rear-engine roadsters competing on either road courses or on oval tracks. For years, Indy-car racing was under the auspices of Championship Auto Racing Teams (CART), but in the 1990s the owner of the Indianapolis Motor Speedway created a competing organization, the Indy Racing League (IRL), which now controls the annual May event at Indianapolis and a number of other races. The rift between CART and IRL has dulled the luster of the Indy 500 as the premier motorsports event in the country, has diminished fan enthusiasm for Indy-car racing, and has therefore been something of a boon to NASCAR. CART also sanctions the PPG–Dayton Indy Lights Championship, a minor league for aspiring CART racers.

Stock-car racing is the most popular motorsport in America today, but *sports*-car racing cannot be far behind. These races are always contested on road courses and, in an interesting departure, feature multiple classes of race car competing on the same track at the same time. The princi-

A

B

C

D

This montage shows four kinds of race car: (A) a "modified" car competing in NASCAR's Featherlite Modified Series; (B) a "sprint" car, one that was raced in the Silver Crown Series and has a young Jeff Gordon behind the wheel; (C) an "Indy" car; (D) a "stock" car, driven here by Frank Kimmel in an ARCA race at Michigan. Modifieds, sprints, and Indy cars are open-wheeled race cars. Only stock cars have fenders that protect the wheels, which therefore allows "fender-rubbing," which would be instantly catastrophic in an open-wheeled racer. And only stock cars look the least bit like the family sedan. Fender-to-fender racing in cars that look like the cars you and I drive is an essential element in NASCAR's appeal. Photo credit: International Speedway Corporation Archives.

pal sanctioning bodies for American sports-car racing are the American Racing Drivers Club (ARDC), Professional Sports Car Racing (PSCR), the International Motor Sports Association (IMSA), and the Sports Car Club of America (SCCA), the latter being the largest and most active of these associations.

Sprint cars are open-wheeled cars built to run on oval speedways; they, too, come in an astonishing array of styles and sizes: sprints, midgets, "Outlaw" cars, quarter-midgets, modifieds, and so on. Some of these classes of competition are sponsored by NASCAR and others by the United States Auto Club (USAC).

Then there is stock-car racing, of course, of which NASCAR is the best-known sanctioning body. NASCAR sponsors twelve different annual racing series. The two most popular are the stock-car series: the Winston Cup championship and the Busch Grand National competition. (Busch and Winston Cup stock cars are essentially identical except that the Busch Series requires a lower engine compression ratio.) Think of the Winston Cup as the major leagues and the Busch Series as the Triple-A minor league. (NASCAR also sponsors the Craftsman Truck Series, the Featherlite Modified Series, the Winston West and Busch North Series, the Goody's Dash Series, and a number of others.) Other important and reasonably well-known stock-car minor leagues include the Automobile Racing Club of America (ARCA), the American Speed Association (ASA), and the United Speed Alliance Racing organization (USAR).

Anything Americans drive, they also race, so there are also organizations that sponsor touring and rallying contests, Legends Car racing, classic-car racing, muscle-car competitions, off-road races of a dozen different sorts, monster-truck contests, tractor pulls, even electrical-vehicle and riding-lawnmower races. There are hundreds of local and regional organizations that sponsor and oversee automobile races, and hundreds more foreign associations that sanction motorsports contests around the world. A complete account must also mention motorcycle and boat racing, both popular, fast-growing sports. Does it look cool and go fast? If yes, then there'll be people racing it—and an association to sponsor the action.

Economics

What does it cost to field a Winston Cup team for a season? "Millions" is an imprecise but reasonable first approximation. Basic expenses include a payroll of forty or so earning an average (let's say) of $50,000 a year, so there's $2 million a year in personnel alone. Add 25 percent for fringe benefits. Then you'll need ten or twenty race cars at $75,000 or $80,000 apiece and, say, fifty engines at $40,000 apiece. So figure on two or three million bucks for your hardware. To get the team and equipment from race to race, you'll need a fully-equipped transporter ($300,000) and a hefty travel-and-expense budget (another half-million, at least). You'll also need a shop (a small factory really) and a budget for testing,

The start-finish line at the Atlanta Motor Speedway. Note the rows of transporters outside the garage areas. The team transporter hauls cars, parts, and equipment from race to race and, fully configured, represents about a $300,000 investment—comparatively speaking, a drop in the budgetary bucket for a competitive team, which will go through about $10 million in a single Winston Cup season.

engineering, and consulting. Once you get to the race, you can figure on using up ten or fifteen sets of tires in qualifying, practice, and the race itself; each set of Goodyear Racing Eagles costs $1300, so over a thirty-seven-event season, the tire bill alone will exceed a half-million dollars. Out-of-pocket costs to run each weekend, including the motors, will run somewhere between $75,000 and maybe twice that figure.

Add it all up and you are talking at least $6 million a year to race in the Winston Cup, and that's if you scrimp. Realistically, to be competitive, you'll need something closer to $8–10 million (more if you spend lavishly or have bad luck). Hendrick Motorsports fields three teams with 200 people on staff and an annual operating budget of $29 million. Amortize the cost of your race shop over its useful lifetime, allow for other unanticipated expenses, and you can easily get the cost up to $10 million a season.

Where does all this money come from? Basically, four sources: sponsors, race winnings, auxiliary income, and the owner's personal fortune. On average, major corporate sponsors of Winston Cup teams cough up

$4-6 million per year to get their names on the cars. Most top teams have one major sponsor and a handful of minor (or associate) sponsors, each good for another million, give or take. So sponsors supply most of the money.

Race winnings also add income to the team. In the 1998 season, thirty-two drivers won a million dollars or more; each of the top ten drivers won two million dollars or more; the champion, Jeff Gordon, brought home more than $9 million. Depending on the driver's contract, from 50 to 90 percent of these winnings revert to the team's coffers.

Race teams have various auxiliary enterprises that also bring in income. If you buy a Jeff Gordon T-shirt, the profit goes to Gordon (the team may also get a share), but if you buy a Du Pont Racing Team T-shirt or a Hendrick Motorsports cap, the income goes to the team. Most teams also sell off old equipment and parts to local racing operations. Most of the cars that compete in ASA and ARCA events, for example, were once Winston Cup cars. According to Huff, used parts sales alone can add up to $150,000 a year.

If sponsor dollars, race winnings, and auxiliary income are not enough to cover expenses, team owners must make up the difference out of their own pockets. But most teams turn a profit in most years. Team owner Felix Sabates stresses that Winston Cup racing "is not a hobby. I've been in it eleven years. I've made money just about every year."[10]

If you are thinking about getting into Winston Cup racing, there is one bright spot in the economics that I need to mention. Unocal provides the racing fuel (108 octane gasoline) for free. Otherwise, it's pay as you go — and to go fast, you pay in the millions.

Lost in the Land of Cotton

▓▓▓▓ The lore and literature of Darlington, fourth stop on the *Fixin'*
▓▓▓▓ *to Git* Road Tour, filled me with expectations, not all of them
hopeful. The first of NASCAR's superspeedways, Darlington hosted the inaugural Southern 500 in 1950. The 1999 event would mark the 50th anni-
versary of that famous race at the 1.366-mile oval, "The Track Too Tough
to Tame." Stroker Ace called Darlington "the cradle of southern stock
car racing . . . first of the big tracks in the Southland, the granddaddy of
them all."[1] But legendary engine builder and owner Smokey Yunick re-
calls, "Even at Darlington, if you wanted to take a piss, you had to stand
in line for an hour; there was one toilet. . . . The only drinking water available at Darlington was a spigot. There was one telephone. If you wanted
to make a call, you had to get in your car and go to a gas station."[2] A
shrine or a shit-hole? Darlington, it turns out, is plenty of both.

Chris and I left for South Carolina on Friday, September 3, and got to
Darlington around midday on Saturday, an hour after the Busch race had
ended. We pulled up to the track with no tickets in hand, no room reservations, no *nothing*. The whole weekend was a test to determine whether,
with no advance planning, you could just head off to one of NASCAR's
premier events and worry about the details once you got there. And the
fact is, you can.

Our fallback position was simple and attractive. We were planning to spend a few days after the race to lounge on the South Carolina beaches, head up the coast to Charlottesville, where we'd spend a few more days with friends, then take in the Exide Batteries 400 at Richmond on the 11th. If we couldn't get a room or tickets to the race, we'd just head directly to Myrtle Beach and spend Sunday there instead—worse fates could be imagined. My friend Steve already had our Richmond tickets, so the trip east would not be a waste even if Darlington tickets never materialized. But, of course, they did, and the happy result was my first fortnight of back-to-back Winston Cup races.

Darlington is farther off the beaten path than most NASCAR venues. You take I-20 east out of Atlanta past Columbia, South Carolina, then exit onto a two-lane highway (US 401) about fifteen miles before you get to Florence. We saw our first impromptu ticket vendors ("Tickets Bought, Sold, Traded") right at the US 401 exit and passed another twenty or thirty of them on our way to the track. There were tickets everywhere. We had no sooner parked, four or five blocks from the track, than we were offered two seats in the main grandstand overlooking the start-finish line. Price: Face value, $105 apiece. Foolishly, I turned these tickets down (the offerer looked like an extra from *Deliverance* and, I thought, just the sort of fellow who'd be passing counterfeit tickets) and went to the official ticket office to see what advice they would have for a fan in my situation. Surprisingly, over-the-counter tickets on the backstretch were still for sale. We bought two seats in the Colvin grandstand for $70 each and figured out later that the $105 tickets on the other side of the track would have been, far and away, the better bargain.

Backstretch tickets in hand, we then asked our ticket agent if she knew of any motel rooms still available in the area. She consulted a large chart labeled "LODGING" and told us there were rooms to be had at the Fairfield Inn in Hartsville, about fifteen miles away. A call on the cell phone got us a confirmed reservation in less than five minutes. For all the fretting I'd done on the drive over, we had a clean, convenient room and tickets to the Southern 500 within an hour of arriving at the track.

I've since learned that tickets to Winston Cup events are *always* available. You often pay a scalper's mark-up, but that's capitalism. Many of these tickets must originate as corporate comp tickets given to people with no interest in racing, who then gladly sell them to scalpers at, say, 80 percent of face value. The scalpers mark them up to 120 percent or so of the face value and make decent money on the deal. As the green flag nears, prices drop, and if the race has already started, any remaining tickets can be had cheaply. But selection falls off rapidly, too. Indirectly, corporate sponsors fuel the informal economy in tickets; street entrepreneurs and their customers, fans like me, benefit from the arrangement.

Despite all the races I'd been to over the years, Saturday night at the Fairfield Inn was my first night in a motel full of race fans. And full of race fans it was: in the bar, the lobby, the little coffee shop, the hallways, the parking lot—nothing but race fans everywhere. No one asked if you were in town for the race—there was no other reason to be there. No one asked who you were rooting for—fans' gimme hats, T-shirts, and other race paraphernalia made everyone's preferences clear. No one asked if you'd seen last week's race at Bristol—anyone who hadn't been at Bristol was certain to have watched the race on TV. No, these conversations were about important, nonobvious stuff. Such as, had anyone found a cheap place to buy beer? One guy mentioned a grocery store, about a mile from the inn, that was running a special on Budweiser suitcases, and a small caravan of fans set out at once—redneck Jasons in search of their Golden Fleece.

Poor souls such as we who'd missed the Busch race were treated to expressions of sympathy so sincere you'd think the hound dog had died. "Oh, that's a shame, it was a great race! I'm really sorry you had to miss it." (The possibility that you just weren't interested in the Busch race would never have occurred to anyone.) One corpulent middle-aged woman in head-to-toe Rusty Wallace gear let it be known that tomorrow would be her first time at a Winston Cup event, and no sooner had the words left her mouth than a dozen fans began telling her what to watch for, who to follow, what great fun she was going to have. One fan, himself in Jeff Burton regalia, asked her why she was rooting for Rusty Wallace. Answer: "O-o-oh, he's so *cute!*" Saturday night at the Fairfield Inn was a NASCAR Family reunion. And it's like that everywhere the Winston Cup goes racing.

By a wide margin, the number one topic of fan conversation at the Fairfield Inn was the "Earnhardt-Labonte incident." At Bristol the previous weekend, Earnhardt had bumped race leader Terry Labonte on the final lap, Labonte's car had gone into a spin, and Earnhardt had motored around to take the victory. Labonte's postrace comments had been acerbic, and Earnhardt himself had been contrite. The predominant fan opinion seemed to be that the Intimidator had stepped over the line—and to NASCAR fans, that line, between fair play and foul, although thin, is still important. So, while there seemed to be as many Earnhardt fans at Darlington as there were everywhere else we went in 1999, they were much more sedate than usual. I overheard one Kyle Petty enthusiast explaining to a Dale Earnhardt supporter just why Earnhardt's bump-and-run maneuver was unsportsmanlike and dangerous. The Earnhardt fan replied, "Oh, hell. It's that kind of shit that makes guys like you and me come to these races!" The Petty guy breathed a deep sigh, took a long draw on his frosty Coors—and agreed.

Some fans were also talking nostalgically about the popular California driver Ernie Irvan, who had just announced his retirement from Winston Cup racing, effective immediately. He had debuted at Richmond in 1987 and had wracked up fifteen wins in 313 Winston Cup races. But, five years before, Irvan had blown a tire at the Michigan Speedway and rammed head-on into the retaining wall at over 180 mph. His condition had been critical for a week, and race fans had waited nervously for the announcement that Irvan was dead. But a miraculous recovery and a year's rehabilitation had gotten him back behind the wheel and driving well enough to win three more races. Still, he had crashed a few more times since, including at Michigan just two weeks before Darlington, and each time, he said, the pain was worse and the recovery harder. Irvan had stared into the belly of the beast once too often, and finally he flinched.

As if to compensate for the loss of Irvan, Indy 500 legend A. J. Foyt had also announced earlier in the week that he and his Conseco sponsors would field a Winston Cup team in the 2000 season. (Weeks later, fans learned that the Foyt team would race Pontiacs and by season's end Craftsman Truck racer Mike Bliss had been named as Foyt's driver.) But no one I talked to seemed interested in the A. J. Foyt news. On the other hand, there was a great deal of animated conversation about STP's announcement that it would end its historic sponsorship of the Richard Petty entry midway through the 2000 season, a move fans at the inn found incomprehensible and even vaguely sacrilegious. General Mills, the breakfast-cereal giant, would become the team's new primary sponsor. To herald and promote its presence in the Winston Cup, General Mills had created the "Betty Crocker Racing Family," a group of women, mostly wives of drivers, who would work to recognize female interest and presence in the sport. So STP was getting out of the Winston Cup, Betty Crocker was getting in, and no one I talked to rejoiced at this development.

The green flag for the next day's race wouldn't fall until 12:30 P.M. but we were up at six, on our way to the track by seven, and parked in the lot adjacent to Darlington Raceway by 8:30, along with twenty or thirty thousand other fans. I try to avoid the trackside parking lots, but given the track's location, we could go any which way after the race and run into an interstate to the coast. Besides, trackside parking was free. So we sat by the car for a couple of hours in folding lawn chairs, reading books, solving crossword puzzles, and observing the goings-on around us.

Judging by the number of cars that were already there, I'd guess fans started showing up in serious numbers around 6:00 or 6:30. By 8:30, half the fans near us were fixing breakfast on charcoal or propane grills. The smell and sizzle of bacon and sausage filled the air, and there were pans of grits and skillets of scrambled eggs everywhere. A few lonesome souls struggled with campfire coffeepots, but the breakfast beverage of choice was beer. A huge, pre-race NASCAR tailgate party—what else would you expect? We watched one fan tow a portable hog-roaster behind his shiny black Dodge Dakota. The roaster (not the pickup) had chrome exhaust pipes and mag racing wheels and was painted black and decorated to resemble Dale Earnhardt's car. The owner could have roasted a couple of whole hogs with that rig and fed three hundred people—and maybe that was the plan. It was soon obvious that many of these fans intended to linger in the lot for hours after the race was over, cooking a second round of food, drinking a second cooler of beer, and having a good time waiting for the race traffic to clear. I had to admit, this strategy seemed at least as sound, and probably a great deal less stressful, than my customary approach to the problem.

From our vantage point, I could make out the license plates and models of about three- or four-dozen vehicles—one Toyota truck and the rest American products. You'll see more Japanese cars in the parking lot of a Chrysler die-casting plant than in a NASCAR parking lot. A third of the cars were from northern and midwestern states. The driver of the Toyota was wearing a T-shirt announcing that he was "Insured by Smith and Wesson." Another T-shirt I saw later said, "Gun control is being able

NASCAR fans kicking back before the race. Race-day parking is always a problem, so many fans come to the track hours before the race, get parked, pitch a tent or dining fly, fire up the charcoal grill, and while away the time drinking beer and socializing with other fans. Many fans will also hang around for a few hours after the race, barbecuing and drinking more beer while traffic clears. These pre- and postrace parking-lot tailgate parties go on at every Winston Cup venue.

to hit your target." You've got to love the gun nuts, especially when they're also race fans. But my nominee for the *Fixin' to Git* 1999 Southern 500 T-shirt of the Race Award was sported by a thick young guy seated down and to the right of us, whose apparel announced, "If you're gonna be stupid, you'd better be tough." Oh, great, I thought, just what we need — more tough, stupid guys.

Stroker Ace described Darlington race fans as a bunch of cotton-picking goobers and low-life white trash. "Every other one has a wooden match in the corner of his mouth and a bottle in a brown paper bag between his feet."[3] Chris's impression at the pre-race tailgate party was just the opposite. These people, she said, "have money," they're "middle class." I had to agree: I saw more Lincolns and Cadillacs streaming past than broken-down, clay-encrusted pickup trucks. Sure, there were plenty of what looked to be long-haired country boys, factory workers, and construction hands, but everyone looked like they were making decent money. The crowd scene outside the Darlington Speedway looked and felt surprisingly affluent.

We hung out in the parking lot for the better part of three hours then headed into the track for a quick concession-stand lunch. Although "track food" is something you might find revolting, the concession-stand offerings at most tracks are surprisingly varied and good. You'll not find anything that resembles health food: no salads, nothing with avocado or sprouts, in fact no vegetables at all except sautéed peppers and onions to go with your kielbasa; but there's lots of the food you'd expect to find at a good county fair: the predictable line-up of burgers, hot dogs, fries, and beers, but also pizzas, grilled bratwurst, smoked or Italian sausages, fried chicken, Philly cheese-steak sandwiches, hot pretzels, barbecued-pork and -beef sandwiches, and, my personal favorite, corn dogs (hot dogs impaled on a stick, dipped in a cornmeal batter, and deep-fat fried). So lunch at the track is something I look forward to. But the concession-stand menu at Darlington was brutally simple. Hamburgers, hot dogs, chips, Pepsi, and beer. Period. For what was always billed as one of stock-car racing's premier venues, I was surprised and, I confess, disappointed by how primitive everything seemed. (It occurred to me later that the offerings on the other side of the track might have been more varied.) We wolfed down a couple of gray, tasteless burgers and repaired at once to our seats.

Except for the shiny new grandstand along the main straightaway (more courage or a quicker decision the day before and that's where we would have been sitting), everything about Darlington looked old, faded, decrepit. The facility showed every one of its fifty years—and not grace-fully. With seating for fewer than 100,000 and relatively primitive facili-ties and accommodations, I wondered whether one of the two annual Darlington dates might not be sacrificed to the Winston Cup's impending expansion. But then I remembered that the facility is now owned outright by the France family, so I thought, Nah, probably not.

The view from our seats was decent but not outstanding. At Darling-ton, some of the slower qualifiers pit on the backstretch (that has since changed), and we had a fine view of the Darrell Waltrip, Dale Jarrett, and John Andretti pit operations. Andretti, of course, drives the Richard Petty Number 43 Pontiac and with my binoculars I could see the King clearly, high up in his observation deck overlooking the pit. He sat motionless

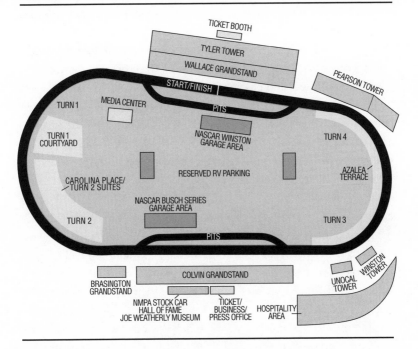

most of the day, legs crossed, occasionally mumbling something into the mike on his head set, his facial expression stolid and unchanging. So the usual problem with backstretch seats—that you can't see any of the pit action—was not a problem here. Also, Darlington's high banks gave us a reasonably clear view of the racing action in the corners. But, because we were down fairly close to the track, we could see practically nothing on the main straightaway.

In 1997 the track was reconfigured: the start-finish line was moved to what had been the backstretch, Turns One and Two thus became Turns Three and Four, and vice versa. The reason for the reconfiguration was compelling: Darlington needed to add seats and the speedway owned plenty of land on the far side of the track where new grandstands could be built. The reconfiguration would put all the new seats right along the main straightaway where they'd fetch top dollar. The problem, of course, was that the same move turned once-prime seats along the start-finish line into cheap seats on the backstretch. And there were plenty of fans around us in the Colvin Grandstand, including the fellow seated next to me, who had had season tickets to Darlington for twenty years and who were not happy in the least that their once-excellent seats were now mediocre. Why not upgrade, I asked? "I've tried to," he said, "but every year they tell me, Ain't no upgrades available." He figured all the new seats—all the *good* seats—had been gobbled up by track owners and officials, corporate sponsors, and possibly NASCAR itself. "Ain't gonna give a fan no break, that's for damned sure." The man was angry that he had been consigned, probably for the rest of his life, to seats on the backstretch, and yet, for all that, he had no intention of boycotting the race. "Where else wouldja wanne be," he asked, "on Labor Day weekend?"

The 1999 Southern 500 was standard Darlington fare—which is to say, wild and wooly all afternoon. The lead changed hands twenty times among ten different drivers, there was hot neck-and-neck racing all over the track, and six yellow flags kept the field tightly bunched. But the remains of Hurricane Dennis were still in the area: light rain had delayed the start and ominous clouds hung low over the track all afternoon. The field was red-flagged for rain at about 4:00, then restarted twenty-five minutes later. After seven more laps, the rains returned, this time in earnest, and the race was red-flagged again. Jeff Burton was in the lead at the time; his brother Ward was second—the Burton boys had been dueling all afternoon. (Ward had finished second to Jeff once before in the 1999 season.) Jeremy Mayfield, Mark Martin, and Kevin LePage rounded out the top five. The predicted, or hoped-for, blood duel between Earnhardt and Labonte never materialized. At the red flag, Earnhardt was down two laps in twenty-second, and Labonte was the last car on the lead lap, in seventeenth.

The feeling in the stands and on the MRN radio broadcast was that the rain would probably clear in an hour. It would take another hour to dry the track. That would leave an hour or more of daylight to complete the remaining ninety-six laps. But the clouds were thick and dark, the rain was heavy, and there seemed to be a lot of wishful thinking in the folk meteorology being played out all around us. So, despite an unspoken pledge never to do so, I decided to get a leg up on the postrace traffic and leave. It proved to be the right decision: the race was never restarted and Jeff Burton was declared the winner about 6:30—his second rain-shortened victory at Darlington that year. (He was also leading the TranSouth 400 in March when the race was called because of rain.)

With most fans still in their seats hoping for a restart that never came, our exit from Darlington was quick and easy, and by the time the race was officially over, we were well on our way to the beach. Since moving to Louisiana, I'd driven widely all over the South, but this was my first time on the back roads of South Carolina. Now, if you get off the beaten path in states like Virginia or North Carolina, you'll come across any number of prosperous little communities, the stretches of road between them dotted with small farms and suburban housing developments. Here and there, widely dispersed, you'll find occasional knots of that gritty, ramshackle, rural poverty that, even a decade or two ago, was emblematic of life in the South. Even in states like Mississippi and Alabama, which I drove through frequently, many of these grim pockets of deprivation are gone. But in South Carolina (and in Louisiana, too), they remain defining features of the rural landscape. The roads in and out of Darlington were thick with scraggly fields of cotton and rusting mobile homes — never had the phrase "cotton-pickin' white trash" seemed so, well, *literal.*

In 1999 the state's big political controversy, which ran through the South Carolina body politic like a nasty infection, was whether the state should continue to fly the Confederate battle flag over its capital building. This festering sore even oozed into the 2000 presidential primary, with the Tweedledees taking a principled stand on one side of the issue and the Tweedledums staking out an equally principled position on the other. Surely symbolic of something, the controversy lasted quite a bit longer than the Confederacy itself. Southern people seem to have an affection for lost causes.

The Confederate flag issue is a sword dangling over NASCAR's head. With the possible exception of Civil War battle reenactments, there's no place in America where you'll see more Confederate flags flying than at a Winston Cup race. The near-universal discrediting of the Stars and Bars as a politically incorrect, if not racist, symbol has obviously not yet reached every Winston Cup fan. Either that, or they just don't care. And, as you might imagine, there was no pussyfooting or self-flagellation about the point among fans at the Southern 500, which was adorned by a profusion of Confederate flags the likes of which I had not witnessed at any other track.

Darlington, alas, has been the most Confederate of the NASCAR tracks since its opening in 1950. Two years before the track opened, the state's then-junior senator, Strom Thurmond, had led the walkout of prosegre-gation Southern Democrats from the party's convention, the begin-ning of the Dixiecrat movement that swept the South in 1948 and made Thurmond a presidential candidate and national symbol. Thurmond made a point of attending the inaugural race at Darlington and most races thereafter, always spewing his vile rhetoric, and in short order the Con-federate flag came to symbolize both the race itself and the enthusiasm of many Southern working-class whites for continued racial segregation. Now, a half-century later, the track still carries some of that early politi-cal baggage. How can NASCAR pretend to be diversifying, to be reaching out to African Americans, Hispanics, and other ethnic minorities, when there are Confederate battle flags all the hell over the place?

When South Carolina refused to lower its flag, the NAACP announced a boycott. Could a national NAACP boycott of the Winston Cup be next? That probably wouldn't affect the gate—there aren't that many black people in the stands anyway—but it sure would be an embarrassment. The heart of NASCAR's problem is that Southerners who defend their flag as a symbol of valor, honor, heritage, and regional tradition are largely rural, blue collar, and white—demographic categories that also contain large numbers of stock-car racing fans. The Mike Luckovich cartoon that I discussed in the prelude illustrates the conundrum.

Luckovich's cartoon got me to thinking: Why not a NASCAR-sponsored Confederate flag buy-back like the gun buy-backs now so popular in the big cities? Why not let race fans turn in their Stars and Bars for official NASCAR checkered flags—no questions asked? I can fore-see little booths all around the track: Confederate Flags Redeemed Here. Maybe Winston could throw in a carton of smokes just to sweeten the pot. Tomorrow's newspapers could run photographs showing the num-ber and variety of flags that had been collected. The world, or at least the NASCAR world, would be a better place. (Note to political eager-beavers: *it's a joke.*)

On the other hand, NASCAR itself may have hit on a better solution. At Daytona and, I believe, several other tracks, NASCAR now requests that all the infield flags be lowered before the start of the race, so as not to obstruct the view of fans or TV cameras as they pan across the infield. I don't really think the purpose here is to improve the fans' view of the far side of the track. The purpose is to get the Confederate flags off national television.

But I digress. Darlington Speedway, like South Carolina herself, is an anachronism, a place caught out of its own time; an enigma both alluring yet strangely disturbing; proud, defiant, unrepentant—and vaguely ridiculous in her pretensions. Darlington is to Winston Cup racing what the Huey P. Long Bridge is to Mississippi River crossings: a grand old lady, long past her prime, ready to be replaced, perhaps, but still serviceable and, in her own way, still an adventure. The state and her premier speedway, I've decided, deserve a second look. Why? Because "where else wouldja wanne be on Labor Day weekend?"

4

The NASCAR Subculture

You don't have to go to very many races to realize that stock-car fans are, well, *different*. Not *bad* different, like the guys you run into if you do studies of imprisoned felons or streetcorner drug dealers (both of which I've done). NASCAR fans are the nicest bunch of folks you'd ever want to meet. True, there's the occasional nasty drunk, racist half-wit, and rude, slobbering idiot, but these are people you find anywhere there's a lot of beer being downed, which includes stock-car races. And not *weird* different, like you'd expect at a grunge convention, punk-rock concert, or Hell's Angels rally. Away from the track, you could dress 'em up in their Sunday-go-to-meetin' clothes and they'd fit right in anywhere. But still, *different*. To a guy like me, race fans are instantly recognizable as a *subculture*.

There is no universally agreed-on definition of a subculture, nor is there an unambiguous difference between a real subculture and just another offbeat group. One sure sign of a subculture is a clearly discernible boundary between in-group and out-group, between *us* and *them*, a boundary created and maintained by a distinctive language or argot, by visible differences in dress, regalia, and insignia, and by a characteristic package of beliefs, norms, and values. Subcultures arise to gratify their members' special and otherwise unmet needs — needs that may be incomprehensible to outsiders but form a taken-for-granted element of social life within the subculture. The gratification of these common but special needs is the subculture's raison d'être.

Stock-car fans openly discuss and even buy T-shirts that proclaim their "Need for Speed," and this is the special need that binds the sport's enthusiasts into an extended clan. There's no sense trying to explain the "need for speed." If it's something you intuitively grasp, terrific. It is a preternatural, subconscious, inexplicable, at times overwhelming desire to experience firsthand the thrills and dangers of an automobile race. It's the sort of desire that lurks deep in the limbic system, in the reptilian portion of the brain. John Shelton Reed captures something of the essence: "The noise, the speed, the vivid colors, the pit crews' feverish work—all of this has a visceral appeal to anyone whose inner child is an East Tennessee sixteen-year-old."[1] Or a small-town kid from the Indiana boondocks. In the fictive but revealing words of Stroker Ace, "There are folks who wet their pants every time they hear one of these big bastard NASCAR machines roar to life."[2] Oh, yeah.

There is something addictive about being at the tracks. Maybe race fans have a special neuroreceptor whose euphoric chemistry is only activated when there are fast race cars somewhere in the field of vision. Television can mollify but not slake this hunger; every so often, you just have to be there. NASCAR fans will say they "need a race" in exactly the same sense that booze-hounds will say they "need a drink." There's an ache deep in the soul to see, to hear, to *feel* the heavy hitters fire up and go racing.

NASCAR writers evoke the imagery of addiction with telling regularity. Peter Golenbock writes in *American Zoom:* "If baseball is chess with a bat, ball and glove, stock car racing is chess on wheels. . . . Once understood, Winston Cup racing is an utterly captivating sport, peopled by some of the most interesting, funny, warm, witty, disciplined, passionate, and talented participants in all of professional sport. I have become addicted to the Winston Cup race circuit. . . . And now that CBS, ESPN, and TNN televise every race, I know I can get my racing fix if I so desire."[3] Mark Howell's *From Moonshine to Madison Avenue* recounts the same: "Winston Cup racing is a sport of addiction. Once you experience it firsthand, you feel compelled to keep following it."[4] The allusion to addiction is only partly metaphorical. Ask my wife.

The NASCAR fan's need for speed is what brings six-and-a-half million of them to the Winston Cup races every year—200,000 to the May and October events in Charlotte, 200,000 more to the February and July events in Daytona, maybe 300,000 to the August event at Indianapolis, and sell-out crowds to every other venue, whatever its seating capacity. Winston Cup crowds dwarf the attendance at other major sporting events. I've read that the average NASCAR fan travels 200 miles to go to a race, spends $400 or $500 for the weekend's entertainment, and goes to four or five races every year. My averages in the year I was writing this book were a little higher: I averaged more than 600 miles of travel (one-way) to get to each event, dropped between $800 and $1,000 every race weekend, and when the season was done, I had attended eight races (and regretted not getting to more).

It is not just the need for speed that brings the stock-car millions to the tracks or binds them into a subculture. The weekend Winston Cup event merely highlights an extended four- or five-day celebration of speed, spectacle, and traditional American virtue that begins when the transporters first start showing up in the middle of the week and doesn't end until the last car has left the parking lot and headed home. In between, there is an endless procession of on- and off-track events to amuse the descending hordes. Away from the track, fans scout out driver appearances, attend parties and hospitality functions put on by sponsors or even by drivers themselves, check out book signings, go to see race cars on display, even get into the groove with live remote radio broadcasts or country music concerts, all of which have a racing theme. These off-track events are astonishingly popular. During the weekend of the 1999 Pepsi 400 at Daytona, Darrell Waltrip made an appearance at the local K-Mart, Waltrip's major sponsor. We learned from a newspaper ad that Waltrip would be at the store from 10:00 to 12:00. We showed up about 10:05 and the line of fans already stretched completely around the perimeter of the store. As we entered, we were advised that the line was more than two hours long, that people just now lining up would probably not make it to the front before Waltrip had to leave. There were easily a couple thousand people there, each with a T-shirt, hat, or some other item of racing memorabilia for Waltrip to sign. At Indy, I met a fan who had paid for a $200 bag of marijuana with a pair of complimentary tickets to a Rusty Wallace hospitality party. Cash, you see, meant little to this fan's drug dealer, but a Rusty Wallace hospitality party? Now, that was *something!*

But the off-track action pales in comparison to what goes on at the track itself. The Winston Cup race is only the most prominent of several weekend racing events. There may also be a Busch Grand National Race the day before the Cup race, or a Craftsman Truck race, or a Featherlite Modified event, or an ARCA or IROC contest. Local tracks in the surrounding areas will also feature big events over Winston Cup weekends, their crowds swollen by NASCAR fans who just can't get enough racing action. Often, multiple NASCAR competitions precede the grand finale. During the weekend I was in Richmond, the Craftsman trucks raced on Thursday night, the Busch teams raced on Friday, and the Winston Cup cars raced on Saturday. It was easy to find people around us in the stands who had been to all three races.

And not just to the races. Each race is preceded, over a period of several days, by qualifying and practice sessions. It is not unusual for tens of thousands to show up at the track and pay to see first-day qualifying for a Winston Cup race. Happy Hour also draws crowds in the tens of thousands. (As an aside of some significance, Winston Cup qualifying sessions and Happy Hour are now routinely televised live.) The Busch and Craftsman Truck races also draw large, enthusiastic and growing throngs. A recent NASCAR survey indicated that while the Busch Grand National Series remains less popular than the Winston Cup, it is more popular than either of the major open-wheeled roadster series (CART and the Indy Racing League) and more popular than NHRA and IHRA drag racing.

A Winston Cup race is a major economic and social event in every city the series visits. (According to *Time* for 5 March 2001, the Daytona 500 generates some $240 million to the local economy annually, more even than the Super Bowl.) As a hundred or a hundred fifty thousand fans arrive, the area around the track is transformed. Homeowners turn their yards into parking and camping spaces; vast instant communities of recreational vehicles spring up; enterprising young people sell cold sodas, hot dogs and hamburgers right off the charcoal grill to hungry, grateful fans. Every business that cares about business displays a prominent banner: WELCOME RACE FANS! And anywhere you go within a twenty-mile radius, you can hear that everyone is talking about racing. Like the Muslim faithful in Mecca, everybody is in town for the same reason—to feed their need for speed.

The instant camaraderie that breaks out wherever race fans congregate is the most charming of the sport's many endearing features. What races you been to? Who's your favorite driver? What do you think of this year's crop of rookies? Who'll be the next first-time winner? If you are at Daytona or Talladega (or, for that matter, anywhere else), you can start up a conversation on the pros and cons of restrictor-plate racing; if you're at Bristol or Martinsville or Richmond, you can argue with people about the future of Winston Cup short-track racing. If you are anywhere in North Carolina, you can commiserate about the end of Winston Cup racing at North Wilkesboro.[5] At Indianapolis, the conversation on every fan's lips is the sorry state of Indy-car racing, the CART–IRL dispute, and how NASCAR will never let something like *that* happen to stock-car racing. Being at the races provides the special comfort of knowing you are around people who care about the same things you care about, whose frame of reference contains the same terms and categories as yours, who speak the same language you speak.

The proof positive that a cultural boundary exists is that outsiders experience culture shock when they step across it. *Sports Illustrated* writer Steve Rushin, for example, ran up against a vocabulary and syntax he didn't understand, and he never recovered. Unfortunately, rather than make the effort to understand (if not appreciate) the differences, he saw fit to ridicule them. "Until last weekend, I had never heard the phrase 'tar far' (tire fire), 'cow shin' (caution), or the proper pronunciation of 'gentlemen' (it rhymes with 'cinnamon')."[6] Oh, my. As a good old down-home boy might say, "This here polecat needs hisself a good talkin'-to" — about regional dialects certainly, and little lecture on tolerance probably wouldn't hurt either. As a student from Mississippi explained to me early in my career at Tulane, "Ya see, Perfessor, down here it's you that talks funny."

Green Bay Packer quarterback Bret Favre, honorary starter for the NAPA Auto Parts 300—the Busch Grand National event that took place the weekend of the 1999 Daytona 500—replaced the well-worn standard, "Gentlemen, start your engines" with "Gentlemen, let's get it on," or, as rendered by Rushin, "Jinnamin! Lit's giddit awn!" Now, if you want to criticize Favre for departing from what many fans consider a hallowed tradition, fine. I'm sure there were a lot of fans who wondered, "What the hell did he say?" But poke fun at his Mississippi accent? Perhaps it would have helped to have a bilingual fan around to translate. Roughly:

"Okay, we've had about three hours of pre-race hoopla. The drivers have all been introduced. Miss NAPA Auto Parts 1999 has made her appearance. We've been greeted by sponsors' reps and local elected officials. We've prayed for a safe race and sung the National Anthem. Hell, they've even paraded the wreckers, ambulances, and fire trucks around the track. And my cooler is running dry! But, hey, we came here and paid good money to see a race. Gentlemen, what say we get on with it?" The translation lacks punch but conveys the essential content. It's a matter of cultural differences, you see.

Again, Rushin: "The entire weekend was a linguistic revelation. Pit crew chiefs, I now know, speak in six- and seven-syllable subject-free sentences: Southern haiku. When asked what went wrong with his car's engine on Saturday, one crew chief sighed, 'Just come apart, I guess.' To explain a rival crew's failure to remove loose tires from pit row, another chief said with a shrug, 'Too damned lazy, I reckon.'"[7]

Let's not pause on the poetic possibilities of Southern haiku but stay instead with the subcultural theme. Every race fan would understand at once that the answers Rushin quotes are to questions posed by reporters (otherwise, how would Rushin have heard them?), so detailed technical responses would not have been appropriate. Talking to reporters requires snappy little sound bites since they lack the attention span for anything more substantial. I'd bet dollars to donuts that the first crew chief knew (if not when the question was asked, certainly within the hour) exactly what had gone wrong in the engine and could well have responded, "The connecting rod from the crankshaft to the number-four piston failed, and a two-inch piece of the rod blew through the head. That resulted in a severe loss of compression, and it was no longer possible to continue the race." But what would have been the point? "Just come apart" says all that needs to be said.

If you don't understand the language, you can never get the point, and it is that special NASCAR language that separates stock-car subculture from society at large. Rushin one final time: "By the time Jeff Gordon pole-sat on Sunday, got the green, traded paint, pitted, took gas, drove the tars off his Chevy, was cow-shinned, caught a mirror full of Dale Earnhardt on his rear spoiler, got the checkered, and thanked Du Pont, Pepsi, and Goodyear, I had watched 1,050 miles of racing in 24 hours."[8] He goes on to lament the pointlessness of it all. And yet strangely enough, and, I assume, inadvertently, he provides a not-bad summary of the race. Jeff Gordon was the fastest qualifier and started the race on the inside of the front row ("pole-sat"). It was a hard-fought battle: cars were banging into one another (they "traded paint") and there were frequent yellow flags ("cow-shins"). Dale Earnhardt was right on Gordon's tail for much of the race ("a mirror full of Dale Earnhardt right on his rear spoiler"), but Gordon drove with skill and determination ("drove the tars off his Chevy"), emerged victorious ("got the checkered"), and, of course, expressed his postrace gratitude to the sponsors who make it all possible. It is another telling observation that most NASCAR authors feel obliged to include a dictionary of subcultural argot, a glossary of terms and phrases to guide outsiders through the linguistic maze.[9]

Subcultures are distinguished not just by their special argot but also by distinctive dress, regalia, insignia, and associated differences in lifestyle, preferences, and tastes. Race fans identify themselves to other fans and declare their allegiances with T-shirts, gimme hats, and other race-day accessories. These are, in essence, species markers (maybe useful for mating, for all I know — it certainly wouldn't do for a Dale Earnhardt guy to hook up romantically with a Jeff Gordon gal, that's for sure).

Interestingly, it doesn't seem to matter *what* your allegiance is, so long as it has something to do with racing. You can sport regalia that memorializes certain races (for example, the 1992 Pepsi 400, Richard Petty's last race at Daytona, or any other race that you've been lucky enough to attend, especially one with historic significance), specific tracks ("Bristol Motor Speedway: Feel the Thunder," "Darlington: The Track Too Tough to Tame," "Dover: The Monster Mile"), makes of race cars ("Ford Forever," "Pontiac Excitement"), specific championship seasons, sponsors, or, of course, your favorite teams and drivers. A special cachet attaches to the fan wearing souvenir regalia from last week's race — this marks you as a "two-in-a-row" fan, an honored status. And ditto items from last year's race at the same venue — this identifies you as a track regular. Inaugural paraphernalia are also highly coveted. I have a hat from the 1994 Brickyard 400, the first Winston Cup race ever at the famed Indianapolis Motor Speedway, and I have seen (and envied) souvenir shirts and hats from the inaugural events at Texas, California, and Las Vegas. At the races following the untimely deaths of Davey Allison and Alan Kulwicki, and more recently of Adam Petty, Kenny Irwin, and Dale Earnhardt, thousands of fans—in Earnhardt's case, tens of thousands—wore special T-shirts to honor and memorialize their fallen heroes. Eulogy by T-shirt—now there's a concept.

Some female fans, particularly Jeff Gordon fans, show up in splendid, festive head-to-toe race outfits: matching shirt, shorts, cap, and even coordinated socks and hair scrungies, all sporting the bright colors and instantly recognizable insignia of the Rainbow Warriors (the moniker of Gordon's team). The truly hard-core Jeff Gordon gal will also have little black enameled Number 24s for earrings and—the pièce de résistance— checkered flag fingernails.

The public display of loyalty extends to seat cushions, coolers, and race bags, all of which may also sport the names, numbers, colors, logos, or other insignia of drivers, teams, races, tracks, sponsors, or sanctioning organizations. The need for proper racing *externalia* also extends to your car or truck, even your RV and campsite if, like many fans, you camp out when you go to the races. (When we camped at Indy, we adorned the site with a NASCAR flag and, later, with a WELCOME RACE FANS! banner that we had cadged from a Coors salesman.) Decals, flags, banners, signs—anything that proclaims to the world, NASCAR Spoken Here! John Shelton Reed describes the Darlington infield: "Scores of flags flapped in the breeze, enough rebel ones to give the encampment the look of a lost Confederate regiment, but also plenty of U.S. flags, plus the flags of many states, flags with the colors of favorite drivers, and flags featuring portraits of Hank Williams Jr. and Elvis."[10] NASCAR fans are not coy about and certainly not ashamed of who they are, where they're from, who they like and dislike, or what they believe.

Racing regalia also serves as free advertising for the corporate enterprises that are so heavily involved with the sport. A Tony Stewart fan is, ipso facto, a walking advertisement for Home Depot; a Terry Labonte fan is a virtual Kellogg's Corn Flakes billboard. But the same can be said, of course, of people who wear Tommy Hilfiger jeans.

As I say, it is acceptable to be "for" more or less anything so long as it has something to do with racing. Every so often, you'll see some clueless neophyte wander by wearing a Dallas Cowboys cap or a Baltimore Orioles T-shirt. This is the equivalent of showing up at a fancy party in bib overalls—it simply isn't done. I've even seen a few guys at the track in shirts and ties and had to wonder what planet they flew in from.[11] No,

A properly attired Tony Stewart fan posing with a busty Ms. Coors at a pre-race shin-
dig across the street from the Daytona International Speedway, a few hours before
the start of the 2001 Pepsi 400. (One of these women is the author's wife.) Race-day
regalia (hats, T-shirts, cooler decals, banners, and the like) serve to declare fans' preferences to one another and thus function as conversational aids. On the other hand,
the dozens of guys who lined up for a signed photograph of Ms. Coors seemed (to
me, at least) to have more than stock-car racing or Coors beer on their minds.

if you're going to the races, you've got to sport your colors. If nothing
else, your attire and insignia give fellow fans a gambit with which to open
a conversation, and it is uncivil — downright unsociable — to deny them
these interactional aids.

Just as you can be "for" anything that has to do with racing, so, too, can
your reasons for these preferences be as idiosyncratic as you wish. Being
a fifty-something baby boomer, I like to root for older drivers nearing the
twilight of their careers. For much of the 1999 season, my race day outfit
consisted of a Bill Elliott tie-dyed T-shirt and a NASCAR cap. Elliott broke
into the Winston Cup in 1976, has forty-one victories to his credit, was
the Winston Cup champion in 1988, and has been voted "Most Popular
Driver" by the fans thirteen times, more times, even, than Richard Petty,
who won the honor nine times. I watched Awesome Bill from Dawsonville
(Georgia) win the 1991 Pepsi 400 at Daytona, and it would be an honor
to see him win again. Ditto Darrell Waltrip, another now-retired former

champion whose continuing popularity with fans late in his career belied his often subpar performances on the track. I kept a Darrell Waltrip K-Mart Racing Team gimme hat in my race bag throughout the 1999 season just in case old Darrell made a run to the front (he never did). Ricky Rudd and Ken Schrader are two other old-timers (relatively speaking) whose progress I like to follow closely. And since it is always a special thrill to watch a driver win a Winston Cup race for the first time, I also root for veterans such as Michael Waltrip (Darrell's younger brother, who went winless in 462 career starts before his victory at the 2001 Daytona 500) and Ted Musgrave (winless in more than 200 Winston Cup starts), plus promising newcomers such as Kenny Wallace, Mike Skinner, Ricky Craven, Johnny Benson, and Jerry Nadeau, all of them sufficiently talented to break through to their first win any given weekend. (Until September 1999, I would have included Tony Stewart and Joe Nemechek on this list, but both scored their first victories that month, Stewart at Richmond and

Driver Bill Elliott, "Awesome Bill from Dawsonville." Elliott's thirteen "Most Popular Driver" awards are as impressive as his forty-one victories or his 1988 Winston Cup championship. Elliott was born in 1955 and is thus one of a fairly large number of aging baby boomers who are still competitive in the NASCAR Winston Cup. Photo credit: International Speedway Corporation Archives.

Nemechek the following weekend at New Hampshire. Since these pages were first written, Nadeau has also broken through, winning the last race of the 2000 season.) And there is always a special place in my heart for the Indiana Gang, even Jeff Gordon. So, when the cars come around on the final parade lap to take the green flag, I've usually got some reason why I'm rooting for half the field.

My sister-in-law, Denise, went to her first race at Daytona in July 1999 and her second at Indianapolis a month later. She picked Ernie Irvan as "her" driver in both races, because she liked the colors and paint scheme of the Number 36 M&Ms Pontiac (one of the prettiest race cars ever put on the track). For backups, she picked Michael Waltrip and Joe Nemechek because she liked the purple paint on both of their cars. Laugh if you want, but a fan could do far worse than root for these three drivers. My brother, Kelley, is a self-described "Hoosier redneck" and a serious race fan; like me, he roots for the Indiana drivers, but he doesn't include Jeff Gordon, whom he considers to be a Californian. Kelley is also partial to Pontiacs—and now to the Dodges—regardless of who's at the wheel. I went to the races in Richmond with my pal and collaborator Steve Nock, a native Virginian who was attending his first NASCAR race. For want of a better decision rule, he cheered on fellow Virginians Ricky Rudd and the Burton brothers. I met a fan at Charlotte who rooted for Tony Stewart and Bobby Labonte, not because they both drove Pontiacs, not because they were both promising young drivers who seemed destined to be Winston Cup champions one day (Labonte in fact won the 2000 points battle), but because they both drove for Joe Gibbs Racing and she was a Washington Redskins fan when Gibbs had coached the Redskins to two Super Bowl victories.

It may seem shameless and opportunistic to root for a half-dozen or even a couple dozen drivers in any particular race, and it is probably true that most fans show up at the track with a single favorite they cheer for. But there are a lot of likable drivers and competitive teams, and the more of them you're rooting for, the more there is on the track for you to watch and care about. I can be perfectly happy watching a battle for thirty-fourth position between a driver I care about and a driver I don't. (As a matter of fact, some of the hottest racing to be witnessed takes place from the middle of the pack to the back—it is often dog-eat-dog back there.) Rooting for multiple teams lets me enjoy the action all over the track, whether my favorites are running up front or not.

There's some, but not much, rooting "against" to be found at the races as well. A decade ago, before Jeff Gordon's spectacular ascent to the pinnacle of the Winston Cup, there were large numbers of fans who specialized in rooting against Dale Earnhardt. In his prime, Earnhardt was a villainous character, the "Man in Black" who, in the perception of many fans, would stop at nothing to win (thus, "the Intimidator"). In the early '90s, "Anybody But Earnhardt" T-shirts and buttons could be seen at every race. But by the end of the '90s, Earnhardt, although still a strong competitor, was no longer the dominant force he had been, so negative sentiment shifted to the new kid on the Winston Cup block, Jeff Gordon, whom many fans love and others just despise.

At the end of the 1999 season, Gordon was one shy of fifty Winston Cup wins, a mark reached by only ten other drivers in the entire half-century history of NASCAR. (He nailed his fiftieth victory at the spring 2000 race at Darlington and as of this writing—June 2001—he is up to fifty-five.) Among other active drivers, only Rusty Wallace has as many as fifty victories. (When he retired at the end of 2000, Darrell Waltrip had eighty-four wins, and Dale Earnhardt died with seventy-six.) Gordon drove in his first Cup race in 1992 at age twenty-one, was Rookie of the Year in 1993, won his first race in 1994, and then won the Winston Cup championship in 1995, 1997, and 1998. No other driver in the history of the sport has had such a meteoric rise to the top—not Darrell Waltrip, not Dale Earnhardt, not even King Richard himself. He is young, handsome, talented, successful, articulate, self-effacing, devoutly Christian, and married to a former Miss Winston Cup. No wonder people find him easy to hate.

A favorite slander of Gordon-haters is to raise questions about his "sexual orientation." You see these people in T-shirts emblazoned with sentiments such as "*Fans Against Gordon*" and "*Forget About Gordon.*" Other Gordon-haters will say he went too far, too fast, too easily, forgetting that the guy began competitive racing when he was five years old and has done practically nothing but race ever since. His Rookie-of-the-Year award came in his seventeenth year of organized motorsports competition. His detractors also say (rather, used to say) that his crew chief Ray Evernham was the real key to the team's success, that anyone could win with an Evernham-prepared race car, and that Gordon would be a no-body, an also-ran, with anyone else calling the shots in the pits. Well, Evernham stepped aside as Gordon's crew chief in October, 1999, just after the fall race at Dover, and Gordon responded by going out and winning the race at Martinsville the following weekend. Then the 500-mile race at Charlotte the week after that.[12] Other drivers may envy his success, but none deny his talent and all concede his unparalleled contributions to the sport. One rival, Kyle Petty, acknowledges that "when Jeff goes on the *Letterman* show, he takes all of us with him. His success has been great for NASCAR and for every one of us."[13]

Every subculture is internally stratified. Winston Cup fans used to fall into three roughly equal-sized groups: Jeff Gordon fans, Dale Earnhardt fans, and everyone else. When they were both driving, Gordon and Earnhardt were, by a wide margin, the two most popular and simultaneously least popular drivers on the circuit. Earnhardt fans were "old school," good old boys (and girls), the kinds of folks who drive pickups, sport tattoos, eat pork rinds, hunt, fish, and drink cheap beer. Gordon fans are "pretty boys" (and girls), younger, more attractive wine-and-cheese types who drive sports utility vehicles, are proficient at video games, and jog regularly to stay in shape. Earnhardt, fiercely competitive and enormously talented, was the face of NASCAR past—truly, the last of a breed. Gordon, mediagenic, well spoken, and also enormously talented, is the face of NASCAR future. To the legions of Gordon-haters, I say, Get over it. He is destined to be a dominant force in Winston Cup racing for another two decades.

Part of NASCAR's appeal is that the NASCAR subculture intersects easily and seamlessly with other subcultural strands in contemporary American life. There is, first, the obvious connection to the regional subculture of the South, although, as we have seen and will see again, this is easy to overstate. More important is the strong link to small-town and rural culture and to traditional outdoors pursuits, to hunting, fishing, camping, and guns. In the Great Cultural Divide between city and country, whose importance in American political and social life rivals or even exceeds the divide between worker and owner, rich and poor, male and female, and even black and white, NASCAR people are unambiguously, defiantly, proudly country folk—and that's true even if they live in downtown Atlanta.

The late Dale Earnhardt (right) with competitor Jeff Gordon, two of NASCAR's most successful drivers. Both won Rookie-of-the-Year honors and both went on to win multiple Winston Cup championships (Gordon has four so far, while Earnhardt died with seven). Earnhardt is remembered by many as the "Greatest Stock-Car Driver of All Time," an honorific that may well pass to Gordon once he is through racing. Photo credit: International Speedway Corporation Archives.

The evidence extends from the sponsors of cars to the performers who sing the National Anthem to the leisure-time pursuits of the drivers and fans. Major Winston Cup sponsors with an overt "country" theme during the 1999 season included Jimmy Dean Sausage, John Deere Tractors, Realtree Camouflage apparel, Polaris All-Terrain Vehicles, Skoal snuff, and Remington Firearms. Country performers Brooks and Dunn were associate sponsors of the Number 40 Sterling Marlin machine. Fans who showed up early for the Pepsi 400 in Daytona were treated to a John Michael Montgomery concert. In the pre-race activities at Darlington, the P.A. system blared out a country-western song written specifically about the Track Too Tough to Tame. Can you imagine a grunge anthem to the Daytona 500? A hip-hop paean to Rockingham?

The link between NASCAR and outdoorsmanship is immediately evident in the huge RV villages that spring up around every track as the

Polaris "all-terrain" vehicles being marketed at the NAPA 500 in Atlanta. NASCAR fans tend to be "country folk," even if they happen to live in a city, and Polaris is one among many prominent Winston Cup sponsors whose products are meant to appeal to campers, hunters, and outdoors sportsmen (and women) of all sorts.

Winston Cup weekend nears. Not dozens, not hundreds, not thousands, but *tens* of thousands of campers, pop-ups, tents, come-alongs, vans, and full-scale, fully-equipped motor homes snuggle up side-by-side to create small cities populated exclusively by race fans. These villages spring to life about the same time the team transporters start showing up and sometimes don't start to empty until a day or two after the race. Reminiscent of small-town life elsewhere in America, a favored activity in these impromptu villages is sitting out in lawn chairs on the campground equivalent of the front porch and discussing the one topic that brings everyone together at this time in this place — racing. In our little campground across the street from the Indianapolis Motor Speedway, I watched a fan from Kentucky (our friend Ron, actually) saunter over to the campsite of some fans from Illinois and ask *to borrow a cup of sugar*—Ozzie and Harriet smack dab in the middle of urban America. I've been offered hot bratwurst right off the grill and cold beer right out of the cooler by perfect strangers, people I'd never met and with whom I had but one thing in common—I, too, was a race fan. A sociologist wondering if there is any real gemeinschaft left in postindustrial America would be well rewarded by a visit to one of these NASCAR villages.

You don't hang out in these places long before you realize that NASCAR fans often plan their yearly vacations around the races. There are people who work fifty weeks a year to earn the pleasure of a week at Charlotte in May and another week at Darlington in September. If that seems incomprehensible to you, ask yourself if it is any sillier than two weeks at Disney World. Or, for that matter, in Florence.

John Shelton Reed first called my attention to the question of gun ownership among stock-car fans in his essay on the 1992 Southern 500 in Darlington, a race memorable for three reasons: it was Richard Petty's last appearance in South Carolina, Darrell Waltrip's last Winston Cup victory, and then-Governor Bill Clinton's first appearance at a Winston Cup venue. Reed was, as he says, "impersonating a journalist" and was in the infield when "Clinton, his handlers, gofers, and accompanying press showed up. From thirty feet away, Clinton looked much fatter than I'd thought, almost Kennedyesque. I was startled, until it occurred to me

Two views of the campgrounds and RV villages outside the track at Talladega. These villages ring the entire track and stretch for miles up and down the access roads. These pictures were taken the day before the 1999 Winston Cup race. All those cars in the foreground brought people into the track for the ARCA race and for Happy Hour, the last hour of practice for the Winston Cup teams.

that he probably had a bullet-proof vest under his pullover sport shirt. For his sake, I hoped so: despite the Secret Service men glaring from behind their sunglasses, 20,000 or so of us had a clear shot, and nobody'd checked *me* for weapons."[14]

True—they don't check you for weapons at the races. They'll check coolers to make sure you're not bringing in any glass containers, but you could be packing your .357 in your race bag and nobody would be the wiser. In places like Daytona and Darlington, thousands of fans drive cars and RVs right into the infield (paying, as you might imagine, a dear price for the privilege) and no one searches for weapons, or contraband, or drugs, or anything. While we were sitting high in the Segrave grandstand waiting for the start of the Pepsi 400, Brother Kelley scanned the Daytona infield and wondered out loud how many of those thousands of RVs had a gun in them. "I'd assume all of them" was my reply. I've been involved in research on guns and gun owners for twenty-five years.[15] I know how many American families own guns (about half) and what kinds of people gun owners are (small-town and rural people who are outdoor-sports enthusiasts, people who were born into gun-owning families, grew up around guns, have owned and enjoyed guns their entire lives). They're the same kinds of people as stock-car fans. More than that: they are the *same people*. Any time you and another race fan get tired of talking about racing (rare, but it happens), you can talk about guns.

I mentioned that one of the large U.S. gun manufacturers, Remington Arms, sponsored the car driven by Ted Musgrave in the 1999 season. An outfit with the intriguing name America Remembers markets a line of commemorative Winchester Model 94 .30–30 caliber lever-action rifles honoring top NASCAR drivers. They are handsome guns with carved shoulder stocks, "elegantly decorated and embellished in 24-karat gold and nickel artwork" featuring portraits of the driver and his race car. I've seen ads in *Stock Car Racing* for the Terry Labonte and Rusty Wallace versions of these rifles, and I am certain there are others. Each is offered in "a limited edition of only 1,000 rifles" and retails for $1,850, first come, first served. The magazine also has advertisements for Jeff Gordon commemorative pocketknives at $37.50 a pop ("each knife accompanied by a Certificate of Authenticity [authentically *what?*] and a drawstring pouch") and countless other products that would seem ridiculous to an outsider but for which a large fan market evidently exists. Winston Cup drivers are also regular celebrity guests on the cable channels' hunting and fishing shows. So the links between the American gun culture, which encompasses half the population, and the stock-car racing culture are deep, immediate, and intimate. You can bet your life there are firearms in a lot of those infield RVs. And yet I have never heard of a shooting incident at a Winston Cup event.

In a sport whose premier showcases are the *Winston* Cup and the *Busch* Grand National championships, you'd expect a lot of cigarette smoking and beer drinking, and here, as in so many things, race fans do not disappoint. There are not many places left in America where the tobacco companies can promote their products, much less shamelessly, but stock-car races are one of them. Every race I went to in 1999 featured attractive young "Winston Girls" who stopped passing smokers, had them fill out a form, and dispensed free cartons of Winstons. The lines to redeem completed forms for free cigarettes were always twenty or thirty people long. And needless to add, the distinctive Winston logo, the red-and-white Winston colors, and the company's "No Bull" marketing slogan are ubiquitous at every race. In 1999, Winston was also the prime sponsor of the Number 23 Ford driven by Pennsylvanian Jimmy Spencer. (I gave up cigarettes on my forty-eighth birthday but enjoy an occasional cigar. A Winston Cup race is one place you can fire up a fat Macanudo without asking anyone's permission and be 100 percent confident that no one will take offense.)

The beer companies are also heavily invested in stock-car racing. In addition to Busch sponsorship of the Grand National Series, Miller, Coors, and Budweiser are all prime sponsors of Winston Cup cars, and fans return the favor by consuming these companies' products by the bucketful. From time to time, you'll see a fan taking a hit from a bottle of Jack Daniel's, but beer is the intoxicant of choice by a wide margin. Trackside prices are exorbitant — $4 for a sixteen-ounce can of beer — so most fans haul coolers full of the stuff into the track. I've seen any number of fans drink their coolers dry before the race even began. (This is partly a result of the size limits each track places on the coolers they allow through the gates. At most venues, coolers larger than fourteen inches are banned. This, incidentally, is not an effort to limit beer consumption; rather, coolers larger than fourteen inches or so will not fit between the seats.) And as you would correctly suppose, a bunch of testosterone-

Gate 13 at the Atlanta Motor Speedway. Note the restriction: "No coolers larger than 14 inches. No glass." Identical signs are posted at every gate. The restriction on cooler size is not an effort to limit beer consumption. Rather, coolers larger than fourteen inches will not fit between the seats. Because of the size limitation, it is easy to find fans at every race who drink their coolers dry well before the green flag.

addled guys drinking a lot of beer out in the hot sun equates to a fair number of drunks and even the occasional fistfight, although given the circumstances (a stock-car race is, after all, a celebration of manly virtues and cries out for macho posturing) and the sheer quantity of beer being consumed, face-to-face altercations are surprisingly rare. In the eight races I went to in 1999, I saw only one earnest fistfight but scores of drunk fans, men and women alike, who simply passed out upright in their seats while the race thundered by before them. If you've ever been to a stock-car race, you'll appreciate just how drunk you have to be to sleep through one of the things.

Above all else, subcultures embrace a characteristic package of values. The values of the NASCAR subculture are best described as the traditional American virtues. Starting a race without a benediction and a prayer would be unthinkable, as offensive as forgetting to stand and remove your hat when the singer begins the Star Spangled Banner. NASCAR fans take their Ten Commandments seriously, respect their elders, and are chivalrous to women. And while they'll use "shit" and "fuck" as all-purpose vulgarities (as in "Fuck You, You Fucking Fuck"—that tee-shirt malediction I mentioned earlier, which, I'd like to point out, manages to use the f-word as a verb, adjective, and noun in one pithy sentence), they hesitate to take the Lord's name in vain: "That fuckin' shithead just spun out ol' Dee Dub-ya, gosh-dang it!" NASCAR men are, well, men, women are women, there is no ambiguity about sexual roles or orientation. Given the size of the crowds and the numbers of people who follow the Winston Cup, it would be preposterous to suggest that there are no gay people within the fan base. But I have never seen an openly or (to me) recognizably gay person at a Winston Cup event. Not even lesbian biker chicks, who, you'd think, might be naturals.

Individualism, freedom, community, mobility—these are NASCAR values, important values, the things we stand for as a nation. And fair play. Win, lose, or draw, you have to play fair. The Earnhardt–Labonte incident at the August race at Bristol triggered a debate that raged for months in the stock-car fanzines. Was Earnhardt's "bump" inside or outside the standard of fair play? Most seemed to feel that Earnhardt had gone too far, and even die-hard Earnhardt fans were apologetic, as though they were somehow personally responsible for this lapse of racing etiquette.

And equality of opportunity. What are NASCAR's elaborate rules and minute, finicky inspections if not an all-out effort to guarantee that everyone is equal at the starting line? No one gets an unfair advantage; when the race begins, to the extent possible, everyone is just the same. Differences in the outcome reflect differences in talent, determination, motivation, and luck. Is this not a symbolic representation of America herself—not necessarily as she is, but as we would wish her to be?

A cultural anthropologist would understand a stock-car race as a ritual celebration of values that sustain the social and moral order. Along those lines, more obvious and important, even, than individualism, freedom, fair play, or equality is courage in the face of danger. Tom Wolfe's Junior Johnson essay explains the essence of the sport's appeal: "Here was a sport not using any abstract devices, any *bat* and *ball,* but the same automobile that was changing a man's own life, his own symbol of liberation, and it didn't require size, strength and all that, all it required was a taste for speed, and the guts."[16] Guts. Now there's a manly virtue all but lost in our flabby, self-indulgent age. "Guts" is what a man has when he knows fightin' words when he hears 'em and what to do in response. John Shelton Reed: "When those mighty cars are screaming past you 20 feet away at 150 miles an hour you truly appreciate the bravery of the drivers, whose skill and preparation are the only thing standing between them and death. It takes a real hero—no kidding—to go out and face that every weekend, and to do it with the self-deprecating insouciance so characteristic of these men."[17]

As we enter the third decade of women's liberation and the second decade of the postcommunist era, we've come to expect, even demand, more sensitivity and empathy in our men than bravado or grit, and the traditional manly virtues of courage, bravery, and "guts" strike many as anachronistic at best, even dangerous and moronic. Perhaps they are. But the world remains a dangerous place despite the fall of the Evil Empire, and from time to time the nation sees fit to send its young men and women into harm's way, to defend our honor, promote democracy, protect our interests, or assure our economic well-being. And in such hazardous times, should we not all be grateful for institutions, rituals, and subcultures (stock-car racing is all of these) that glorify courage in the face of danger, that give us heroes to worship and emulate, that reward unflinching bravery in circumstances that would scare lesser men and women out of their wits?

It is easier to show that a subculture exists than to give a precise estimate of its size or composition, most of all when the membership criteria are loose. What makes a person a stock-car racing fan? Is it enough to follow the sport on TV, or do you have to go to the tracks? If the latter, is it sufficient to frequent your local tracks, or do you have to go to the major NASCAR events? And if the latter, does it count if you only go to the Busch races, or do you have to be at the Winston Cup events? Does one race a year make you a fan? One race every two years? When Peter Golenbock reports that "the Goodyear Tire and Rubber Company in 1990 conducted a survey and discovered that a full 26 percent of Americans are race fans, including 14 million women," just what do you suppose that means?[18]

I've located two relatively recent surveys that we can use for some first approximations. The 1993 General Social Survey (GSS) conducted by the National Opinion Research Center asked a representative probability sample of U.S. adults whether they had been to "an auto, stock car, or motorcycle race in the past 12 months." Of the 1,593 people who responded to the question, 245, or 15.3 percent said yes. This, obviously, is an imperfect measure. The survey was done in 1993, and the years since have been major growth years for motor sports in general and stock-car racing in particular, so I'd guess that the percentage saying yes would be much higher now than then. Only adults (over eighteen) are eligible to participate in this survey, but many young people are also rabid fans. For any number of reasons, hard-core fans may not have been able to get to the races "in the past twelve months" and would be compelled to say no despite their enthusiasm for the sport. Finally, the question lumps all kinds of motorsports together, so it is not possible to separate stock-car fans from other racing aficionados. Still, taking what the question gives us, in 1993 nearly one U.S. adult in six had been to a motorsports event sometime in the previous year.

The second survey is the 1998 Southern Focus Poll conducted by the Institute for Research in Social Science (IRSS) at the University of North Carolina in Chapel Hill (UNC-CH). Of the forty Winston Cup teams whose shop addresses are given in Richard Huff's *Insider's Guide,* three are in Virginia, one is in South Carolina, and the remaining thirty-six are in North Carolina, so it is appropriate that UNC-CH researchers would be the ones to ask racing questions in their surveys. The 1998 survey has several questions useful for our purposes. One asks whether the respondent "had *ever* been to a NASCAR stock-car race." Twenty-two percent of Southern respondents and 24 percent of non-Southern respondents said yes. (The survey document before me gives all results separately for South vs. non-South since the main point of the Southern Focus Poll is to describe regional differences. So I'll follow that convention in my presentation as well.) This question differs from the GSS question in two important ways: first, it asks for attendance over the respondent's lifetime, not just in the past year.[19] And second, it asks specifically about going to NASCAR stock-car races, not "auto, stock car, or motorcycle races." So the results of the two surveys are not entirely comparable. Still, nearly a quarter of U.S. adults, regardless of region, had by 1998 been to a NASCAR stock-car race at least once in their lives. If we added kids, the number might be higher. If we added stock-car races sponsored by organizations other than NASCAR, the number would certainly be higher. Either adjustment would get us close to and perhaps a ways beyond Golenbock's 26 percent.

Just as there are rabid pro-football fans who have never gone to a pro-football game, so too are there rabid Winston Cup fans who have never made it to a race. Going to the races is an expensive proposition. With even the cheap seats priced at $65 and up, it is far more costly entertainment than going to the movies or even to a fancy restaurant. The Southern Focus Poll asked, "Do you ever watch NASCAR on TV?" Among Southerners and non-Southerners alike, 45 percent said yes. Watching "ever" is not the same as watching every weekend; watching the main event on Sunday is different from tuning in for qualifying, Happy Hour, and anything else racing-related the networks choose to put on the air; and catching the opening and closing laps of the Winston Cup race is different from watching every lap of every event that flickers across the TV screen.[20] But if the criterion for stock-car fandom is watching televised NASCAR events at least from time to time, then the category includes nearly half the U.S. adult population.

The IRSS survey document also breaks down responses to these questions according to selected characteristics of respondents, and these cross-tabs, as they are called, give us some tantalizing hints about the differences between NASCAR fans and the rest of the population. As already reported, the aggregate regional difference is small, not statistically significant, and in the opposite direction of what might be expected (non-Southerners are slightly *more* likely than Southerners to have ever attended a NASCAR race). In both regions, whites were more likely than nonwhites to have ever attended a race (26 percent to 4 percent in the South; 29 percent to 21 percent outside it). Southern blacks, as can be seen, are especially unlikely ever to have attended a NASCAR stock-car race. The gender difference is surprisingly small, although in the expected direction: among Southerners, 24 percent of men and 21 percent of women had been to a NASCAR race, among non-Southerners the numbers being 29 percent and 21 percent respectively. Contrary to conventional wisdom, the likelihood of having ever been to a NASCAR race tended to *increase* with both education and income in both regions, although college graduates were somewhat less likely to have ever attended than high-school graduates or those with some college but not a college degree. The same general differences were observed on the question that asked about watching NASCAR on TV, with the exception that the differences by gender were more pronounced. In the South, 55 percent of men but only 37 percent of women watched televised stock-car races; in the North, it was 62 percent of men and only 32 percent of women.

The GSS survey is older and the question is less specific, but it provides an opportunity to replicate the results from the Southern Focus Poll and to explore some additional variables. First the demographics: like the IRSS data, the regional difference in having attended a race in the last year is small (South, 14 percent; non-South, 16 percent), insignificant, and in the "wrong" direction. (The difference according to the region where one was raised was also trivial.) Although the IRSS differences by age were small, the GSS data show motorsports fans to be relatively young: among those eighteen to twenty-nine, 26 percent had been to the races in the past year; among those thirty to fifty-nine, 16 percent; and among seniors over sixty, only 5 percent. The GSS gender difference is more pronounced than the IRSS data showed: 23 percent of men but only 10 percent of women responded yes to the question about having attended a race in the last year.[21] On the other hand, the racial difference was less pronounced: 16 percent attendance among whites, 13 percent among nonwhites. As with the IRSS data, attendance was highest among those with high-school degrees and those with some college, and lower at the extremes of the educational distribution; and there was again a tendency for attendance to *increase* with income (granted, these differences were small).

The GSS asks a number of questions that the other poll does not. One question asks respondents to describe themselves as either "working class" or "middle class." It will come as a surprise to persons who think of America as a middle-class society that a small majority of U.S. adults (52 percent) describe themselves as working class. Those who do are about twice as likely to have been to a race in the last year as those who describe themselves as middle class (20.1 percent to 10.5 percent). So, taking all this into account, we'd not be too far off in saying that the "average" NASCAR fan is a young, white, working-class male of middling education and higher-than-average income. Which, if you've ever been to a race, is about what you'd expect.

The GSS also has some revealing questions about "country" and "outdoors" themes. There is a 3:1 difference in going to the races between small-town and big-city residents (18 percent for those from towns of 50,000 or less; 6 percent for those from cities over a million); a nearly 2:1 difference between gun owners (20 percent had been to the races in the last year) and nonowners (12 percent); almost a 3:1 difference between hunters and nonhunters (33 percent to 12 percent); another 3:1 difference between those who had been "hunting or fishing in the past 12 months" and those who had not (27 percent to 9 percent); a 2:1 difference between people who go "camping, hiking, canoeing" and those who do not (21 percent to 11 percent); and—don't you just love surveys?—almost a 3:1 difference between people who like country music "very much" and those who hate it (21.3 percent to 7.6 percent).

Statistical tendencies are not categorical differences. In both surveys, there are at least *some* race fans in every category of analysis. Even 8 percent of the people who hate country music went to a car race last year. So it is evident that the NASCAR subculture reaches into every corner and every segment of contemporary American society. Still, it is the tendencies that impart the flavor, the flair to a subculture. And the flavor of the stock-car racing subculture is very much that of young, white, working-class guys who left school for jobs in the factories, make good money, hunt, fish and camp whenever the occasion arises, and get to the races whenever they can. You won't see many of these guys up in the Winston Tower, but if you wander through the RV encampments or sit in the cheap seats on the backstretch, you meet them by the thousands. They comprise the sport's heart and soul.

The day before I started working on this chapter, my colleague Joel Devine forwarded the following, and it's as good a wrap-up of NASCAR subculture as any. Caution: To paraphrase Jeff Foxworthy, if you get most of these, you may be a stock-car fan yourself.

Top Ten Signs You're at a NASCAR Fan's Funeral
10. The casket is adorned with STP decals and has the number of the deceased's favorite driver painted on the lid.
9. The deceased is referred to as "being out of provisionals."
8. A heart-stirring eulogy is delivered by Dr. Jerry Punch.
7. "Amazing Grace" is performed by a nine-year-old girl from Bristol, Tennessee—who has all of her teeth.
6. Only the fastest forty-three cars are allowed into the procession.
5. The hearse is referred to as "the pace car."
4. The cars in the procession weave back and forth to keep heat in the tires as they make their way to the cemetery.

3. Cars caught speeding as they leave the church are ordered to the rear of the procession.

2. First-time mourners have a yellow stripe across their rear bumpers.

And the Number One sign you're at a NASCAR fan's funeral:

1. No coolers over fourteen inches allowed in the chapel.

Short-Track Showdown

The run up I-95 from South Carolina to Virginia takes you past a peculiar but well-known Southern landmark, the South of the Border gas-station-cum-restaurant-cum-discount-curio-shop-cum —what?—motorist megamall. South of the Border signs—immense, tacky, bright-yellow billboards featuring outrageous puns and Pedro, a stereotypical little Mexican fellow in sombrero and serape (just the sort of thing that riles those of advanced ethnic sensitivities)—start showing up a hundred miles out, and by the time you get to the thing itself, curiosity compels a quick stop-over, just to see what it's all about. South of the Border and its only serious competitor, the JR Discount Outlet, are cavernous retail outlets just off the interstate where you can buy gas, food, country hams, whole slabs of bacon, unfinished furniture, country crafts, discount clothing, tacky souvenirs, bags of peaches and pecans, NASCAR merchandise—and, in the case of JR, unbelievably cheap premium imported cigars. We rummaged around for an hour or so at the J-R outlet, scored four boxes of premium smokes, fueled up, and headed north to Charlottesville and our old friends Steve and Daphne.

Theirs is a gorgeous, comfortable home nestled on a crest of Virginia's Eastern Range overlooking the Blue Ridge Mountains. Richmond was a Saturday race and we'd planned to scout out track logistics on Friday, but that gave us two days to walk around the University of Virginia, which was designed by Thomas Jefferson and is certainly one of America's loveliest campuses, and drive along the Blue Ridge Parkway that meanders for 500 miles down the spine of that famous scenic range. It was our first visit to the eastern mountains in a dozen years, and they were spectacular.

Steve is a Virginian by birth and temperament, has taught at the University of Virginia for nearly twenty years, misspent his youth as a confirmed motorhead, and drives a Corvette, yet he had never been to a Winston Cup race. Daphne, too, had been raised in the South but had little interest in and no previous exposure to the stock-car racing scene. They'd accompanied me once or twice to the modified races at Riverside Park in Massachusetts, but that was twenty-odd years ago. Still, they're the kind of people who'll try anything once, just for the hell of it, and they seemed to be looking forward to Saturday's race.

Being an academic, Steve had asked me a month earlier what he should read to prepare himself for the race weekend. I shipped him a copy of Huff's *Insider's Guide* via Amazon.com. Homework is not compatible with my idea of going to the races, but we'd be going to this race with Steve's niece Liz and her husband, Brian, both serious Winston Cup fans, and he didn't want to seem uninformed. So we spent our evenings catching up on old times and friends and going over racin' basics and track protocol. A local mall had a fine though pricey selection of NASCAR gimme hats. Steve had heard of fellow Virginian Ricky Rudd, so we got him a Tide Racing Team hat and touted Rudd's improbable sixteen-season winning streak. He was satisfied that a Rudd victory was well worth cheering for, so he was all set. Daphne felt no need for a race favorite, so we got her an Ernie Irvan M&Ms hat and explained why it would soon be a valuable NASCAR collectible. Well, a collectible anyway. By race day, both looked and could even talk like semiserious Winston Cup fans.

Friday's check into race-day logistics revealed a near-certain parking disaster in the making. Richmond International Raceway sits on the Virginia State Fairgrounds, north of downtown but definitely within the city of Richmond, an urban setting that would certainly complicate our parking and exit strategies. The NASCAR trucks had raced there Thursday night and the Busch cars were scheduled to run on Friday, so by the time we got to Richmond, all the race-day signage and routing were already in effect. And, clearly, the traffic control folks had their own ideas about

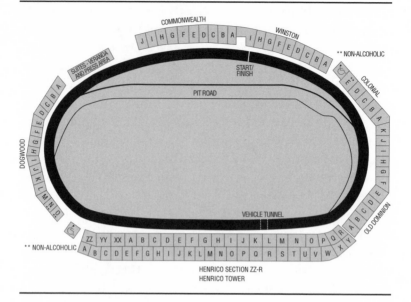

how people would get to the track and where they would park once they got there. So we resolved to do as we were told, park where we were directed to park, and slog our way out late Saturday night after the race was over.

Saturday dawned bright and clear, and we headed back to Richmond about noon. Sure enough, by 2:00, we were being directed along a back road into a peripheral lot that had school buses to shuttle fans to and from the main gate. We parked in an open grassy field along with what seemed like 50,000 other fans, found a cool spot near a stand of trees, and spread out the picnic lunch we had brought with us from Charlottesville. That shady stand of trees, it turned out, was an enticement to race fans who were unwilling or unable to wait for a vacant Port-A-Potty, so we munched on barbecued chicken and cole slaw while fan after fan, male and female alike, sauntered by to seek relief under the oaks, each a bit embarrassed but none deterred. Many had been tossing back brewskis for hours—we knew this from the urgency in their step. We picnicked for a couple of hours, then headed to the track about 4:30 for the 7:30 start.

Richmond's speedway is a three-quarter-mile track, one of only three short tracks remaining on the Winston Cup schedule (the others are

Bristol and Martinsville). It is a clean, attractive, modern, well-appointed facility, seating just under 100,000. The infield is barely large enough to accommodate the transporters, garages, inspection stations, and pits, so unlike the larger tracks, there are no camping or parking spots in Richmond's infield. To compensate, virtually every lawn within a mile or two of the facility had been turned into a makeshift campsite.

As befits its location, the atmosphere outside the track was reminiscent of an old-time country fair. Red, white, and blue bunting was everywhere. Just inside the main gate of the Fairgrounds was a large barnlike structure featuring rural crafts (quilts, cane furniture, hand-spun yarn) and farm goods (homemade jellies and jams, pickled vegetables of every description, fresh apple and pecan pies). Across the way, there was a large livestock show-barn, where Virginia's budding grangers could strut their stuff. There were kids in shorts with Mickey Mouse backpacks and bouffants of cotton candy bigger than their heads, plump moms slurping ice creams cones and carting throwaway cameras and bags of souvenirs, sunburned dads staring resolutely forward, feigning oblivion to the chaos all around them. A few clowns and stiltwalkers made their way through the crowds, and here and there we'd see people, mostly black people, scalping race tickets (the only nonwhite people in evidence). All in all, the mood was lively and convivial, the theme unmistakably All-American, and even though this was a night race, no one was yet falling-down drunk.

Richmond also gets high marks for its concessions, which offered a more varied selection of goodies than any other track I'd been to, including a corn dog that may well rank among the world's best, draft beers (in addition to the customary cans), a Mexican booth with what looked like passable nachos, burritos, and enchiladas, even a Chinese concession where you could get hot egg rolls and pork-fried rice. This, I thought, is a track to come back to, year after year.

Between the main gate and the entrance to the track were the phalanxes of souvenir trailers. At most tracks, these trailers are tucked off in some relatively out-of-the-way spot so you can avoid them if you want to. Not so at Richmond, where everything seems shoehorned into its space. Huge crowds milled around the trailers, drinking beer and lemonade, munching on concession-stand goodies, talking about the race. Most fans whooped it up, Gordon fans shopped for fresh garb (you will *never* see a serious Jeff Gordon fan in a faded or rumpled T-shirt), and the

Jeff Gordon fans shopping for fresh regalia outside Gordon's souvenir trailer. Gordon was NASCAR's hottest star in the 1990s, wining the Winston Cup championship in 1995, 1997, 1998, and 2001. Born in 1971, Gordon notched his fiftieth Winston Cup victory early in the 2000 season; as of summer 2001, his tally was up to fifty-five. He is the only active NASCAR driver with a realistic chance of notching 100-plus wins in his stock-car career, a mark that has been reached only twice in NASCAR's entire history.

four of us bought a race program and some beers and made our way to our seats.

Because of its size and layout, Richmond offers an unobstructed view of the entire track from nearly every seat. We were in the middle of the Old Dominion grandstand, about midway between the third and fourth turns, not far from the entrance to Pit Road. Tickets were $75 apiece. Binoculars were unnecessary: our seats offered a clear, naked-eye view of everything happening on the track. Maybe it was the great view, maybe night-racing under the lights, maybe the rare pleasure of my friends' company, maybe my first short-track racing experience, and maybe the race outcome—rookie Tony Stewart's first Winston Cup victory—but I enjoyed the Exide 400 more than any previous race of the season.

From where we were seated, we could easily see a steady stream of fans walking across the track and into the infield. I'd been bragging to Steve and Daphne that NASCAR lets fans in the pits before each race. I had neglected to add that you need special passes for the purpose, passes that are usually included in hospitality packages distributed by corporate bigwigs, passes we didn't have and weren't sure where to get. But we saw that a surprising numbers of fans, all clutching yellow pit passes, were being turned away. Apparently, their corporate benefactors had failed to alert them that no shorts are allowed in the pits. (This is a safety issue. No open-toed shoes are allowed either. When a Winston Cup engine is fired up, the exhaust is more than hot enough to burn exposed flesh, so no exposed flesh below the waist is allowed.) It was a simple matter to beg unused passes from four forlorn fans and, minutes later, we were walking along Pit Road.

Nothing in my previous racing experience had prepared me for the intricacy and excitement of Pit Road an hour before the race. Every fan knows that the cars go through a lot of tires. But I hadn't realized (I had never thought about it) that each team's supply of tires would be set out in precisely ordered rows and columns behind the pit stalls, or that each tire would have its ultimate location predesignated in yellow chalk letters (LF, RR: left front, right rear), or that the air pressure in each tire would

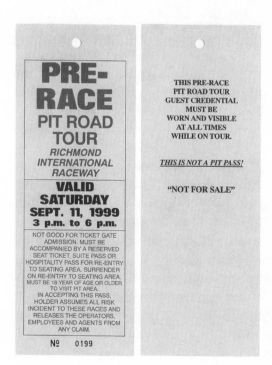

Pit tour pass (front and back) for the Exide Batteries 400 at Richmond. Note that the prohibition against wearing shorts in the pits is not mentioned, which made it possible for the *Fixin' to Git* research team to snag passes and go on its first pit tour.

be checked and rechecked to be sure it was perfect, or that before each race, a member of the pit crew had to glue five lug nuts to every wheel. I watched a young guy gluing lug nuts and realized that one small, innocent mistake on his part—a poorly-glued nut that might fall off at just the wrong time—could cost his team the race. There must be hundreds of similar details to tend to before each race, every one critical to the outcome. That NASCAR allows fans to mill around the pits during these last-minute preparations is remarkable.

On TV or from the stands a half-mile away, the men and machines of the Winston Cup are at best images, ephemeral symbols more than steel, rubber, flesh and blood. The pits made the racing experience more palpably real to me than ever before. We got close enough to Richard Petty's Pontiac to read the dials on the dashboard gauges, and all of a sudden Petty's driver, John Andretti, became a living, breathing human being to me—not a sports hero or a media presence, not some talking head hawking products on the postrace interview, but a real, live thirty-six-year-old guy from Indianapolis who, in about sixty minutes, would be strapping himself into this very fast pale blue hot rod—*this car right here!*—and, along with forty-two other guys, going out on Richmond's three-quarter-mile D-shaped oval to risk life and limb for my amusement. I always figured the pits would be a hoot. But an epiphany? Who knew?

Half past seven rolled around, and as the National Anthem echoed through the raceway, we waited eagerly for the fly-by that never came. *No fly-by!* Every race I'd ever been to had a fly-by, so I had just assumed that Richmond, too, would feature its own version of this noisy, patriotic display. Come on, folks: The Naval Air Station at Norfolk is only ninety-three miles away—they'd be over and back in less than an hour. But this was the only demerit on an outstanding night of Winston Cup action.

Our neck of the grandstand had the predictable contingents of Gordon and Earnhardt enthusiasts and included what was for me a first—a Jeff Gordon gal in full regalia accompanied by an Earnhardt supporter, her husband. This was about as close to an interracial marriage as NASCAR fans get. I wondered: Did this odd couple know each others' racing enthusiasms before they got married? Or did they find out later? "Oh my God! You're a Jeff Gordon fan?" This would, I believe, constitute grounds for annulment in most of the Southern states.

The main topic of fan conversation at Darlington — the Bristol "incident" — was old news by now. Whatever remorse Earnhardt fans may have felt a week or two before was long gone, and they had returned to their loudmouthed, boisterous ways. Sons of Virginia Ricky Rudd and Jeff and Ward Burton enjoyed larger-than-usual fan cohorts, but fellow Virginian Rick Mast was also in the field and I didn't see a Rick Mast T-shirt all night. By the time the green flag dropped, plenty of fans around us were already tipsy, but only one was falling-down drunk, a tough-looking, wiry country boy who took hits on his bottle of Jack Daniel's between puffs on his Marlboro cigarette. He lasted until about Lap 50, then passed out upright in his seat.

Fans, particularly male fans, cheer on their favorite drivers with a peculiar repertoire of gesticulations that is hard to describe in words. As the field comes around, fans stand up and with their left hands (the up-track hand) point to their favorite car, as if to separate that car from the herd. Then, as the cars near, fans wave them through with a long sweep of the left arm, like a crossing guard waving children through an intersection, but with much greater animation. Then, as the cars pass, fans turn to face the crowd behind them and pump their fists in the air, grunting "Oo-oo-oo," Tim Allen style or screaming "You da man, you da man." I sometimes think these guys believe that they actually communicate their enthusiasm directly to the drivers with these gestures. Female fans have a variation on the routine: they stand, bite their knuckles, and then when their favorite driver thunders by, they do a little shimmy and shake all over — a once-a-lap mini-orgasm, maybe fake, maybe real, and maybe not mini.

On the track, rookie Tony Stewart had the strongest car all night long; after a couple of near-misses, he'd found the place to win his first Winston Cup race. He started beside Mike Skinner on the outside of the front row (another Lowe's–Home Depot confrontation) and led 333 of the 400 laps, including the final 144 — as dominant a performance as any driver had turned in all season. I had seen first-time winners twice at the Pepsi 400 at Daytona; a first-time win makes any race a memorable occasion, but this one was even more so because Stewart was a fellow Hoosier. (He went on to win two more races in 1999, a rookie-season record.)

With my attention focused on Stewart, I lost interest in how my other drivers were doing. Jeff Gordon blew a transmission at Lap 311 and finished fortieth; Earnhardt finished sixth; his son, Dale Earnhardt Jr., finished tenth—his first top ten showing in four Winston Cup events. The four Virginia racers finished back in the pack: Jeff Burton at thirteenth, Rudd at twenty-seventh, Ward Burton at thirty-fourth, and Mast at forty-first. All in all, a disappointing night for the state's favorite sons. (On the other hand, Mast ended the 1999 season as the only driver to start *and* finish every one of the season's thirty-four races.) The total purse for the night: $1,939,896. The winner's share: $136,160. The *Fixin' to Git* T-shirt of the race: "Losing is nature's way of saying YOU SUCK!"

Lines for the shuttle buses were prohibitively long, so we walked back to our cars about 11:00, determined to make the best of what promised to be a slow, frustrating creep-along back to the interstate. But traffic control cleared the parking lots with commendable efficiency, with every available lane being used to move cars away from the track. Richmond is the only track I've ever been to that realized the need for traffic control *inside* the parking lots as well as at the exits. At one point, I should have changed lanes but didn't, and the result was a five-mile detour; even with that, we were southbound on the interstate by midnight, making our way toward Charlotte, Atlanta, and home.

Short-track racing is very different from the racing at Charlotte, Daytona, Indianapolis, and Darlington. Since you can see the entire track without binoculars, the action is much easier to follow. But it's not just that you can see more, there's also more to see. At tracks like Indy or Daytona, it doesn't take long for the cars to get into single file, and they will sometimes run in single file for twenty or thirty laps. Ho hum. On the short tracks, the cars are more tightly bunched, so there is more side-by-side racing and passing. Also, given the shorter distance, the lead cars come around on the field more quickly—in a matter of ten or so laps, slower cars are fighting with the leaders to keep from going a lap down and that, too, adds to the excitement. (At Richmond, only eight cars finished on the lead lap.) More side-by-side racing also produces more wrecks, caution periods, pit stops, tweaking, and strategy. Short tracks put a premium on braking and handling. There simply isn't enough straightaway to accelerate to superfast speeds, so the speeds are slower but the action is more continuous and more intense. At the big tracks, there comes a time in every race when the mind begins to wander. Not so at Richmond.

Not all Winston Cup fans are enamored of short-track racing. Before the race we bought beers from a concessionaire who said he was looking forward to the day when this "little track" would be demolished and a superspeedway erected in its place. "Hell," he added, "these boys can only do 125 or so here—I want to see some *speed*." NASCAR's fabulous popularity may grant this fan his wish. Since more grandstand seating can be erected around a big track than a small one, racing economics favor bigger tracks. The short track at North Wilkesboro was sacrificed to create open dates for new superspeedways in New Hampshire (1.058 miles) and Texas (1.5 miles). The last short track added to the circuit was Bristol in 1961; Martinsville hosted a "Strictly Stock" event in 1949, NASCAR's first season of competition; Richmond opened in 1953. Since Bristol opened, fifteen new Winston Cup venues have been added to the schedule, all of them a mile or more in length. And all the tracks currently under discussion as possible Winston Cup expansion sites are being built as relatively flat mile-and-a-half superspeedways.

Although the crowd for the Exide 400 was the largest for any sporting event in the history of Virginia, the place seats barely 100,000 and grandstands rim nearly the entire perimeter. In contrast, the average gate for a Winston Cup race is now 180,000 and climbing. Let's see . . . eighty thousand extra fans at $75 or $100 a pop—my sakes, that's a lot of money.

NASCAR's first stock-car race was contested on a three-quarter-mile track at Charlotte, and short-track events have been featured in championship stock-car racing ever since. Short tracks are more intimate and the racing's more exciting. They add variety to a sport that critics claim is already too homogenized. Would NASCAR sacrifice the tradition, lore, variety, and excitement of the remaining short-track races just to add some more millions to its already bulging coffers?

Don't bet against it.

5

The Yankee Invasion

▨▨▨ Early in *Days of Thunder,* in the scene that introduces Cole
▨▨▨ Trickle (Tom Cruise), the following exchange takes place between Tim Deland (Randy Quaid), Harry Hogge (Robert Duvall), and
the owner of rival Rowdy Burns' car:

OWNER: "S' Harry, where'd you say your driver's from?"
DELAND: "Uh — Eagle Rock . . ."
OWNER: "'At's up around–uhh — Wilkesboro, idn't it?"
DELAND: "No, Glendale. [Pause] California."
HOGGE: "He's a Yankee?!?"
DELAND: "Not exactly. If you're from California, you're not a Yankee.
    [Pause] You're not really anything."
HOGGE: "You said it."

In its earliest years, NASCAR was on its way to becoming a national
sport. There were tracks, drivers, and fans all over the country. In
NASCAR's first three seasons, a fan could have gone to a championship stock-car race in any of fifteen states: North Carolina, Florida, Virginia, New York, Pennsylvania, Ohio, South Carolina, Indiana, Alabama,
California, Arizona, Georgia, Michigan, New Jersey, and Connecticut. If
you're counting, that's six states in the South and nine states elsewhere.
    And so, too, today. Whether the measure is going to the races or fol-

lowing the Winston Cup on TV, there is no hint of a regional gradient in the contemporary fan base. To the contrary, surveys show that the proportion of race fans is actually a touch *higher* among non-Southerners than Southerners, and since a much larger fraction of the U.S. population lives outside the South (by about 3:1), non-Southerners must comprise the sizable majority of stock-car fans at the present time. In 1999, a fan could have witnessed a Winston Cup event in any of seventeen states, eight of them Southern states and nine non-Southern, and in that same year, twenty-four of the top fifty drivers hailed from the North.

So why on earth do people think that stock-car racing is a *Southern* sport?

There's no doubt they do. Fairly or not, Winston Cup racing is more closely identified with the lore, legends, and legacy of the Old South than any other sport except, possibly, professional bass fishing.[1] Our leading commentator on things Southern, North Carolina sociologist John Shelton Reed, includes entries on stock-car racing, Junior Johnson, Richard Petty, and the Darlington Speedway in *1001 Things Everyone Should Know about the South*. That the sport was "too Southern" to attract a national audience is often cited as a principal reason for the networks' three decades of indifference toward championship stock-car events. And, certainly, the vivid display of Confederate battle flags at Winston Cup events adds to the impression that stock-car racing is (or was until Jeff Gordon came along) a Southern sport contested mainly by Southern drivers and enjoyed mainly by Southern fans.

As we will see, there is a simple answer to our question. Although championship stock-car racing enjoyed a national presence and fan base in its earliest years, by the 1960s the nascent national following had been largely abandoned and NASCAR's Grand National Championship series had become a sport of mainly regional interest. Between 1959 and 1971, NASCAR simply stopped racing (more or less) outside the South. The resulting stereotype of Winston Cup racing as the quintessential Southern sport has been with us ever since.

Like all stereotypes, this one has a substantial basis in fact. NASCAR's first non-Southern champion, Bill Rexford of New York, was crowned in 1950, in NASCAR's second season. The second non-Southern champion, Alan Kulwicki of Wisconsin, wasn't crowned until 1992. So Southern drivers have literally dominated the competition over the years, and

An off-the-back-of-the-pickup flag vendor displaying his wares at the 2001 Pepsi 400 in Daytona. In addition to American and Confederate flags, state flags featuring the Stars and Bars were also being offered, along with an assortment of driver, beer, NASCAR, and Florida State banners. Excepting (perhaps) Civil War battle reenactments, there are more Confederate flags to be found at a Winston Cup race than anywhere else in America, a fact that NASCAR's critics seize on with predictable regularity.

to a significant extent they still do today. Still, NASCAR's regional parochialism began to break down in the late 1960s with the opening of new venues in Michigan and Delaware, and by the mid-1970s, the marketing needs of major corporate sponsors essentially mandated that NASCAR widen its geographical base. In the past three decades, NASCAR's strong (at times, near-exclusive) regional focus has been abandoned, numerous venues outside the South have been added, non-Southern drivers and teams have flourished, and Yankee fans have flocked to the sport in the tens of millions. The influx of Yankee drivers and fans—what I will call the Yankee Invasion of NASCAR—is largely responsible for making Winston Cup racing America's fastest-growing sport.

NASCAR Eras

By convention, NASCAR's fifty-one year history is divided into premodern and modern eras, the former lasting from 1949 until 1971, the latter beginning in 1972 and continuing to the present day. It proves useful to my presentation to divide the premodern era into the formative years (1949–1958) and the sixties (1959–1971). As we will see shortly, NASCAR's retreat into regional parochialism was a development of the sixties. I've also divided the more recent years into the early modern era (1972–1989) and the nineties (1990 to date).

Championship stock-car racing was a different sport in the premodern era than it is today. Until 1972, the Grand National season was comprised of as many as fifty or even sixty events, many of them short races (100 miles or less) on dirt tracks and often pitting a handful of top NASCAR stars against local competition. (In the beginning, NASCAR was almost exclusively a dirt-track series. One of Big Bill France's many profitable insights was his recognition that NASCAR's road to respectability would be surfaced with concrete or asphalt, not clay.) The longest season ever was 1964, when sixty-two Grand National Championship races were held. On a few occasions, multiple championship events were even staged at different venues on the same day.

During this era, the eventual champion was often the driver who towed his car to the most races and entered the most events. To illustrate the point (which we'll take up again in the next chapter), the 1958 champion Lee Petty ran in fifty of the season's fifty-one events. Runner-up Buck Baker (Buddy Baker's father) ran in forty-four; no other driver competed in as many as forty. This was not an uncommon pattern. Ned Jarrett's championship season of 1965 saw him compete in fifty-four of the year's fifty-five events. Runner-up Dick Hutcherson and eleventh place finisher Wendell Scott competed in fifty-two, and two other top ten finishers competed in fifty-one. No other driver competed in more than forty-seven; the fifth-place finisher, Californian Marvin Panch, competed in only twenty. In the premodern era, it was not unusual for 200 or more drivers to qualify for and run in at least one of the season's events, the large majority of them competing in just one or two races. In contrast, in the 1998 Winston Cup season, only sixty-eight teams competed in at least one event and seventeen teams competed in *every* event.

Many NASCAR records set in the premodern era will never be duplicated under present rules and format. Richard Petty's 200 total wins will never be equaled; ditto his record of twenty-seven wins in a single season (1967) or his record ten wins in a row (also in 1967). Not to speak ill of Petty's talents, which (to understate) were considerable, but seasons that were fifty or even sixty races long and races that were often run against local competition certainly helped the King amass these spectacular numbers.

In the modern era, the seasons have featured between twenty-eight and thirty-four races, all of them pitting the same fifty or so top teams against one another. (In 2001, the season was expanded to thirty-six events, and there is talk of going to thirty-eight.) Fewer races and stiffer competition ensure that many of Petty's records will stand for all time. Jeff Gordon's 1998 championship season, with thirteen wins, was as dominating a feat as any in the modern era. A driver who won thirteen races every season (an inconceivable feat given the present-day level of competition) would need more than fifteen seasons to amass 200 victories. In the modern era, we are amazed, and rightly so, by a streak such as that of Ricky Rudd, who managed to win at least *one* race sixteen seasons in a row.

The onset of NASCAR's modern era was marked by three significant changes. First, in 1972, NASCAR's founder and organizing genius, Big Bill France, turned over the reins of the organization to his son Bill France Jr. That same year also saw the arrival of big-bucks corporate sponsorship (a topic we'll take up in detail in the next chapter), STP, Coca-Cola, and, of course, Winston cigarettes being the pioneers. Finally, also in 1972, the current seasonal format was adopted, and with a large infusion of cash from the R. J. Reynolds Tobacco Company, NASCAR's championship series was renamed the Winston Cup. Not coincidentally, the modern era has also witnessed a Yankee resurgence in the sport.

The Venues

Before television coverage, NASCAR fans would have been found mainly in the states where NASCAR races were staged. In the early years, being a fan meant going to the local tracks. And, before the advent of corporate sponsorship, which picks up travel expenses, the same would have been true for the competitors, or at least many of them. We saw earlier that wherever NASCAR chose to compete in its early years, local drivers showed up to meet the challenge, no doubt bringing local fans with them. There were drivers and fans from Pennsylvania, New York, and other

Percentage of Winston Cup (Grand National) Races Run Outside the South, 1949–1999.

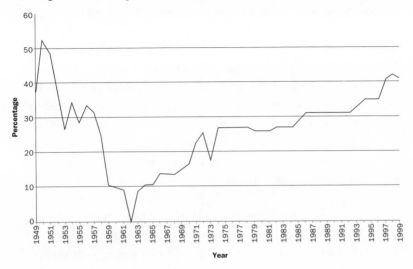

nearby states, even in that first 1949 season, because NASCAR chose to race in those states. So, throughout the premodern era (and, to some extent, even to this day), the venue itself determined the regional flavor of the sport.

So where has NASCAR chosen to race over the years? The graph above charts the percentage of championship events held outside the South for each season through 1999.[2] There was a healthy representation of non-Southern venues in the first three seasons and a reasonable non-Southern presence for most of the fifties. From 1949 to 1958, 131 of 381 races (34 percent) were contested at Yankee tracks. Even in the 1958 season (the low point for Yankee venues in the formative years), there were thirteen races outside the South: four in New York, three each in New Jersey and Pennsylvania, two in California, and one in Toronto, Canada. (Trivia buffs will appreciate that the 18 July 1958 stock-car race in Toronto marked Richard Petty's NASCAR debut. Yep, the King started his Grand National Championship career *in a foreign country!*) In other of the formative years, fans could have attended NASCAR championship races in Connecticut, Ohio, Indiana, Michigan, Illinois, Wisconsin, South Dakota, Nebraska, Iowa, Oklahoma, Arizona, Washington, and Oregon, as well as at the usual venues throughout the Old South. In the late fifties, however, the percentage of races held outside the South plummeted, reaching an all-time

The Yankee Invasion 185

low in 1962, when *every* race of the season was staged at a Southern track. The relative exclusion of Yankee venues persisted throughout the sixties: from 1959 to 1971, only 83 of 661 races (13 percent) were held in non-Southern states. The modern era, in contrast, has witnessed a slow but steady growth in NASCAR's non-Southern presence: in every year since 1986, more than 30 percent of NASCAR's events have been held outside the South, and for the past three seasons, that number has climbed to more than 40 percent. For convenience, I will refer to the precipitous decline in non-Southern venues during the sixties as the "Yankee Hiatus" and the slow growth since as the "Yankee Resurgence." It was during the Yankee Hiatus, of course, that NASCAR acquired its reputation as a Southern sport.

The 1962 season is the only one in NASCAR's entire history with no events outside the South. Eighteen of the year's fifty-three races were held in North Carolina, followed by ten events in South Carolina, eight each in Georgia and Virginia, four each in Florida and Tennessee, and one in Alabama. It was no coincidence that between 1951 and 1983, *every* NASCAR stock-car championship was won by a driver from one of these seven Old South states. The string was broken by Texan Terry Labonte in 1984 and again by Missourian Rusty Wallace in 1989, but aside from these two interlopers, Old South drivers continued to utterly dominate until Alan Kulwicki's championship season of 1992.

Except in 1962, Yankee venues were never *entirely* ignored, with some five to eight non-Southern races in most years of the sixties. NASCAR's most consistent non-Southern presence was in California, where there was at least one race in every year except 1962. Altogether, twenty-one of NASCAR's eighty-three non-Southern races in the era of the sixties were run in California. There was also a fairly consistent presence in New York, which hosted seventeen races between 1959 and 1971. Otherwise, the non-Southern venues amounted, at best, to a thin scattering here and there. The contrast with the formative years could scarcely be sharper, when NASCAR's championship series made regular visits to tracks throughout the East, Midwest, and West.

The graph on the page before contains the answer to the question with which we began. The idea that stock-car racing is a Southern sport clearly arose in the sixties, when, for all practical purposes, it was. But why the bail-out from non-Southern venues? Why a Yankee Hiatus? Surprisingly, the available histories of NASCAR are silent on this point. So far as I can tell, no one has ever even noticed the pattern, much less have they provided a compelling explanation for it. At least initially, the Yankee Hiatus seems mysterious. To all appearances, the non-Southern races of the formative years were as popular, well attended, and profitable as the Southern races. Why, then, did NASCAR just stop racing (more or less) outside the South? Why abandon the non-Southern fan base that had been developed in the formative years?

Was it an effort to reduce the travel burden on struggling, underfunded race teams? Nah. If that was it, you'd expect the California venues to be the first to go. Nothing about the race schedules in the years of the Yankee Hiatus suggests a concern with travel costs. For example, in 1961, there were five non-Southern races, four of them in California (the fifth was in Massachusetts). The first of the California races was at Hanford on March 12. The series returned to California for a race at Riverside on May 21 and another race at Los Angeles on May 27, then returned again for a race at Sacramento on September 10. An economy-minded scheduler would have had the teams run these four events on consecutive weekends, don't you think?

Nor did the teams capitalize on their westward travel by picking up additional events en route. The race before Hanford was in North Carolina and the one after was in Atlanta; the two races on either side of the May swing through California were both in Charlotte; the week before Sacramento, the series raced in Virginia, and the week after, in Atlanta. Again, that's not the kind of schedule you'd come up with if you were trying to contain travel costs.

No decent or suitable tracks outside the South (and California) for the teams to race on? Nope, not that either. NASCAR had had no trouble finding suitable Yankee venues throughout the formative years in states all over the East, Midwest, and West. In 1962, with no Yankee venues at all, twenty-two of the fifty-three events were run on dirt tracks of a half-mile or less, and the same was true in most other years of the premodern era. Tracks of this general description could be found in every state in the country.

Here as in many things, our answer lies in politics and economics. *Pere* France controlled NASCAR with a heavy, dictatorial hand throughout the premodern era. Even the most sympathetic of France's biographers are compelled to rationalize and apologize for his seemingly arbitrary, non-negotiable, often self-serving rulings.[3] No one who has studied NASCAR's early years will have any trouble believing that France scheduled races wherever he damn well pleased.

And, beginning in 1959, he "damn well pleased" to schedule the large majority of NASCAR events in the racing venues of the Old South. This, I believe, was for two reasons. First, although a native of Washington, D.C., France had gone South early in his adult life and was something of a Southern chauvinist. The best evidence for this proposition was his service as the chairman of the Democrats for Wallace campaign in Florida in the 1968 presidential election. (George Wallace carried the state by a wide margin and, in exchange for France's assistance, had some highways built out in the middle of rural Alabama that made France's Talladega superspeedway economically viable.) So it is a fair conclusion, I think, that Big Bill's personal views would have predisposed him to venues in the South.

More importantly, with NASCAR on a firm initial footing, France set out to build the sport's premier showcase, the Daytona International Speedway, in the mid-1950s. (He had broached the idea of the speedway with Daytona officials as early as 1949.) By all accounts, France was fixated on the superspeedway concept. He believed that the future of championship stock-car racing lay not in the short dirt tracks where the sport had originated but in the immense, paved, high-banked tracks that allowed cars to pass in the turns and to run at speeds approaching the then-unthinkable speed of 150 mph. France felt that such superfast tracks, of which Daytona would be the prime example, would attract fans in the hundreds of thousands — a brazen but, as it turned out, correct view. (NASCAR's first superspeedway, the 1.366-mile high-banked oval at Darlington, had opened in 1950 and was the sport's most popular venue until Daytona opened in 1959.) France's superspeedway vision gave us NASCAR as we know it today.

France took huge risks and incurred enormous personal debt to get the speedway built. But, with his characteristic perseverance and with financial assistance from Clint Murchison and Pepsi chairman Don Kendall, build it he did. The Daytona track was at the time unique in all of motorsports, nearly twice as long as the stock-car track at Darlington, with banking in the turns three times steeper than the venerable Brickyard at Indianapolis. Then as now, people marveled at the sheer immensity of the thing. And yet, despite the size, nearly every grandstand seat afforded a clear view of the entire track. France's superspeedway at Daytona permanently transformed the sport.

Daytona International Speedway opened in 1959. It was not only one of the largest race tracks ever built, but it could also accommodate vastly more fans than any previous venue. From that point forward, France had a clear economic interest in building up the sport of stock-car racing in states whose residents could, in a weekend's worth of driving, get to Daytona, watch the race, and get back. For much of the sixties, France's economic well-being depended on sell-out crowds at every Daytona event. And what better way to insure this outcome than to promote the sport most heavily in the nearby areas, that is, the Southeast?

By 1959, France's associates throughout the South were also heavily invested in stock-car racing and venues. France was an active race promoter in the thirties and forties and had pals, business associates, and cronies everywhere in the region, many of them owners of the very tracks that soon became NASCAR staples. He was instrumental in making Harold Brasington's track at Darlington a success and took a direct hand in promoting NASCAR's first 500-mile race there in 1950. South Carolinian Jim Hunter had been France's vice president of administration and marketing for eleven years before becoming Darlington's director of public relations in the mid-60s. In 1982, France's International Speedway Corporation bought the Darlington speedway lock, stock, and barrel. So, in addition to his interests in Daytona, France and his associates always had racing interests in the Carolinas. He and the ISC also built the Talladega superspeedway in Alabama, which opened in 1969, and eventually came to own controlling interests in the tracks at Watkins Glen, Phoenix, and Miami, as well as a tenth of Penske Motorsports, which owns the Michigan and California Speedways. Another France crony, Enoch Staley, owned the track at North Wilkesboro. France's old friend, one-time driving partner, and sometime nemesis, the notorious wild man and moonshiner Curtis Turner, was a co-founder with Humpy Wheeler of the track at Charlotte. Another of the Charlotte principals, Bruton Smith, eventually built the track in Loudon, New Hampshire, which hosted its first Winston Cup event in 1993. Longtime France associate Charles Moneypenny designed both the Daytona and Talladega superspeedways and the three-quarter-mile short track at Richmond, as well as the two-mile track in Michigan that opened in 1969. Fact is, hardly anyone associated with stock-car racing in the forties, fifties, and sixties was unknown to France or failed to profit from his friendship, vision, and business acumen. While he also had friends and associates in California, New York, and elsewhere, France's social and business circle and his own economic interests were heavily concentrated in the Southeast. And so, too, was NASCAR racing throughout the sixties. These decisions made France (and his pals) millionaires many times over, but they also delayed the maturation of championship stock-car racing into a truly national sport by at least a decade.

By the time France opened his second superspeedway at Talladega, his Daytona debts had been long since retired; he was making money hand-over-fist, so it was possible at last to loosen the Southern stranglehold on the sport. In the first year of the modern era, eight of thirty-one races (26 percent) were held in non-Southern venues, the highest percentage since 1957. Between 1972 and 1989, 29 percent of NASCAR's races were contested outside the South, and in the nineties the figure jumped to 36 percent and continues to climb, exceeding 40 percent in the most recent seasons.

The 1999 season was contested on twenty-one tracks in seventeen states, eight of those being Southern venues, nine being non-Southern. The pace of the Yankee Resurgence is seen in the histories of these twenty-one tracks. The oldest still on the schedule is Martinsville, the only remaining venue from the inaugural 1949 season. The superspeedway at Darlington, the second oldest venue, opened in 1950. The three-quarter-mile short track at Richmond opened in 1953. Then, in succession, came Daytona (1959); Charlotte and Atlanta (both in 1960); Bristol, Tennessee (1961); and Rockingham, North Carolina (1965). Heralding the onset of the Yankee resurgence, the first two non-Southern venues on the current schedule—those at Brooklyn, Michigan, and Dover, Delaware—opened in 1969 along with France's superspeedway at Talledega. The next six new venues were all located outside the South: Pocono, Pennsylvania, in 1974; Watkins Glen, New York, in 1986; Phoenix in 1987; Sears Point, California, in 1989; Loudon, New Hampshire, in 1993; and Indianapolis in 1994. In the last years of the nineties, two Southern venues (in Ft. Worth, Texas, and Miami, Florida) and two non-Southern venues (in Las Vegas and Fontana, California) were added. In 2001 new tracks at Chicago and Kansas City hosted their first Winston Cup events. Along the way, the road course at Riverside, the famous California track in Ontario, the Texas World Speedway in College Station, Texas, and the short track at North Wilkesboro, along with countless other previous NASCAR venues, have fallen by the wayside.

As the NASCAR venues approached regional parity, so, too, did the fan base, and by the 1990s, any Southern "distinctiveness" in fan support for championship stock-car racing had long since disappeared. So, if NASCAR has suffered over the years by its now-stereotypical association with the Old South, they have no one but themselves to blame. The Yankee fans were always there for the taking; it was the Yankee *races* that turned up missing.

The Competitors

Ditto the Yankee drivers. The loss of NASCAR venues outside the South in the era of the sixties was matched by a decline in the number of non-Southern drivers (see table 1). The peak of Yankee involvement came in NASCAR's second season, when twenty-four of the top fifty drivers, six of the top ten, and the national champion himself all hailed from the North. In NASCAR's formative years, an average of about twenty non-Southern drivers finished in the top fifty each year (an average of 2.0 finished in the top ten). In the sixties, the Yankee presence among the drivers fell by nearly half (with an average of just over eleven non-Southern drivers among each year's top fifty). As Yankee venues were added after 1969, the number of Yankee competitors increased, up to an average of 15.4 in the top fifty in the early modern era, and up again to 18.9 in the nineties. Finally, in 1999, there were again twenty-four non-Southerners among the year's top fifty, which equaled the 1950 figure. So the Yankee Hiatus cost NASCAR not only its non-Southern fans but also its non-Southern drivers.

More than 3,000 drivers have competed in NASCAR's stock-car championship series, but at the end of 1999 only 153 drivers had ever won a Winston Cup or Grand National race. (By the end of 2000 that figure was 157, and as this is being written, it's up to 162.) Of the 153 winners as of 1999, eighty-four (54.9 percent) hailed from the South, sixty-eight (44.2 percent) from the North, and one from Canada. Given the reduced

Table 1. Yankee Performance in the Winston Cup (1949–1999)

Year	Number in Top Ten	Number in Top Fifty	Highest-Ranking Yankee
1949	1	17	7th
1950	6	24	1st
1951	1	25	8th
1952	2	2	5th
1953	1	16	3rd
1954	3	27	4th
1955	1	18	7th
1956	2	17	8th
1957	1	20	2nd
1958	2	19	9th
1959	2	12	6th
1960	0	10	11th
1961	0	11	16th
1962	2	11	7th
1963	2	12	3rd
1964	1	8	10th
1965	3	8	2nd
1966	1	11	5th
1967	2	12*	3rd
1968	1	11*	6th
1969	1	11	5th
1970	2	14	6th
1971	1	16	5th
1972	1	13*	7th
1973	1	13*	9th
1974	2	16*	6th
1975	3	16	2nd
1976	2	17	6th
1977	1	17	6th
1978	2	18	5th
1979	0	15	12th
1980	1	12	9th
1981	1	16	9th
1982	2	11*	6th
1983	1	15*	10th
1984	1	18*	9th
1985	1	14*	5th

Table 1. Continued

Year	Number in Top Ten	Number in Top Fifty	Highest-Ranking Yankee
1986	2	15*	3rd
1987	0	15*	13th
1988	1	15	6th
1989	1	21**	9th
1990	3	20*	3rd
1991	1	18	5th
1992	1	19	1st
1993	1	20	6th
1994	1	17	8th
1995	2	19	1st
1996	2	18	2nd
1997	1	18	1st
1998	1	21	1st
1999	3	24	4th

* Includes one foreign driver. ** Includes two foreign drivers. Formative years average: 203 / 10 = 20.3; Sixties average: 147 /13 = 11.3; early modern average: 277 / 18 = 15.4; Nineties: 170 / 9 = 18.9. The table shows for each year from 1949 to date the number of non-Southerners who finished in the top ten and in the top fifty each season. The number of non-Southerners racing in NASCAR tends to track closely with the number of NASCAR events held in non-Southern states. The modern era has been characterized by an increasing number of Yankee drivers, a trend that accelerated in the 1990s.

number of Yankee drivers and venues throughout much of NASCAR's history, those sixty-eight Yankee winners represent, I think, a respectable showing.

The graph on the next page shows the states of origin for the 153 race winners through 1999. North Carolina has produced the most winners, with twenty-six. California is second, with nineteen, a function of NASCAR's nearly continuous presence in that state throughout the organization's history. Georgia has produced eleven winning drivers, and South Carolina has produced ten—that's it for the double-digit states. Among non-Southern states other than California, New York is notable for having produced nine winning drivers and my home state of Indiana for having produced eight (even though, I might add, Indiana had no consistent NASCAR presence until the series went to Indianapolis in 1994). Over the years, thirty of the fifty U.S. states have had a native son

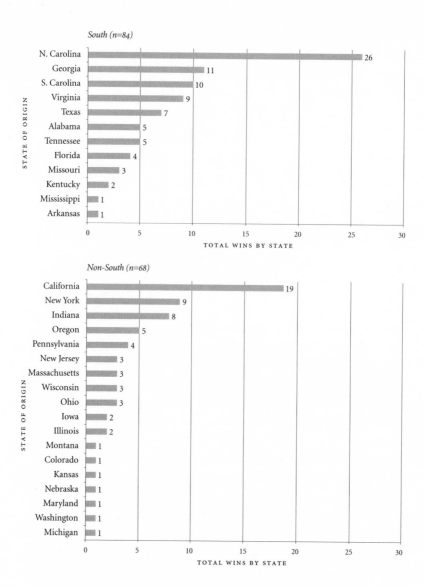

South (n=84)

State	Total Wins
N. Carolina	26
Georgia	11
S. Carolina	10
Virginia	9
Texas	7
Alabama	5
Tennessee	5
Florida	4
Missouri	3
Kentucky	2
Mississippi	1
Arkansas	1

STATE OF ORIGIN

TOTAL WINS BY STATE

Non-South (n=68)

State	Total Wins
California	19
New York	9
Indiana	8
Oregon	5
Pennsylvania	4
New Jersey	3
Massachusetts	3
Wisconsin	3
Ohio	3
Iowa	2
Illinois	2
Montana	1
Colorado	1
Kansas	1
Nebraska	1
Maryland	1
Washington	1
Michigan	1

STATE OF ORIGIN

TOTAL WINS BY STATE

NASCAR Winston Cup or Grand National Winners by Region

in NASCAR's Victory Lane, another indicator of stock-car racing's broad national appeal.

Of the fifty-one champions crowned by NASCAR between 1949 and 1999, only five have been Yankees, three hailed from Texas and Missouri, and the remaining forty-three have been from the Old South. North Carolina again leads the list: twenty-six of the fifty-one championships have gone to drivers from the Tarheel State, with North Carolinians Richard Petty and Dale Earnhardt securing fourteen championships between them. South Carolina comes in second, with seven championships. Tennessee, Georgia, and Indiana all have three; Alabama, Texas, and Virginia have two; New York, Wisconsin, and Missouri have one apiece. As I have already pointed out, the first Yankee champion, New York's Bill Rexford, was crowned in 1950; the second, Wisconsin's Alan Kulwicki, was crowned in 1992. The third, fourth, and fifth Yankee championships went to California-born and Indiana-raised Jeff Gordon, who won the Winston Cup championship in 1995, 1997, and 1998 (and who will probably win it a few more times before he hangs up his helmet for good).

That's a mere five Yankee champions in NASCAR's first fifty-one years —but that's also four in the eight years and three in five years leading up to 1999. And that's as clear a sign of the Yankee Invasion of NASCAR as I have found. Some portion of the fan animosity toward Jeff Gordon must be that he, like Cole Trickle, is a *Yankee*. More than that: he is to the Yankee invasion of NASCAR what General Sherman was to that earlier Yankee invasion more than a century ago. (The 1999 champion, by the way, was Dale Jarrett from North Carolina, the 2000 champion was Texan Bobby Labonte, and the 2001 champion was again Jeff Gordon.)

The future of the Yankee presence in NASCAR seems assured. Gordon was the top rookie in 1993, and six of the seven Rookies of the Year crowned since have hailed from Northern states: Ricky Craven (Maine), Johnny Benson (Michigan), Mike Skinner (California), Kenny Irwin (Indiana), Tony Stewart (Indiana), and Matt Kenseth (Wisconsin). (How 'bout them Hoosiers!) The only Southern Rookie of the Year since Jeff Gordon entered the scene was Virginia's Jeff Burton in 1994. Other up-and-coming Yankees include Jerry Nadeau (Connecticut), John Andretti (Indiana), Kevin LePage (Vermont), Rich Bickle (Wisconsin), Dave Blaney (Ohio), and Steve Park (New York). The large number of talented young Northern drivers has caused at least a few Southern fans to express fears about an emerging Yankee monopoly, but there are plenty of talented young Southern drivers as well: Dale Earnhardt Jr. (North Carolina), Buckshot Jones (Georgia), Eliot Sadler (Virginia), Jeremy Mayfield (Kentucky), and numerous others. If all the drivers I have just named live up to their potential, I predict there'll be regional parity among Winston Cup competitors for at least the next couple decades.

In his *Time* article, Steve Lopez asserts that "NASCAR didn't go national until a Yankee [Jeff Gordon] became its star, and resentment is the breeze that keeps those rebels flags flying."[4] But as we've seen, NASCAR "went national" in its first three seasons and was a national sport, or at least was trying to be, throughout its formative years. True, the sport also "went South" for a decade, but this was a relatively short-lived aberration. The beginning of the end of NASCAR's regional parochialism can be dated to 1969, when the new speedways in Delaware and Michigan were opened. Not to pick nits or anything, but that was two years before Jeff Gordon was even born. The Yankee Resurgence is by no means a recent development. It has been under way for three decades and has been a defining feature of NASCAR's modern era.

The Legends

While there've been championship stock-car races held outside the South in every year but 1962 and never fewer than eight non-Southerners among the top fifty drivers, the sport's legends have always been dominated by Southerners. Peter Golenbock's *American Zoom,* one of the best books ever written about stock-car racing, is based on transcripts of interviews with a couple dozen of the sport's living legends. Of the twenty-five legendary figures featured in the book, eighteen were born and raised in the South and four more, although born elsewhere, were associated for most of their careers with the South or with Southern owners and teams.[5] The only "pure" Yankees featured in the book are Dave Marcis and Alan Kulwicki (both from Wisconsin) and Derrike Cope (born in California, raised in the state of Washington), and these three are featured less because they are NASCAR legends than because they are curiosities: Marcis is featured as one of the last of the independent owner-driver teams whose major claim to fame is "racing on a shoestring"; Kulwicki, because he was the first Yankee Winston Cup champion in more than forty years; and

Cope, because he won the 1990 Daytona 500 (he won a race at Dover later the same year but has yet to win again). In addition, most of the legendary NASCAR figures who are not given chapter-length treatments in Golenbock's book—the Allisons, the Yarboroughs, David Pearson, Darrell Waltrip, Dale Earnhardt, Fireball Roberts, Joe Weatherly, Curtis Turner—were also Southern boys through and through. So, despite the realities of the Yankee presence over the years, the myths, legends, and lore of NASCAR are all distinctively, overwhelmingly Southern.

Why?

Perhaps for lack of raw material. To form the basis of a good legend, a man has to have a renegade streak, a bit of the outlaw in him, and the best of the Yankee drivers simply didn't. Take Freddie Lorenzen from Illinois, who was the winningest Northern driver in NASCAR's history until Jeff Gordon came along. Lorenzen broke into the championship circuit in 1956, racking up twenty-six wins and eighty-four top ten finishes in 158 starts through 1972. Like many of NASCAR's drivers in the sixties, Lorenzen drove Fords out of the famous Holman-Moody stable. In his time, he was obviously a top competitor, yet he figures in NASCAR's legends mainly as a foil in stories told about others. For example, his hotly contested fender-to-fender duel with then-teammate Curtis Turner in the 1961 Rebel 300 is remembered mainly because Turner was so incensed by his eventual loss that he rammed his car into Lorenzen's as Freddie was taking his victory lap, an episode recreated with liberal embellishments in *Days of Thunder*. The wild-eyed moonshiner Curtis Turner is the object of this legend, while the talented but uncolorful Lorenzen is just a sideman.

Then there was Lorenzen's win over Glenn "Fireball" Roberts at Darlington in 1964, which is memorable primarily because Roberts died from injuries suffered the following weekend in a crash at the World 600 in Charlotte. Roberts was burned horribly in the crash, hung on for two months, then lapsed into a coma and died. At the funeral, one of Fireball's relatives was heard to remark, "Want to hear about bad taste? Glenn gets burned to death and the mortuary sends the family a smoked ham! That's the goddamn South for you." True or false, this is the sort of story from which good legends can be crafted—and rarely the sort of story you hear about Yankee drivers.

Lorenzen's engine builder, Waddell Wilson, reminisced to Golenbock,

"Fred gave everything he had to racing. He was very hyper, but smart. I ran around a lot with Freddy and had a lot of respect for him. He didn't chase women or booze it up. . . . He had a one track mind—that race car." A great driver and a fierce competitor, yes, but not a womanizer, not a booze-hound, and thus just not the stuff of legend. In fact, his potential status as a NASCAR legend seems to have suffered precisely because of his origins. Bud Moore admits in his *American Zoom* interview that Lorenzen "*was* a good race driver . . . [but] Freddy came from USAC, ran up North. He was a Yankee coming down South." Legendary crew chief Bob Tomlinson remembers him as "the Golden Boy. . . . He presented a good image but with the equipment Freddie had . . . he should have won a lot more races."[6] Lorenzen himself apparently felt that being from the North was a handicap. He is quoted by Mark Howell to the effect that "down South, drivers were brought up at 10 or 11 years old to learn how to drive a car. . . . They were all brought up on the back roads. . . . There's no comparison."[7]

Then there's Californian Marvin Panch. Who? My point exactly. Panch had seventeen wins and 126 top ten finishes in 216 starts from 1951 to 1966, which makes him the most successful of the California drivers and, among drivers not currently active, the winningest non-Southerner other than Lorenzen. (Among active Northern drivers, only Jeff Gordon and New York's Geoff Bodine have more wins than Panch had.) But, once again, Panch was more a sideman in NASCAR's legends than a principal character. His 1961 victory in the Daytona 500, for example, is remembered more as a win for car owner and chief mechanic Smokey Yunick. In fact, Panch is best remembered for a race he *didn't* run. In 1963, then driving for the Wood Brothers, Panch was badly burned in a sports-car race about a week before the Daytona 500. Tiny Lund from South Carolina was chosen as the replacement driver and went on to win the race—Lund's first NASCAR victory and thus the beginning of the Tiny Lund legend. Car owner Leonard Wood: "It was a very emotional victory for everybody, especially after Tiny took over for Marvin. It was a Cinderella story."[8] And there you have it: Panch the older stepsister to Lund's Cinderella. Yunick remembers Panch as "a real, real nice guy and a good driver, but not a super driver."[9] *A real nice guy?* That is hardly the stuff of legend.

Other top Yankees over the years have included Dick Hutcherson from

Iowa (fourteen career victories), Paul Goldsmith from Michigan (nine wins), Indiana's Darel Dieringer (seven wins), and Oregon's Herschel McGriff (four wins). McGriff ran his first championship stock-car race in 1950 and his last in 1993 at the age of sixty-six (which I believe is the record), but aside from his longevity as a driver, nothing much is ever said about him in any of the NASCAR histories. "Goldy" Goldsmith came into NASCAR from motorcycle racing and is known to have hung out with gamblers and other seedy types, but his potential as a legend clearly suffers because, according to old Smokey, he "was very, very quiet, a very likable guy. He'd work on the race car with you. He had good manners."[10] Good manners? Good grief! North Carolina's Herb Thomas, a legitimate NASCAR legend, had "the manners of a pig"—when you're crafting legends, that sort of thing seems to help.

The best of the Yankee drivers over the years have tended to be capable men who took what they did seriously but who were not nearly as "colorful" as, say, a Buck Baker or a Curtis Turner or a Fireball Roberts or a Joe Weatherly. With the exception of Ohio's Tim Richmond, and possibly one or two others along the way, none of the top Yankee drivers could meet or even approximate the standards of wild drunkenness and sustained hell-raising set by these legendary Southern figures.

Many winning Yankee drivers over the years—Dick Rathmann (thirteen wins), Dan Gurney (five wins), Parnelli Jones (four wins), Mark Donahue, Jim Hurtubise, and Mario Andretti (one win each)—are racing legends, true, but not for their accomplishments in stock cars as much as for their achievements in the Indianapolis 500. Hurtubise turned the first 150-mph lap at Indy. Jones was the first to *qualify* for the race at a speed greater than 150 mph and will be forever remembered as the Andy Granatelli driver whose revolutionary turbine engine failed in the 1967 race with just four laps remaining. And while Mario Andretti is still the only racer to have won a Triple Crown—an Indianapolis 500, a Daytona 500, *and* a Formula One championship—he is known to stock-car fans primarily as an Indy driver and as John Andretti's uncle. Well into the 1960s, it was common for top drivers to race at Indy *and* to compete in the NASCAR championship series (many also raced sports cars, often successfully), but the drivers who enjoyed successes in both venues are almost all remembered for their Indianapolis exploits, rather than for their stock-car racing prowess. In the fifties and sixties any Indiana boy could tell stories about the premier Indy competitors. But successful Hoosier stock-car racers such as Darel Dieringer, Charlie Glotzback, or Larry Frank—gee, who knew? I'd never even heard of these guys until I started the research for this book.

Young boys everywhere worship their local sports heroes, and professional sports came late to the South. In the fifties and sixties, Northern boys idolized baseball players Mickey Mantle and Ernie Banks, football stars Y. A. Tittle and Jim Brown, basketball standouts Oscar Robertson, George Mikan, and Jerry West, and hundreds of others. Even when these sports legends hailed from the South, they played for Northern teams; there were no Southern teams in these professional sports until the late 1960s.[11] So, years before Georgia boys could cheer for Hank Aaron and the Atlanta Braves, they rejoiced in the racing exploits of the legendary Flock brothers, just as Carolina boys rooted feverishly for their state's stock-car champions long before they followed the Charlotte Hornets. If one assumes that the number of sports legends is some simple, constant function of the number of young boys worshiping regional sports heroes, then the Southern prominence among the legends of stock-car racing must reflect, at least partly, the lack of competition for the affection of young Southern boys from other professional athletes.

But there are other, less prosaic reasons why NASCAR's *legendarium* is dominated so emphatically by Southern drivers and teams. Like pro sports and much else, literacy came later to the South than to other regions. Oral traditions thrive where people can't yet read and write—in the backwoods hollows of Appalachia, throughout the Mississippi delta, on Native American reservations, in the inner-city ghettoes, and throughout the American South. The English Department at Tulane University, for example, offers courses on the Southern storytelling tradition and storytellers remain a featured attraction at Southern festivals and fairs. And when the region's storytellers belly up to the wood-fire and begin spinning yarns, one hardly expects them to recount or memorialize the accomplishments of Yankee carpetbaggers and scalawags. Legendary characters, we should remember, are not those who do legendary things but those about whom legendary stories are told and retold. In the North, a person who "tells stories" is a liar, but throughout the South, even to this day, a "storyteller" is an honored member of the community—the keeper of history, the repository of community lore, the storehouse of tradition.

The Southern wing of the NASCAR community has been no different over the years.

It would be wrong, even preposterous, to see in every Winston Cup race an allegorical replay of the Civil War, but large swaths of the *legendarium* are hard to see in any other light. What is that oft-told saga of Carolina moonshiner Curtis Turner ramming the victorious car of his Yankee opponent Freddie Lorenzen if not a metaphor for a proud, defiant, defeated South striking a last futile blow against the Northern foe? One hears in these grand tales the muted but still audible voice of the Vanquished Nation, herself a legend that breeds legends — a brave, chivalrous, outlaw nation brought to heel by Union cannon and Yankee bayonet. Does no part of her nineteenth-century audacity live on in the stories of rebellious, talented, courageous Southern drivers? Do these Southern legends not exist at least in part as compensation for the region's grim history?

John Shelton Reed was once interviewed by a Yankee reporter who wanted to know why Richard Petty is so admired throughout the South. "I finally figured out that he wanted me to say that we like Petty because we lost the Civil War and he gives us something to be proud of." Reed lists three reasons why this probably does not comprise the core of Petty's appeal: "(1) we're not stupid enough to believe that anyone will think better of us for having good stock-car drivers, (2) Southerners who are looking for something to be proud of are found in Atlanta fern-bars, not at the Darlington Raceway, and (3) I'm not sure that most race fans are aware we lost the war."[12] Fair enough. Still, there's no denying that guys like Petty, and certainly King Richard himself, are visibly Southern men, proud Southern men, gritty down-home people without a shred of artifice, and men whose lives display the traditional virtues of "skill, courage, humility, and sly humor," as Reed has it. It just so happens that these virtues are admired by working-class people in all regions and settings, from the smallest villages to the most immense megalopolises, so it has always been easy for NASCAR to lay claim to a large fan following wherever it has chosen to race. But it does not strain credulity — at least, I hope it does not — to suggest that to the sport's Southern fans, heroes like Petty serve as a reminder of what never was but might well have been.

At the same time, there's not much regional chauvinism among today's stock-car fans, not nearly as much as you might expect. The display of

Confederate insignia and sentimentality is the principal remaining exception. At the 1999 fall race at Talladega, one fan from South Carolina had painted a large Confederate flag on the side of his camper and added the solecism, "It Ain't Coming Down." And I've seen numerous good old boys (and girls) with flamboyant tattoos honoring Dixie. Still, Jeff Gordon is booed as loudly at Loudon as he is at Talladega; at the same time, while there were noticeably more Gordon fans at Indianapolis than at other races I've attended, he had plenty of fans everywhere I went. Likewise, I've talked to a lot of Yankee fans over the years who disliked Dale Earnhardt, but no one ever told me it was because he was born in North Carolina.

In a superb spoof (at least I think it is a spoof) on the Southern obsession with collegiate sports, John Shelton Reed recounts a conversation with a group of Chapel Hill students about their long, hard struggle to get lacrosse, of all things, established as an official varsity sport at the University of North Carolina. "Squash? Tennis? Lacrosse? Crew?" Reed laments.

> "It occurs to me to wonder why we'd want to import these la-di-da Yankee sports when we have fine native traditions to build on. . . . Think about it. How about varsity bass-fishing? The university could offer a few scholarships to eighteen-year-old Bassmasters; they'd probably even bring their own boats. Or what about a grant-in-aid for some old boy from Randleman, N.C., who's been racing cars since he could see over a steering wheel? Can you imagine the Tobacco Road 500: UNC, Duke, Wake Forest, and N.C. State fighting it out at Rockingham? Never mind that it's not really Duke's kind of thing. They could hire a team."[13]

Whether or not life imitates art, it always seems to lust after its own ironies, and Reed has given us a fine one. The University of North Carolina at Charlotte, following the lead of Clemson, has recently inaugurated a course of study in high-performance automotive engineering for its students who aspire to a career in motorsports. (At Luzerne County Community College in Pennsylvania, you can earn an Associate of Applied Science degree in motorsports technology — amazing what you can find out surfing the Internet these days.) UNC-Charlotte sponsors a Legends car as part of its overall promotional profile. So does N.C. State, and

I am told that the University of Virginia may soon do likewise. Duke! Wake Forest! Wake up and smell the exhaust fumes! Loyal Volunteer Sterling Marlin honored the University of Tennessee's 1998 national football championship by sporting a UT logo on his race car throughout the 1999 season. Jeff Gordon and former crew chief Ray Evernham have spoken to freshmen engineering students at Princeton, 90 percent of whom had viewed a Winston Cup event. Mark Howell reports that universities such as Clemson and Tennessee, and even Michigan, Colorado, and Penn State, have given serious consideration to sponsoring their own Winston Cup racing teams. Yahoo! The Tobacco Road 500 may not be a spoof after all. Will the day come when hungover sports fans can choose between football and the intercollegiate stock-car championship race for their New Year's Day entertainment? One hopes so.

But in the spirit of this chapter I am compelled to report that the true pioneer here, the first institution of higher learning to align itself with a Winston Cup team, was not the University of North Carolina at Chapel Hill, which you'd have to expect, nor any of the fine universities in South Carolina, Georgia, Alabama, or Tennessee. No, pride of place goes to a Yankee school, the University of Nebraska, who co-sponsored Lake Speed's Number 9 Thunderbird for the 1996 racing campaign. The deal was set up with funds donated by former Cornhusker football player Trev Alberts. The university took pains to assure its faculty, students, and alumni that it was not frittering away its own money on racing engines or pit-crew expenses. I guess Nebraska alums needed some assurance that the university would only fritter away their millions on football. But say what you will, the program got Nebraska's name, colors, and logo on national television for each of the season's thirty-two Winston Cup events, generating February-to-November exposure across the nation — a college marketer's dream. Could as much be said for the average university's football or basketball program?

Nebraska? Hmm. The only Nebraska native ever to win a NASCAR stock-car championship race was Omaha's Bob Burdick, who won the Atlanta 500 in 1961 in a Pontiac. This was Burdick's sole victory in fifteen career starts between 1959 and 1961. It was a crisp day late in March. Californian Marvin Panch was on the pole. All in all, something of a bright spot for non-Southern drivers early in the Yankee Hiatus. . . .

Nantahala Interlude

▞▞ Chris and I spent the drive from Richmond to New Orleans chatting about how much we had enjoyed being back in the mountains. Louisiana's vistas are flat in every direction. Not including the buildings, the highest elevation in the city of New Orleans is Monkey Hill in the Audubon Zoo, which towers all of nine feet above sea level. And even that little topographical bump is artificial, a WPA project of the 1930s bulldozed into place to show New Orleans children what a hill is supposed to look like. Why not spend October somewhere in more interesting terrain, experiencing real hills and a real fall for the first time since moving to New Orleans? My sabbatical and a leave of absence for Chris removed all the usual barriers, and, conveniently, all four of October's races (Martinsville, Charlotte, Talladega, and Rockingham) would be within driving distance of the Great Smokies. So, with western North Carolina as the target destination, a few days of Web-surfing had turned up a lovely little cabin in the Nantahala Gorge near Bryson City, some two hundred miles west of Charlotte. A month in the mountains it would be.

The hopeful idea that I might take in all four of the October races quickly came a cropper. A wedding shower kept us in New Orleans until the Martinsville Sunday (October 3), so Martinsville was out. And some close friends were planning to visit us at the cabin the weekend of the 24th, so Rockingham was also out. On the other hand, we had invited

Chris's parents, Bud and Jo, to spend a week in the mountains with us, and they had picked a Wednesday-to-Wednesday itinerary that would make it possible for Bud to go to Talladega; my brother and his wife were also planning to "do Talladega" then spend a few days with the rest of the family at the cabin. So Talladega on the 17th was a definite go. And there didn't seem to be anything standing in the way of the UAW-GM Quality 500 at Charlotte on the 10th either.

Nothing, that is, but the weather.

Charlotte

My tentative plan for race day was to rise well before dawn and make my way to Charlotte. (Chris planned to stay behind and tend to the dog and cats). Under normal conditions, we had been told, it would be three and a half hours by car to the Charlotte airport. The airport is south of the city, the speedway another thirty or so miles to the north. Add a half hour for the extra miles and another hour for race-day traffic congestion. The total run, I guessed, would be five hours, give or take. Once I got to the track, I'd need to find parking and score a ticket. Add another hour for these essentials and a final hour of fudge factor "just in case." I'd need to leave the cabin by 6:00 A.M. to be reasonably certain of getting to the speedway for the green flag at 1:00 P.M.

It had been raining in eastern North Carolina for a month, and there was talk all day Saturday of rain that might delay or even postpone Sunday's race. I got up about 4:30 Sunday morning and the rain outside the cabin looked like it was being poured out of a bucket. The Weather Channel's radar showed an immense dark-green blotch covering the entire state and a fair portion of the surrounding states. The "chance of rain" in Charlotte was given as 100 percent. (At 100 percent, there is no longer "a chance" of rain — it's raining.) With visibility near zero; half the distance to Charlotte comprising steep, winding, unfamiliar mountain roads; and a high likelihood that the race would be postponed anyway, I pulled the plug on my Charlotte trip and went back to bed. If they get this race in today, I thought, it'll just have to be one I watch on TV.

Prerace coverage started at 11:00, and the opening footage showed heavy rain at the Lowe's Motor Speedway. Really heavy rain. Huge puddles everywhere. Okay, I thought, good decision to cancel — there's no way they'll be racing at Charlotte today. But then radar images showed some clearing to the west. The general thinking seemed to be that while the start of the race would be delayed by a few hours, there was still a chance (not a *good* chance, just a chance) that the race would happen after all. But it was not to be. Throughout the pre-race hemming and hawing, it was raining. When television coverage shifted over to TBS at 12:30, it was still raining. About 3:00, NASCAR gave up the ghost and announced that the race would be postponed until 11:00 Monday morning. I felt smug, sitting high and dry in my cabin when the announcement was made.

The forecast was for nice weather the next day, and I knew tickets would be plentiful and cheap. (In fact, only 90,000 fans showed up for Monday's race.) But the 11:00 start would roll back my target departure time to 4:00 A.M., which would mean getting out of bed at 3:00. Even the thought of that hurt. Then, too, I would be driving to Charlotte and back on Wednesday to pick up Chris's parents, and I was not eager to make that run twice in three days. So, while I agonized for a while, in the end it was an easy decision to spend Monday watching the race on TV — a decision I've regretted ever since, because that race was one any serious Hoosier race fan would like to have seen.

Nearly all the pre-race buzz was focused on the Indiana drivers. Even out in western North Carolina, you could hear race fans talking about Jeff Gordon and his former crew chief, Ray Evernham, who had left the team two weeks before. While many expected (even hoped) that Evernham's departure would end Gordon's domination of the series, Gordon had gone to Martinsville the weekend after Dover and nailed the forty-eighth victory of his career. Was this a fluke, or was new crew chief Brian Whitesell every bit the head honcho that Evernham had been? The team's performance at Charlotte would go a long way toward answering that question. As it turned out, Gordon got his forty-ninth win at Charlotte. My lassitude cost me the chance to witness the best Yankee driver in NASCAR's history win a race, and not just any race: these back-to-back wins tied Gordon with Rusty Wallace for tenth on the all-time win list and, I should think, removed all doubt about the real force behind Gordon's astonishing Winston Cup record.

Hoosiers Tony Stewart and Kenny Irwin had also been in the NASCAR news since Martinsville, where the two former dirt-track sprint-car foes butted heads in a series of confrontations that led to a $5,000 fine being levied against Stewart for "actions detrimental to auto racing." Twice in the early going at Martinsville, Stewart had tagged Irwin from behind and spun him out. Later in that same race, Irwin had retaliated by bumping Stewart from the back and putting him in the wall. Shades of *Days of Thunder*. Making matters worse, as the field had come around under the yellow, Stewart had banged on the hood of Irwin's car, thrown something through the window, and nearly climbed through the window himself, screaming what I assumed to be obscenities all the while. By the following weekend, apologies had been tendered and accepted and both drivers had assured their fans that there would be no carry-over of hostilities to Charlotte. Still, you couldn't help wondering if the two young Hoosiers might not be rubbing up against each other the whole race. In fact they did not. Irwin started back in the pack at thirty-fourth but ended up fifteenth; Stewart started in the fifth position but finished behind Irwin in nineteenth. Neither seemed to pay much attention to the other all day.

The race itself was an odd one — boring most of the day, then wildly exciting at the end. Bobby Labonte had started on the pole, had led most of the race, and seemed completely in control with thirty laps to go. Gordon started in the twenty-second position and only managed to lead sixteen of the race's 334 laps, but among these sixteen happened to be the final eight. Gordon had managed to "stay close" (stay in contention) all day, and when Labonte was slowed by lapped traffic, Gordon made his run to the front, passing Labonte for the final time on Lap 327. Great competitors always find a way to win, and this race was a testament to Gordon's greatness. Gordon-haters were livid, most of all over a controversial Jeff Gordon pit maneuver that NASCAR later declared to be completely legal. (He somehow managed to block Mike Skinner from getting easily into his pit stall, and the move took Skinner out of contention.) Hoosier race fans, on the other hand, were delighted — even if they happened to find themselves a few hundred miles away.

The most interesting story of the weekend was not the rain or the racing but the heavy-duty security at the track. Hours before the race, bomb-sniffing dogs searched the grandstands, and fans were met at the gates by security officers asking questions and inspecting coolers and bags. The reason: two recent bombings of Lowe's Home Improvement Warehouse stores and a bomb threat at the speedway itself earlier in the week. The motives of the bomber or bombers were unknown. Some speculated that the bombings were a protest against the sale of the speed-way's name to Lowe's (still as controversial in October as it had been in May). Others mentioned possible fan anger that Lowe's had not done more for the victims of a May 1 IRL crash at the speedway that had left three fans dead and eight others injured. Either way, everyone assumed that the bombings and bomb threats had something to do with racing.

I was reminded at once that the Winston Cup bad boys were not the only outlaws-cum-folk-heroes running in North Carolina these days. Somewhere out in the wilds of the western North Carolina mountains — maybe just over the next hill — was the notorious Eric Robert Rudolph, wanted by the FBI for the bombing of the Centennial Olympics Park in Atlanta in 1996 and for three other bombings (at two abortion clinics and a nightclub) that had killed two and seriously injured more than twenty others. Every gas station, gift shop, and convenience store in the Nantahala Gorge (Rudolph's suspected whereabouts) sported a poster announcing a $1,000,000 reward for information leading to his arrest; despite this he had remained at large, living off the land and success-fully evading a massive federal manhunt for more than two years. No one doubted for an instant that he had been abetted in this evasion by local people who admired his pluck, his politics, and his righteous defi-ance of the feds. North Carolina mountain-folk are a feisty lot, and there was plenty of pro-Rudolph sentiment in evidence in the little hamlets throughout the region, among them Andrews (the town nearest to our cabin and the site of the FBI's local Southeast Bomb Task Force opera-tions center) and Murphy (Rudolph's home town). One rough-looking fellow at an Andrews gas station provided me with the *Fixin' to Git* T-shirt of the race in absentia: "Eric Robert Rudolph: Western North Carolina Hide and Seek Champion, 1998–1999."

Talladega

Talladega would complete my tour of the legendary NASCAR superspeed-ways: Charlotte, Daytona, Darlington, and now the monster supertrack in central Alabama, which features "the biggest track, the closest finishes, the fastest speeds, the coolest fans" (copy from a speedway marketing brochure). Biggest and fastest are indisputable; at 2.66 miles, the place is even bigger than Daytona, and it holds all the records for fastest Win-

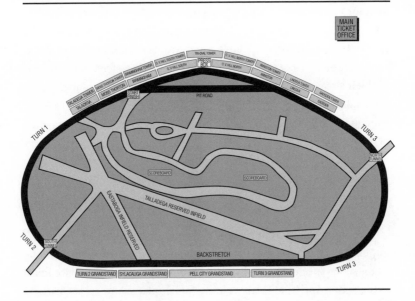

ston Cup laps ever turned. The track was built to resemble Daytona and it does: huge, wide, towering corners, mile-long straightaways, a vast infield, surrounded by parking and RV camping lots stretching for miles in all directions. Somehow I was expecting Talladega to be raw and primitive—a bigger and faster Darlington. But it was much more like Charlotte and Daytona: modern, clean, well appointed, amply adorned with concession stands offering every imaginable treat, a fine place to hunker down for a 500-mile race.

In contrast to the aborted effort to get to Charlotte, my Talladega plans came off without a hitch. Bud and I headed out early Saturday morning about 7:00, with a plan to meet Kelley and Denise at the Airport Holiday Inn in Birmingham, where we had a pair of rooms for the night. Along about 11:00, we stopped for gas, picked up a race brochure, and realized that we could probably get to the track in time for the ARCA race scheduled to start at 1:00. We drove straight in, parked free at trackside, dropped $70 for a pair of general-admission tickets, and by about 1:15 or so we were in our seats along the main straightaway trying to orient ourselves to the race that had just started.

As Winston Cup racing has achieved new heights in fan popularity, interest in the stock-car minor leagues has also surged. I never saw a gate total for the Saturday event but I'd guess there were fifty or sixty thousand people in the grandstands. For an ARCA race! I was dazzled. The race was a 300-mile (113 laps) affair and was just about as wild as stock-car racing gets. Forty cars started the event — only sixteen finished. One car blew a rear end, three more blew engines, a fifth went out with clutch problems, and the remaining nineteen cars wrecked, six of them badly enough to send their drivers to the hospital. (All recovered.) Forty-seven of the 113 laps were run under yellow — on average, a caution period every ten or so laps. For most of the afternoon, Talladega looked more like a junkyard than a speedway. If you're the sort of fan who likes big, high-speed crashes, then — believe me on this one — you owe yourself an ARCA superspeedway race.

Most of the fans in our section of the grandstand seemed to be rooting for Shawna Robinson, the only woman in the race. Shawna's 1999 ARCA super-speedway tour had been impressive — a second-place finish in the season opener at Daytona and a fourth-place showing at Charlotte (a race I attended) — and her eighth-place qualifying effort at Talladega gave her a good shot at winning the race. The speedway also sponsored a "Hit the Jackpot with Shawna" sweepstakes for the Saturday event — $100,000 to a lucky fan if Robinson was victorious. Alas, Shawna's Number 1 Bob Evans car got caught up in a wreck and left the race at Lap 66. At thirty-four, the clock is ticking on a Winston Cup career for this likable and attractive mother of two, but I've seen her race twice in person and both times she was a competitive fan favorite. (There were also plenty of Shawna Robinson fans at the June 2001 race at Michigan, where she became the first woman since 1989 to run in the Winston Cup.) The good ol' boys all around me let out an audible sigh of disappointment when it was announced that she would not be returning to the contest.

Fifty-year-old Bob Strait was the eventual winner of the ARCA race, his first-ever superspeedway win and yet another victory for aging baby boomer race fans everywhere. Winning drivers at all levels of competition often do 360-degree spins (a.k.a. "donuts") at the start-finish line when the race is over — stock-car racing's answer to the flamboyant end-zone celebrations that now routinely accompany NFL touchdowns or the chest bumps now common when basketball players execute a winning play. Donuts are a big crowd favorite, very noisy, and they create towering

Shawna Robinson, one of a very few women currently active in big-time stock-car racing. Shawna raced in the ARCA series during the 1999 season while this book was being written. Since then, she has attempted to qualify for several Winston Cup races and made the field for the June 2001 race at Michigan—the first female driver in the Winston Cup since 1989. When not racing, Robinson spends her time decorating baby nurseries (or so I've been told). Photo credit: International Speedway Corporation Archives.

plumes of smoke from squealing tires. After an embarrassing false start, winner Strait popped three very flashy 360s, but as his car spun through its own cloud of tire smoke, the cockpit filled with fumes and Strait was overcome, unable to make it to Victory Lane. It seemed an appropriate climax for the day's wreckfest to have the race winner himself be unable to walk away under his own power.

With the ARCA race over, a few fans left but more showed up for Happy Hour, including one young fan wearing the *Fixin' to Git* T-shirt of the race: "Fuck milk! Got pot?" This spoof on the American Dairy Association's "Got Milk?" advertising campaign was especially ironic because Jeff Gordon is one of the celebrities featured in the campaign. I'd seen plenty of potsmokers at other races, long-haired country boys who delighted in flouting convention and authority (at least to the point of wearing T-shirts out in public with FUCK printed on them in large block letters). All of a sudden it dawned on me that a strand of hippie culture lives on in NASCAR, not on the track but in the stands—and for some bizarre reason, out there in the middle of Alabama, that felt good to me.

Bud and I stayed for some of Happy Hour, marveling at a sport so popular you can get tens of thousands of paying customers to watch the competitors *practice*. It was about 4:00 when we made our way to Birmingham, some forty miles to the west. As it turned out, Kelley and Denise had spent most of the morning at the track trying to find tickets for the Winston 500 and had left at just about the time we had arrived there. Kelley had accepted the assignment to acquire tickets and had come through with excellent seats in the Tri-Oval Tower, about four rows down from the top. The bad news: those superb seats had cost us $165 apiece, a mark-up of $40 over the face value. It was the most I had ever paid to see a Winston Cup event, but Sunday's race also proved to be the most competitive I had ever witnessed.

The Airport Holiday Inn at Birmingham was completely full, and if there were people in the hotel who were not race fans, I never saw them. Shortly after checking in, we went down to the bar for a few beers. Just like the motel in Darlington, the place was packed with fans decked out in their NASCAR regalia. We went to dinner at a tacky little beanery about five miles from the motel, and everybody in that restaurant was also in town for the race. There may have been retail establishments somewhere in Birmingham that did not display a WELCOME RACE FANS! banner, but I never saw them, either. Like practically everywhere else I had been on the Road Tour, the cities and towns within a thirty- or forty-mile radius of the track had been transformed into what I can only describe as a gigantic family reunion. It felt good to be back home.

The buzz at the bar, the restaurant, and (I imagine) wherever NASCAR fans congregated that weekend focused on Jeff Gordon's two-in-a-row winning streak following Ray Evernham's departure. As always, the fans were in two camps: those who felt that a Gordon victory on Sunday was inevitable, and those who felt it was impossible. I also overheard fans discussing the points race. Leader Dale Jarrett had won the fall race at Talladega a year before, and a win on Sunday would pretty much lock up the championship for him. If, on the other hand, Jarrett had early trouble and second-place driver Bobby Labonte did well, then Labonte could put a significant dent in Jarrett's points lead and use Talladega to launch a late-season charge to the championship. The year's two first-time winners, Tony Stewart and Joe Nemechek, also cropped up in conversations. Did either of them have the car or the moxie to pull down a Talladega win? Nemechek had qualified on the pole and looked like he might have the car to beat. But then Ricky Rudd had the second-fastest qualifying speed and would start next to Nemechek on the front row. Would Sunday bring a victory to extend Rudd's sixteen-season winning streak? Meanwhile, over in the other corner, Earnhardt fans were crying in their beers about the Intimidator's unintimidating twenty-seventh place qualifying effort. Would he find a way to push to the front? We retired Saturday night about 11:00 pondering these questions with the same anticipation with which a six year old retires on Christmas Eve, wondering what Santa will bring.

We had resolved to rise at 5:30 A.M. and be on the way to the track by 6:30 for the projected noon start. The Airport Holiday Inn featured a free continental breakfast and at 6:00 there was already a line — all race fans, of course. We wolfed down what we could scavenge from the breakfast bar and got on the road about 6:15. Fans had started leaving the hotel parking lot at 5:00, and by the time six o'clock rolled around, we were already behind more traffic than we wanted to be behind. We had chosen a route to the track that avoided the interstates altogether, but even with that we were in bumper-to-bumper traffic for the larger share of an hour. We parked about a half-mile away, with our vehicles pointed in the direction we'd want to go, and by 9:00 we were in our seats.

Although it was overcast and chilly early in the day, by 10:00 it was warm and sunny and by noon the temperature was well into the 80s. People all around us were shedding sweatshirts to bask in the spectacular October sunshine. The crowd was a quarter-million strong, with 190,000 or so in the grandstands and give or take another 60,000 in the infield. From what I could see through my binoculars, the pre-race action in the infield was uncharacteristically sedate. I witnessed none of the drunken shenanigans for which Talladega is infamous — no drunken bubbas careening around in pickups, no topless Daisy Maes. Our view was magnificent, as good as Daytona. The seats atop Talladega's Tri-Oval Tower are considered by racing connoisseurs to be the best in all of motorsports, and I would not disagree. We could see the whole track clearly, every corner, all of Pit Road. About 11:30, a half hour before race time, I saw Joe Nemechek pushing a baby carriage through the pits and toward the garage area to his waiting wife, Andrea — the NASCAR Family incarnate. About ten-to-twelve, a black man belted out a solo jazz interpretation of the National Anthem on his trumpet that had the crowd cheering, and as at Richmond, I awaited the fly-by that never came. Nope, no fly-by at Talladega, either. If anybody ever pens a Winston Cup fan's bill of rights, I'd put the right to a fly-by somewhere near the top.

The author and his father-in-law waiting for the start of the Winston 500 at Talladega, the most competitive race in the 1999 *Fixin' to Git* Road Tour. This picture was taken about two hours before race time. Note the crowds walking along Pit Road and, in the background, the infield campgrounds.

The start of a restrictor-plate race (you'll remember that Daytona and Talladega require restrictor plates on the carburetors to hold down the speeds) is unlike the start of most Winston Cup races. At most races, when the green flag drops, you actually see the cars "jump" as the drivers get on the gas and accelerate to racing speed. The faster cars up front jump a little more forcefully than the slower cars at the back, so the cars begin to thin out almost immediately. At the restrictor-plate tracks, the cars don't jump to top speed but slowly creep up on it, all of the cars accelerating at about the same rate.

The effect is eerie. You have a pack of forty-three cars who, after a lap and a half, are all running wide open at close to 200 mph. They are side by side, bumper to bumper, a large gaggle of fast, beefy dancers joined at the hips. In effect, they are forty-three parts of a single physical entity. The volume and pitch of the engine noises build steadily as the pack approaches, then fall off dramatically as the field whizzes by, the well-known Doppler effect. Then there is near-silence — just a distant hum as the cars pass through the first two turns and head down the backstretch — until midway through Turns Three and Four, when the noise begins to build to another roaring crescendo. This *danse macabre,* this high-speed, death-defying, full-metal mambo, goes on for dozens of laps. And sometimes for the whole race: when the Winston 500 ended at Lap 188, half the field was still running fender-to-fender, nose-to-tail, in the lead pack.

The track at Talladega is wide enough and steep enough to run three-wide through the corners and four- or even five-wide in the straight-aways. As the pack fans out off the corners, drivers must make continuous split-second decisions about which cars to follow or which lines to run. At Talladega more than at any other track, drafting is *everything,* and if you get caught without a drafting partner, you'll get shuffled back in the pack. A driver who is highly skilled at drafting is said to "see the air" and can gain a half-dozen positions or more in a single lap. Those who make the wrong drafting decisions lose positions just as quickly. To illustrate, Kevin Lepage was running in second place when he got out of the draft on Lap 180; eight laps later, without wrecking or losing a cylinder or brushing the wall or anything, he finished the race in eighteenth. In the vernacular, he got "hung out to dry." Talladega is like that. The lead changes hands often, and usually when the leader gets passed, he is passed by a group of drafting cars that can be six or eight strong. Going from first place to back in the pack in a single lap is an average day of racing at Talladega.

True to form, the 1999 Winston 500 featured thirty-two lead changes among sixteen drivers. There were only three caution periods for a total of seventeen laps, so the average speed was fast: 166.632 mph. When the dust settled, it was Dale Earnhardt leading the high-speed train of cars to the checkered flag to claim his tenth Talladega victory and his third (and final) win of the year. Earnhardt and Jarrett dueled for the lead for the last twenty laps, but in the end Earnhardt "saw the air" better than anyone else. Amazingly, as the lead pack exited Turn Four for the last time and headed down the main stretch to the start-finish line, the outcome was still in doubt; Earnhardt's winning margin over Jarrett was one-tenth of a second. Flag to flag, it was the most exciting, most tightly contested Winston Cup race I'd ever seen. Most of the crowd spent the entire three hours on their feet, for fear that if they sat down even for a minute they'd miss something exciting.

Jarrett's second-place finish widened his point lead over seventh-place finisher Bobby Labonte and nearly locked up the 1999 championship.

Rudd was in contention all day and finished third, a strong run but, alas, not a victory. Rookie Stewart finished in fifth; Jeff Gordon wound up twelfth; Joe Nemechek thirtieth. At the checkered flag, thirty-eight cars were still running (practically unheard of at Talladega, where huge multi-car wrecks are common), twenty-one of them on the lead lap.

Earnhardt fans were always single-minded in their expressions of enthusiasm for their favorite driver, and by race's end they were whooping it up with the kind of beer-soaked macho posturing that would make you think *they* had just won the race. Kelley in his Tony Stewart hat and I in my Bill Elliott T-shirt were a little annoyed by the clamorous celebration, but Bud enjoyed it—he had always been a big Earnhardt fan himself. Denise was just happy to have seen someone other than Dale Jarrett win a race.

I'd spent years going to Daytona and wondering if racing ever got any better than that. Then I saw my first short-track Winston Cup race at Richmond and decided that the short-track action is as good as racing gets. But Talladega, I concluded, is a thing apart. The track geometry and restrictor plates keep the lead cars tightly bunched from green flag to checkered, and while you do see equally tight racing on the short tracks, you do not see it at 190 mph. A fan seated near me had a gimme hat proclaiming: "NASCAR: "Raw *American* Power." And that's Talladega. Raw power, incredible speed. Everything about the place—the immense size, the vast and immaculate grounds, the speed, the competition—is breathtaking. Allah commands all devout Muslims to make a pilgrimage to Mecca at least once in their lives. Every true stock-car fan likewise owes his devotion a weekend at the gigantic megaspeedway in the rolling hills of central Alabama. It cleanses one of error and purifies the soul.

6

Alcohol, Tobacco, and Firearms: Why Corporate Sponsorship Has *Improved* Winston Cup Racing

We're not big on smoking around here, Shaft, but . . . we called up Cliff at the Federal Bureau of Alcohol, Tobacco, and Firearms. And don't those sound like the ingredients for a great camping trip? — Cecil Adams, *The Straight Dope Tells All*

The U.S. Bureau of Alcohol, Tobacco, and Firearms (ATF) is the bête noire of the country's gun nuts and, given the NASCAR subculture's evident enthusiasm for beer, cigarettes, and guns, is probably not your average race fan's favorite federal agency either. The agency has the unenviable job of regulating commodities near and dear to the hearts of many Americans, and certainly to the hearts of stock-car racing fans. Alcohol, tobacco, and firearms may kill a half-million Americans a year, but they have also given us championship stock-car racing as we know it today. And if that doesn't strike you as a bargain, you've been reading the wrong book.

No sport on earth is more dominated by corporate sponsorship than Winston Cup racing—a domination so total that it is obvious to every observer. Steve Lopez refers to Winston Cup stock cars as "extremely mobile billboards," and who would disagree? Stock cars in the 1950s and 1960s would have a number painted on the side and maybe MERCURY OUTBOARDS or the name of a local car dealer, gas station, or restaurant in block letters down their rear fenders, and that would be it. Bob Latford's *Built for Speed* features a photo dated 19 June 1949 showing three cars racing at the Charlotte Speedway in NASCAR's first Strictly Stock event. All that can be seen on the cars are the numbers: Number 22, Number 41, and Number 47. (Number 47 appears to have some text along the side, but I cannot tell what it says.) Contrast this with modern Winston Cup cars, whose most prominent features are the logos and insignia of their corporate sponsors. What stock-car fan can think of Tony Stewart's Number 20 Pontiac without having the orange-and-white logo of Home Depot spring immediately to mind? Who thinks of the Jeff Gordon car without thinking of Du Pont Automotive Finishes? Newcomers to stock-car racing will know who sponsors a particular car long before they figure out who's driving it or even what make it is.

Cars, teams, drivers, and their corporate sponsors have come to share a common identity and serve a common purpose: to move product. Sometimes it seems that the whole point of running well or even winning races is to get the sponsors' cash registers ringing, a point that NASCAR's critics seize on at every opportunity. Steve Rushin makes a telling observation: "A NASCAR driver will emerge on fire from a 16-car pile-up and still thank Goodyear, Dura-Lube and the good people at Winn Dixie before passing out from the pain."[1]

A Winston Cup stock car sports decals promoting forty, even fifty separate products. Some of these decals hawk high-performance automotive parts and products that the teams actually use (generally, the manufacturers provide these products gratis in exchange for the publicity). Others are displayed to qualify the car, team, and driver for various contingency prizes that are awarded at every race. For example, all the cars sport a Gatorade decal because Gatorade awards a $10,000 bonus to the driver who is leading at the halfway point of each race. The Gatorade decal makes a car eligible to receive this bonus. Other prominent sponsors of contingency awards — and whose decals will therefore be found somewhere on nearly every car — include Budweiser, Exide Batteries, MCI, Raybestos, Goody's Headache Powders, True Value Hardware Stores, and Union 76.[2] Finally, you have the colors and logos of the team's primary and associate sponsors, who pay millions each year for the privilege. The primary and associate sponsors are also prominently featured on the uniforms of the driver and crew, on the transporters that haul the cars from race to race, on pit walls, toolboxes, garage areas, and every other available flat surface, not to mention on the regalia of fans (slower than the cars but mobile billboards just the same). A Winston Cup race is a marketing bacchanalia, an orgy of salesmanship, a festival of American consumerism.

These days, or so critics allege, the race and its outcome are almost incidental, merely the means to accomplish larger corporate goals. While there's no point quarreling with the *fact* of corporate domination, the interesting questions concern its history and effects. How did championship stock-car racing come to be dominated so completely by its corporate sponsors? What do the sponsors get for their millions? And what has been the effect on the sport and its fans?

Many stock-car enthusiasts write long, impassioned letters to the fanzines bemoaning corporate domination. The corporate megamillions are described as a corrupting influence that has transformed stock-car racing —and not for the better. In the words of fan Jeff Brock (in a letter to NASCAR *Winston Cup Illustrated*), "It seems to me that it is coming down not to driving skill but the amount of money your car owner has." Pepsi and Burger King and Bell South can hardly afford to have their products associated with wild-eyed drunks, so all the wild-eyed drunks of the "good old days" have been cast aside in favor of bland, uninteresting, *uncolorful* characters whose chief asset is that they make good corporate pitchmen. Who cares if they can drive or not? If they're handsome and well-spoken, get 'em behind the wheel—and in front of the camera.

The argument churns forward: Corporate involvement has driven up the price of racing. Without major sponsorship, it is well-nigh impossible to compete. This has driven out the smaller, independent competitors and has reduced the level of competition. Not just the drivers but even the races themselves have become insipid and prosaic. Just a few top teams, the five or ten with the best-heeled sponsors, now win all the races. The rest of the field is there to create the illusion of a competitive race. In the words of Fetzer Mills ("my buddy Fetzer" in John Shelton Reed's essay on the 1992 Southern 500), Winston Cup racing has become "a watered down, bloodless version of the sport I grew up with. This is all due to the massive influx of corporate sponsorship in racing."[3]

Although there is some truth to this line of criticism, the larger part is sheer nostalgia. Corporate domination of Winston Cup racing has *changed* the sport dramatically—of that there can be no doubt. But the further conclusion that these changes have somehow been bad for the sport is much less obvious to me. Indeed, I'll make just the opposite case: that corporate sponsorship has made Winston Cup racing better for the fans and probably for the competitors, too.

Warning: The Surgeon General Has Determined . . .

Our story begins in 1964 with the Surgeon General's report *Smoking and Health,* which unequivocally identified cigarette smoking as a health hazard. The report put the federal government's imprimatur on the long-suspected association between cigarette smoking and poor health. This was by no means the first official government report to raise questions about smoking. Pride of place here goes to England's King James I, who issued an edict declaring tobacco smoking as evil, harmful to health, and offensive to religion in 1604. Three and a half centuries later, the evidence associating tobacco use with an assortment of lung and cardiovascular diseases was overwhelming. The immediate practical effect of the 1964 report was to get Congress thinking about how to reduce the American affection for cigarettes.

Six years of warfare between Congress, the tobacco companies, and an assortment of antismoking groups eventuated in a 1970 requirement that all cigarette packaging contain the now-famous warning: "The Surgeon General Has Determined that Cigarette Smoking Is Dangerous to Your Health." The following year, all cigarette advertising on radio and television was banned. Antismoking public-service announcements began running on radio and TV, and as a result of all this, the nation's smokers, once numbering as many as three quarters of all adults, have dwindled to fewer than one in four.

Whatever the long-term effects of these rulings on the tobacco industry (the cigarette companies have remained remarkably profitable), the immediate effect of the ban on radio and television advertising was to free up literally hundreds of millions of dollars that the companies had been spending annually to promote their products. Enter that Last American Hero, Junior Johnson. Johnson's old backwoods mountain buddy, Ralph Seagraves, was a higher-up in the R. J. Reynolds Tobacco Company, and the two pals had talked from time to time about R.J.R. sponsorship of a

The Winston Thunder Theater and a Winston show car, two of a large number of promotions that R. J. Reynolds features at all the Winston Cup races. Stock-car races are one of the few places left in America where tobacco companies can market their wares openly and shamelessly. Note the "proof of age" restriction — a fan has to be at least eighteen to visit the Winston Thunder Theater — and the Surgeon General's warning. Not visible in the photo are "the Winston Girls," attractive young women who work the pre-race crowds and give out coupons redeemable for cartons of Winston cigarettes to passing smokers. The 1971 prohibition against advertising cigarettes on TV and radio led to a flow of marketing dollars from the tobacco companies into NASCAR and gave us championship stock-car racing as we know it today.

race car. At first the company was hesitant to identify itself with something as hazardous as stock-car racing, no small irony considering that tobacco kills 400,000 people each year in the United States alone. But then came the 1971 advertising ban. Junior Johnson in his interview with Peter Golenbock: "In 1971, I was looking for $800,000 to sponsor my race team. I went to talk to R. J. Reynolds. I was the first person to talk to them. . . . I told them I was looking for $800,000. They told me they were looking to spend $300 or $400 million! . . . They had money coming out of their ears, so I suggested they talk to Bill France, Sr. and see what they could work out as far as sponsoring the sanctioning body, and that's what they did."[4]

If there's anything more closely associated with North Carolina than stock-car racing, it would have to be Big Tobacco, which carried and continues to carry a big stick in the state (and region). So the eventual coalition of tobacco and racing was perhaps inevitable. Still, there is little doubt that this lucrative linkage literally saved the day for championship stock-car racing. From the founding of NASCAR up through the sixties, stock-car racing was fueled mainly by the car and tire companies, which were motivated by the NASCAR mantra, "Win on Sunday, sell on Monday." But in the 1960s, Detroit's dominance of the domestic automobile market was being seriously challenged by German and Japanese imports, profits were falling, and the value of being publicly identified with big, fast, gas-guzzling cars was suddenly in some doubt. In 1964, in a dispute with NASCAR about its infamous Hemi engine, Chrysler dropped its sponsorship of Grand National Racing; General Motors got out in 1965; Ford did likewise in 1969. Humpy Wheeler, cofounder of the Charlotte Motor Speedway: "All of a sudden Junior Johnson and Bud Moore and the rest of the car owners were left with only the equipment. They had no sponsors, and for a few years they were able to run with the equipment they had."[5] The very survival of NASCAR was in some doubt.

Enter Junior Johnson, Ralph Seagraves, and Winston cigarettes. Even in the sixties, money—lots of it—was the lifeblood of big-time racing. And starting in 1971, huge barrels full of cash were being invested in the sport by the R. J. Reynolds Tobacco Company, maker of Winstons. Dollars that had formerly gone to purchase radio and television time were now being used for prize money, NASCAR promotions, car and race sponsorship, and just about everything else for which money could be used to strengthen and promote the sport. In exchange, in 1972 NASCAR's Grand National Championship series was renamed the Winston Cup Grand National Series. (In 1986, the "Grand National" was dropped, and the series became simply the Winston Cup.) More than any other single factor, the tobacco industry's promotional millions ushered in NASCAR's modern era. Cigarettes may be hazardous to health, but they've been damned good for stock-car racing.

"Before Reynolds became involved, most of the sponsors were automotive-related sponsors—Champion spark plugs, Goodyear, Firestone, Moog transmission companies, service stations," Jim Foster says in *American Zoom*.[6] Judging from old photographs, local sponsors often got involved in nearby races: car dealerships, gas stations, auto-parts stores, even an occasional restaurant. But Winston's near-instant promotional success with its NASCAR sponsorship soon caught the eye of other national companies.

Unlike the tobacco companies, the beer makers were never driven off radio and television, but Winston's success was enviable and NASCAR's demographics and ambience were irresistible, so Miller and Anheuser-Busch soon followed R. J. Reynolds's lead. Pepsi had been instrumental in helping Bill France Sr. build his superspeedway at Daytona and has been the track's official soft drink ever since; France had offered Coca-Cola the same deal, but Coke declined; it later compensated for its obvious marketing boo-boo by affiliating itself with the tracks at Darlington, Watkin's Glen, and Charlotte and by sponsoring the Bobby Allison race team.

Sponsorship support from the tobacco, beer, soft-drink, and automotive industries carried the sport handsomely through the 1970s. Then came a 1984 marketing study revealing that nearly half of older race fans were women and that there were female fans at all age levels, so all of a sudden the makers of candy, laundry detergent, film, breakfast cereals, fast foods, and even pantyhose were vying for advertising space on Winston Cup stock cars. Once in, most sponsors have stayed in and even increased their level of commitment to the sport.

The arrival of big-time corporate sponsorship transformed the sport of championship stock-car racing in many ways. National corporations seek national exposure for their products and nationwide promotional venues. (Beyond not wanting to be associated with something dangerous, by the way, R. J. Reynolds also hesitated at first because they were concerned that stock-car racing would only be a useful promotional tool in the South). Thus, the involvement of national companies in Winston Cup racing marked the end of the Yankee Hiatus. The influx of leading corporations was more influential than any other factor—indeed, more consequential than all other factors combined—in transforming stock-car racing from a regional to a national pastime. NASCAR "went national" because national corporations discovered they could use the sport to bring national exposure to their products.

Joe's Bar and Grille in downtown Charlotte will derive value from having its name on the side of a car racing at Charlotte, but coughing up the cash to send the Joe's Bar and Grille Mercury to race in California or Michigan would be pointless, of course. In contrast, national corporations who are investing millions each year in their racing programs want maximum promotional exposure for the investment over the widest possible geographical area. If you have millions invested in the STP Pontiac, well, there are potential STP consumers everywhere, so now it does make sense to send your team to compete in every race on the schedule.

As I have said before, the premodern era featured a handful of relatively well-funded top national teams racing against literally hundreds of underfunded local competitors. Table 2 shows that throughout that period, the annual championship usually went to the team that competed in the most events. The annual champion was also first or tied for first in the number of events entered in fifteen of the twenty-three years of the premodern era and always competed in at least three quarters of the races.[7] Before 1972, a team could win the championship this way simply because few teams could afford to race in every event. After 1972, nearly *all* the competitors were national teams, backed by national sponsors and competing (or at least making the effort to compete) in every race on the schedule. It is by no means obvious that the result has been a less competitive or less interesting sport.

Table 3 shows just how immediately the effects of big-time sponsorship took hold. For each season since 1949, the table shows the total number of races scheduled and the number of drivers who competed in all of them. In the twenty-three seasons from 1949 to 1971, there were but two (1953 and 1968) in which at least one driver competed in every race. Since 1972, there have never been fewer than six teams who competed in every race and often twenty or more who did so. Conversely, in the premodern era a couple hundred drivers competed in at least one race (each season), whereas since 1972 there have rarely been as many as seventy-five. So, one effect of corporate sponsorship has been a smaller number of teams, each competing in a larger proportion of races.

Has the result been a less competitive Winston Cup? We'll tackle this question head-on a bit later, but even in the material already presented we can see that there is no simple answer. The trends shown in table 3, which are a direct result of big-bucks sponsorship, are responsible for reducing the total number of annual competitors from a few hundred to several score, so national corporate sponsorship drove out many local teams and in that sense reduced the level of competition. On the other hand, the teams that remain now compete on a much more equal footing.

Table 2. Number of Races Entered by Champion Drivers (1949–1971)

Year	Champion	NTOTAL*	NCHAMP**	Rank among All Drivers in Races Entered	
1949	Red Byron	8	6	1	(T)***
1950	Bill Rexford	19	17	1	(T)
1951	Herb Thomas	41	35	1	
1952	Tim Flock	34	33	1	
1953	Herb Thomas	37	37	1	
1954	Lee Petty	37	34	1	(T)
1955	Tim Flock	45	39	3	
1956	Buck Baker	53	40	1	(T)
1957	Buck Baker	53	40	4	
1958	Lee Petty	51	50	1	
1959	Lee Petty	44	42	1	
1960	Rex White	44	40	1	(T)
1961	Ned Jarrett	52	46	2	
1962	Joe Weatherly	53	52	1	(T)
1963	Joe Weatherly	55	53	2	
1964	Richard Petty	62	61	1	(T)
1965	Ned Jarrett	55	54	1	
1966	David Pearson	49	42	5	
1967	Richard Petty	49	48	1	
1968	David Pearson	49	48	5	
1969	David Pearson	54	51	4	
1970	Bobby Isaac	48	47	1	(T)
1971	Richard Petty	48	46	2	

*NTOTAL = number of races run each season. **NCHAMP = number of events in which the eventual champion competed. ***Tied with one or more other drivers for highest N of events entered. This table lists the twenty-three NASCAR Grand National champions crowned between 1949 and 1971, the number of races run each season, the number of events in which the eventual champion competed, and the champion's ranking among all competitors in terms of number of races run. Until the onset of the modern era, the eventual champion each season was usually the driver who competed in the most races; after 1972, all the top teams competed (or attempted to compete) in virtually every race. Before heavy corporate sponsorship, a few top teams traveled to most of the races and beat up on local competition, a very noncompetitive pattern that ended when corporate sponsorship spread throughout the sport.

Table 3. Running in Every Race

Year	No. of Races	Drivers in Every Race	Year	No. of Races	Drivers in Every Race
1949	8	0	1975	30	7
1950	19	0	1976	30	14
1951	41	0	1977	30	11
1952	34	0	1978	30	12
1953	37	1	1979	31	12
1954	37	0	1980	31	14
1955	45	0	1981	31	12
1956	56	0	1982	30	15
1957	53	0	1983	30	16
1958	51	0	1984	30	17
1959	44	0	1985	28	22
1960	44	0	1986	29	16
1961	52	0	1987	29	20
1962	53	0	1988	29	21
1963	55	0	1989	29	21
1964	62	0	1990	29	22
1965	55	0	1991	29	24
1966	49	0	1992	29	26
1967	49	0	1993	30	24
1968	49	4	1994	31	18
1969	54	0	1995	31	25
1970	48	0	1996	31	22
1971	48	0	1997	32	21
1972	31	6	1998	33	17
1973	28	6	1999	34	32
1974	30	6			

From 1949 until 1971, it was very unusual for *any* team or driver to compete in every championship stock-car event on the annual schedule. One driver (Herb Thomas) accomplished this feat in 1953 and four drivers did so in 1968. In the modern era, many teams compete in every event on the schedule, most of all in the 1990s, when it was unusual for fewer than twenty teams to compete in every event.

As Mark Howell has pointed out, "corporate sponsorship made racing teams more evenly matched."[8] Every team (or nearly every team) can now afford what only a few of the top teams used to afford: the best equipment, the top people, the luxury of being able to compete in every race on the schedule, no matter how far-flung. Once all the teams were well funded, it was no longer possible for a few top teams to dominate. In that sense, big-time corporate involvement has dramatically increased the level of competition.

A Marketing Dream

It is clear what championship stock-car racing got and continues to get from big-time corporate sponsorship: survival through a couple of otherwise rough and potentially fatal years, as well as unparalleled prosperity in the decades since. But what do corporations get from the deal? Surely, there must be better ways to sell candy than plastering M&M decals all over the side of a race car.

To begin, it must be understood that advertising is less about getting people to *buy* your product than getting them to *recognize* it. The principal point of product promotion is to develop brand awareness and corporate identity. So, the point of advertising M&M candies, say, is not so much to compel people to rush to the store and buy bagfuls of those colorful little goodies but rather to get them to *recognize* the M&M product the next time they are thinking about buying candy and to have positive feelings about the brand and its manufacturer. Thus, an advertising goal for Budweiser is not to sell so many millions of gallons of the product but to ensure that the average American male is exposed to the Budweiser name, logo, or slogan at least ten times every day.[9] Obviously, stock-car fans did not flock to Home Depot in the tens of millions the morning after Tony Stewart won his first race. But Home Depot sponsorship of Tony Stewart's team might well cause race fans to think of Home Depot the next time they need to pick up a sheet of plywood or a gallon of paint. And that is exactly the point.

Truth be told, one beer, cigarette, candy bar, engine oil, or home improvement center is much the same as the next. In modern times, corporations compete less on price or quality than on brand image. The value of product promotion through the Winston Cup, then, lies less in its direct effect on sales (which may be difficult or impossible to measure any-way) than in being associated in the minds of stock-car fans with their favorite sport. (This principle generalizes to all forms of sports advertis-ing.) Stock-car fans buy laundry detergent when they need it, just like everybody else. But one laundry detergent works about as well and costs about as much as any other. That being the case, most people will buy the brand whose name they recognize and associate with something of value. So stock-car fans buy Tide not because Tide's involvement in the Winston Cup somehow makes fans believe that Tide works better than Cheer but because fans recognize the Tide name and logo and identify it as "their" brand. They buy Tide because they understand that Tide helps make Winston Cup racing possible whereas rival soap powders do not.

The point of stock-car sponsorship is *exposure* as much as sales. Throughout the 1970s, the exposure gained through NASCAR sponsor-ship was largely confined to the live crowds at the tracks, but because these crowds often dwarfed the attendance at other major sporting events, the live gate was plenty good enough, so a number of national corpo-rations first got involved in championship stock-car racing during this period, among them Gatorade and Coca-Cola. But the big upsurge in sponsor interest (and money) came in 1979, with the first-ever live telecast of a championship stock-car race, and then again in the middle 1980s, when the various cable channels began offering live telecasts of virtu-ally every Winston Cup event. Once the Winston Cup became a route to national television exposure, sponsors lined up by the hundreds. Accord-ing to Richard Huff, there were 523 companies mentioned or otherwise promoted during television coverage of the 1991 Winston Cup season; by 1996, the number had grown to 689, a 32 percent increase.[10] And the number is certain to have grown further in the years since.

These days, it takes about $10 million to field a Winston Cup team for a season, most of which comes directly from the team's corporate spon-sors. The primary sponsor might invest, say, $4–6 million in the team, and various associate and secondary sponsors might each kick in another million or so. These sums are paid directly to the race team. In addition to the core "deal," most teams have contracts with their sponsors that in-clude various performance bonuses (for winning races or the champion-ship, for sitting on the pole, for finishing in the top five or top ten), since strong performances generate more attention and more coverage. In exchange, the primary sponsor gets to choose the car's color scheme, logo, and name placements on the car, as well as (to some extent) the companies that come on as associate sponsors. In fact, an increasing number of big-time sponsors now pay a single price for the rights to the entire car, then sell off space to other sponsors to offset a share of their original investment.

These direct investments in the race team usually represent the *smaller* share of a sponsor's total racing commitment. A sponsor can and often will spend several additional millions on promotions built around the team. For example, many sponsors host large, elaborate hospitality functions in conjunction with the weekend's race, functions at which customers, employees, distributors, and others are wined and dined at the sponsor's expense. The costs of these promotions are on top of the direct subsidy to the team itself. Some sponsors spring for luxury suites at the tracks. Suites that accommodate twenty-five or thirty people rent for as much as $25,000 per race; even larger suites can cost as much as $70,000. Sponsors also shoulder the costs of bringing show cars and drivers to various public appearances. All the promotional materials, products, commercials, advertisements and "give-aways" that mention the sponsor and its race team are also paid for by the sponsor — even the cost of decorating the team transporter with the corporate colors and logo.

Richard Huff reports that in the course of the 1996 racing season, the Pennzoil corporation, sponsor of the car driven by Johnny Benson, gave away 311,950 driver autograph cards; 14,711 Pennzoil hats; 4,007 credential holders (little plastic things that hang around your neck and hold your tickets); 51,500 pairs of earplugs; 601 life-size cardboard "standups" of Benson; 5,665 Johnny Benson posters; 159,330 Pennzoil racing decals; 1,941 inflatable toy cars; more than a thousand umbrellas; 1,180 rain ponchos; 6,361 WELCOME RACE FANS! banners; and 24,950 post cards.[11] Every one of these items sported the Pennzoil logo and was paid for by the Pennzoil Corporation. Huff says that these ancillary promotional efforts will often double or even triple the sponsor's total investment — that is, for each dollar spent in direct subsidy to the team, an additional one or two dollars are spent in various racing-related promotions.

Fans who pay out-of-pocket for cheap seats in the backstretch probably do not realize just how much corporate salesmanship transpires at

Winston Cup races. I was only dimly aware of it myself until the NAPA 500 in Atlanta, the last race of the 1999 season. My friend Jay Joyner is a regional manager for a company that supplies filters and other products to NAPA's stores, and he and NAPA use NASCAR races for marketing and promotions. The basic marketing package that Jay was distributing to his customers and agents included a ticket to the Saturday ARCA race (face value: $35), a ticket to the Saturday night NAPA Race Party (held in a swank downtown hotel and featuring open bars and buffet lines, attended by several thousand people), a ticket to the NAPA Hospitality Tent on Sunday morning (this ticket was also good for a pit and garage tour), and a ticket to the race itself (face value: $95). Each of these packages must have cost NAPA a couple hundred dollars and the company had thousands of them to distribute. The company also coughed up something like a million more bucks to sponsor the race itself. So, between direct team subsidies, race title sponsorships, and related marketing and promotional activities, major sponsors can easily have $15 or $20 million on the racing table each season. A millionaire's sport indeed.

Corporations can and do get involved in racing for smaller sums. According to Robert Hagstrom, part of NASCAR's marketing genius is that the organization offers a complete sponsorship menu that has something for every corporation regardless of its marketing budget.[12] There are, first of all, twelve NASCAR racing divisions. If the price of getting involved with the Winston Cup is too steep, a corporation might consider the Busch Grand National Series instead, or the Craftsman Truck Series or Featherlite Modified Series; if the price is still too high, then there are regional series such as the Busch North or the Winston West for which the costs of sponsorship are lower. Many corporations experiment with sponsorship in one of NASCAR's lower divisions, then, if they are satisfied with the return on their investment, move up to the Winston Cup.

If you have tons of spare cash on hand, you can have an entire racing series named in your behalf (for example, the *Winston* Cup Series, the *Busch* Grand National Series, the *Craftsman* Truck Series). RJR Nabisco pays about $30 million a year for the privilege of having NASCAR's top series named after Winston cigarettes. The price for the Grand National or the truck series is presumably less, although doubtless still substantial. For much less, a corporation can buy an "Official NASCAR Status," that is, it can become the "official soft drink of NASCAR" (Pepsi), NASCAR's "official beer" (Busch), "official theme park" (Daytona USA), "official film and one-time-use camera" (Kodak), and on through a long list. Being an "official" NASCAR something-or-other costs around $1 to $2 million per year. And, for less than that, a company can sponsor a contingency award.

Corporations also sponsor specific NASCAR events (for example, the *Pepsi 400* at Daytona and Michigan, the *Diehard 500* at Talladega, the *NAPA 500* at Atlanta, the *Exide Batteries 400* at Richmond). Nearly every Winston Cup race now has its own official sponsor, with the per-race price tag ranging from one to several million, depending on the stature of the event, the live gate, and television coverage.

Many companies pony up every way they can. Winston sponsors the top championship series, several lesser series, the Winston 500 (the fall race at Talladega), and The Winston (the spring all-star event); in 1999 it also sponsored the Number 23 Ford Taurus driven by Jimmy Spencer. And while Winston is more heavily invested in stock-car racing than any other corporate entity, annual sponsorship budgets in excess of $10 million are by no means rare.

Eight figures seems like a lot of money just to be associated with stock-car racing. What do the sponsors get in return that justifies these enormous expenditures?

Number one, they get television exposure, the exact amount and value of which are carefully tabulated week-to-week in a publication called the *Sponsors Report*. Every Monday morning during the racing season, gnomes at the *Sponsors Report* review videotapes from the weekend's race and record in painstaking detail every mention of products and every clear, in-focus appearance of corporate names and logos, a daunting task considering that virtually every available surface at a Winston Cup event is plastered with an ad for something. In fact, some sort of corporate or product name or logo is visible somewhere on the TV screen virtually every second of every race. According to Peter Carlson, it takes twenty-five to thirty hours to review a Winston Cup race and tabulate all the mentions and appearances.[13]

The effort generates intriguing data. For example, during the telecast of the May 1999 Coca-Cola 600 at Charlotte, "210 sponsors joined forces to secure four hours, twelve minutes, three seconds of clear, in-focus exposure time, 263 mentions and $25,564,320 of comparable exposure value."[14] Needless to say, the exposure time, mentions, and exposure value are reported separately for each sponsor, so sponsors know in detail just what they get from the deal—race by race, weekend by weekend. Most sponsors look to get at least a four-to-one return on their investment—that is, they want $4 worth of "exposure" for each dollar they invest. And most seem to think they get it. At least, they keep lining up year after year.

Only the terminally naive would be surprised to learn that drivers, crew chiefs, and other team members are encouraged and even coached to mention the sponsors at every on-air opportunity. This leads to the occasional odd locution, such as Dale Jarrett's routine postrace reference to his "Ford Quality Care Ford Credit Ford," or Rich Bickle's mention of the "Ten-Ten-Three-Four-Five Pontiac," or Joe Nemechek's reference to his "Bell South Mobility Lucent Technologies Chevrolet," the latter a fifteen-syllable marketing effusion that means "my car." (Indicative of how rapidly NASCAR changes, all three of the drivers just named now have other sponsors.) During the postrace interview, the winning driver will change hats three or four times to make sure that each major sponsor gets appropriate on-camera recognition. Things get particularly awkward when a driver wins a race sponsored by one of his own sponsor's rivals (for example, when the Pontiac Excitement 400 is won by a Ford, or when a Pepsi-sponsored race is won by a Coke-sponsored driver, or when Miller-backed Rusty Wallace puts his car on the pole and wins the Budweiser pole award), since race and contingency award sponsors expect recognition from the winning drivers no less than the driver's own sponsors.

The crass commercialism of all this does get to be a bit much. Just once, I'd like to see the winning driver say, "Well, yes, I thought I drove one hell of a race!" rather than reel off all his sponsors' names. But drivers, teams, and fans realize that speed costs money and that without the money brought to the table by corporate sponsors, there'd be no Winston Cup. Some bemoan the passing of an earlier, simpler, cheaper era in stock-car racing but the bottom line is that without corporate sponsorship, Winston Cup racing would be a different sport, and not necessarily a better one.

But is there really any benefit, say, in having Kellogg's Corn Flakes "mentioned" in connection with Terry Labonte's race car? Wouldn't a sponsor's millions be better spent purchasing air time and running conventional commercials, the obvious alternative marketing strategy? Well, no, not necessarily. First, there's that 4:1 leveraging that companies look for from their sponsorship ($4 of exposure value for each dollar invested). Yes, it can be difficult to measure the effects of sponsorship on product sales or brand recognition, but the same is true of television commercials, billboard advertisements, and other standard promotional activities. Many sports fans use commercial breaks to run to the fridge or the john, or they'll just hit the mute button until the action comes back on. Having your company and product mentioned and featured as part of the event itself avoids this problem. In this sense, sponsorship may actually be *more* effective than conventional commercials.

And, again, the point is product recognition as much as sales, and there is no doubt whatsoever that race fans recognize sponsors' products and associate them with stock-car racing. In fact, NASCAR fans' abilities in these regards are the envy of the marketing world. Robert Hagstrom expresses the point this way: "Ask any person at a race track, 'Who's your favorite driver?' and then ask, 'Who sponsors him?' You will *always* get the right answer. . . . The emotional bond that exists between fans and corporate sponsors in stock car racing is unlike any other in the world of sport."[15] In contrast, how many pro football fans do you suppose could name the companies that sponsor televised coverage of their favorite NFL team? NASCAR has been stunningly effective in educating fans about the importance of sponsorship to the sport. And that is evidently more than good enough for the seven hundred or so companies that are now involved in Winston Cup racing. (We are probably safe in assuming that these companies—many of them Fortune 500 corporate giants—didn't get where they are by making stupid decisions about how to market their wares.)

NASCAR's demographics are also irresistible to sponsors. Nearly half the adult population of the country watches at least one Winston Cup event on the TV each year, and several million turn out at the tracks to watch the action live. The average paid gate at a Winston Cup event is now approaching 180,000 (up from 75,000 a mere fifteen years ago). According to a number of market surveys, the average NASCAR fan has a family income higher than the U.S. average. About half the fans have kids, two-thirds own their own homes, half work in professional or managerial occupations, and three-quarters are regular credit-card users. A sizable fraction (by some estimates, nearly 40 percent) of stock-car fans are women, a higher fraction of female fans than one finds in any other major-league professional sport. (Women are coveted by marketers because they often control household consumer decisions.) Demographics like these score a direct hit on the target markets for products ranging from breakfast cereal to beer to ammunition — alcohol, tobacco, firearms, and nearly everything else.

The most thorough analysis of the economics of race sponsorship is Hagstrom's *The NASCAR Way*. "Sponsorship," he writes, "works to highlight a company in what is otherwise a vat of indistinguishable media messages. Sponsorship, overall, does increase corporate visibility." Again, the point is not just product sales. Some companies use racing to develop a distinctive corporate image. "Racing is viewed as a fast, tough, exciting, innovative and aggressive sport, and many companies are finding out that being linked to those qualities gives them distinct marketing advantages." Hagstrom also points out that race-team sponsorship often increases employee morale and is used by corporations as an entertainment opportunity to reward old customers and seduce new ones.[16]

Most of all, what a corporation buys with its sponsorship dollars are the most loyal consumers in all of sports. A 1994 marketing study by Performance Research in Newport, Rhode Island, stunned the advertising and marketing world. The study report, *RaceStat,* was prepared for the firm's clients — NASCAR itself had nothing to do with it. Two critical facts about stock-car fans came to light. First, fans know who the sponsors are. Second, they have remarkably strong tendencies to buy the products of those sponsors.

Fans were asked to identify companies that sponsored stock-car racing. Respondents named over 200 companies or specific products that they thought were involved with the sport, of which 99 percent actually were. For comparison, Hagstrom points out that the VISA credit-card company paid $20 million dollars to be the official sponsor of the 1992 Olympics, yet 30 percent of the respondents in a follow-up survey named rival American Express as the sponsor.[17]

"Not only are stock car fans aware of which companies sponsor their sport, they are fiercely loyal to those companies." The Performance Research survey found that three quarters of stock-car fans consciously purchase products made by Winston Cup sponsors. Among tennis and golf fans, the figure is about half (who say they intentionally purchase products made by their sports' sponsors); among baseball, basketball, and football fans, it is barely one in three. The level of NASCAR fans' product loyalty is unparalleled anywhere in professional sports. The survey also showed that stock-car fans were more likely to trust the products of race sponsors than, say, football fans were to trust the products of football sponsors. And finally, the marketing coup de grace, more than 40 percent of NASCAR fans said that they had "purposely switched brands when a manufacturer became a NASCAR sponsor" at least once, a far higher percentage than registered among the fans of other professional sports.

In every way, NASCAR is a marketing dream. The marriage of championship stock-car racing to live television coverage has proven, in particular, to be a potent marketing force. Witness the $467 million *per year* that Fox and NBC coughed up for broadcasting rights to the 2001 season and beyond.

A Fan's Nightmare?

Okay, so the big corporations have found a way to profit handsomely from their involvement in Winston Cup racing, and NASCAR has thrived from the resulting corporate largesse. But what have been the costs? How has big-time corporate sponsorship affected the fans, the teams and drivers, and even the sport itself? Purists argue that corporate sponsorship has corrupted and homogenized the sport and reduced the level of competition, but I'm not convinced.

To all appearances, championship stock-car racing certainly looks to be healthier than ever before. The new TV deal could well *double* the purses at Winston Cup events and has enormously strengthened the financial position of the tracks and of NASCAR itself. (NASCAR gets 10 percent of the TV deal, the tracks get 65 percent, and the remainder goes to the purses.) More and more cities are building world-class racing facilities in the hopes of snagging a Winston Cup date. Fan attendance grows every year and TV ratings continue to climb. Two races into the TV partnership with Fox, NASCAR's Nielsen rating were up 86 percent from the previous year, with a particularly strong showing in the major urban markets. This sounds like a sport at the pinnacle of its success, not one whose heart and soul have been ripped out and sold off to the highest bidder.

Corporate involvement has also widened the fan base. My friend Jay Joyner had no interest in and knew nothing about stock-car racing until he started working for a company that supplies auto parts to NAPA stores. Now, a few years later, he is a knowledgeable and passionate fan who goes to a dozen races a year. Home Depot sponsorship of the Tony Stewart race team makes a potential race fan out of every Home Depot employee and customer (and potential Home Depot customers out of every race fan). No one knows how many fans are in the seats of an average Winston Cup race due to complimentary tickets from their employers, suppliers, sales representatives, and the like, but the number is surely large. There were thousands of fans at the NAPA 500 in Atlanta who had tickets because of their association with NAPA, its stores, and its suppliers, and that is only one sponsor among 700 and one race in a schedule of thirty-four events. I'd not be surprised to learn that one fan in three or four was first introduced to the sport via free tickets copped through some sponsor's promotional deal.

Corporate sponsorship has widened the fan base in other ways. "Through off track marketing, sponsors such as Tide detergent and Kellogg's Corn Flakes have exposed millions of new fans to the sport who otherwise would never have come in contact with the excitement of racing," says Huff.[18] Sponsors feature their race teams in stores and on-air promotions, and this exposes additional millions to the sport. As Huff says, "credit for at least a portion of the boom in racing lies firmly with the sponsors." Fans who come into NASCAR via corporate sponsorship "arrive" with obvious affinities for specific teams, drivers, and cars. While there is no guarantee that every Home Depot employee will root for Tony Stewart, it is a good bet that there is a higher percentage of Tony Stewart fans among Home Depot employees than among any other definable fan grouping. So, as it has worked out, corporate sponsorship has also created a batch of "races within races" that have made stock-car racing intrinsically more interesting. Let me explain.

If you have become a race fan or are attending an event because you have some affiliation with Home Depot, then if nothing else you'll want the Home Depot car to do better than the Lowe's car, since Lowe's is Home Depot's chief competitor. So even if you don't give a hoot about racing, or about how the championship battle is shaping up, or about any other aspect of the day's contest, you still keep your eye on Tony Stewart in the Home Depot Pontiac to see how he's doing in comparison to Mike Skinner in the Lowe's Chevrolet. Home Depot versus Lowe's becomes a corporate "race within the race" that can be of interest even if both cars are running well back in the pack.

Corporate involvement in racing creates dozens of these mini-competitions all over the track. You can root for the Pontiacs to beat the Fords, the Pepsi teams to outdo the Coke teams, or the Budweiser car to best the Miller's and Coor's entries. If breakfast cereal is your thing, you can root for the Cheerios car to whip the Corn Flakes car. And if motor oil matters to you, well, you can hope that Valvoline bests Havoline, Pennzoil, and Quaker State. Do you have a preference for Exide, Interstate, or Die Hard batteries? If yes, then there's a car to root for and two to root against. Do you have a preference for Wendy's over Burger King or McDonald's? Ditto.

The advantage of paying attention to these little mini-competitions (each of them a metaphor for the competitive essence of corporate America) is that they give you plenty of racing action to follow even if your favorite drivers are doing poorly. If it is important to you that Home Depot beat Lowe's, then you'll have as much fun watching Stewart and Skinner joust for twenty-eighth position as you'd have if they were running one and two. If you got complimentary tickets to the race because you manage a McDonald's restaurant, then of course you'll be interested in how the McDonald's-sponsored entry fares against the rest of the field.

The unexpected conclusion is that corporate involvement has made Winston Cup racing more interesting to more fans because these corporate mini-competitions give fans more to get excited about. If you have a preference for a particular beer, battery, gasoline, long-distance service, motor oil, candy bar, breakfast cereal, whole-hog sausage, soap powder, car maker, auto-parts store, engine additive, brand of tool, supermarket chain, soft drink, headache remedy, or fast-food restaurant, then somewhere on the track of every Winston Cup race you'll find something of interest going on. Compare this with any other major sport, where your choices are restricted to rooting for this team or that one. When I combine all my preferences for drivers, teams, and sponsor products, I usually have at least some reason to root for half the entries in the field.

Corporate sponsorship arrangements have also increased the level of contact between the stars and the fans. Say what you want about drivers becoming corporate spokesmen, as corporate representatives the drivers are out in public as often as possible, meeting people, signing autographs, shaking hands. Top drivers are in nearly year-round demand by their sponsors to appear at corporate events, stores, and sales meetings; in fact, many are under legal contract to get out and meet the public. The accessibility of drivers to the fans is one reason NASCAR has become such a popular sport.

Naturally, a driver's demeanor and appearance matter when corporations are trying to decide which drivers, teams, or cars to sponsor. No corporation is going to pay millions to be associated with some slobbering, toothless fool or a vulgar, foul-mouthed drunk. So, yes, today's drivers are probably more presentable and better-spoken (less "colorful") than drivers in the fifties and sixties. (Contracts with sponsors and obligations to their teams also keep today's drivers busy year-round, so today's drivers have much less time to drink, carouse, and raise hell than did the drivers in earlier eras.) But let's not exaggerate. No one is going to strap a man into a $200,000 racing machine and let him run it around a track at 200 mph just because he's good-looking.

Purists lament the transformation of top drivers into corporate *spokes*men, but when drivers are featured in sponsors' product commercials, as they frequently are, they often have no spoken lines. There are many exceptions, of course, but in a surprising number of cases, the viewer sees the driver but does not hear him speak. The reason is not hard to fathom. Many top drivers have thick, nasal, high-pitched Southern accents or goofy-sounding Hoosier accents that make them less than ideal as voices for their corporate sponsors. For the most part, the drivers are corporate *looks*men, not spokesmen. No sponsor ever put money down on the Bill Elliott racing program because Awesome Bill *sounds* good when he's behind the microphone pitching products.

A few of today's Winston Cup stars are strikingly attractive men. Chad Little is often described as "disarmingly handsome," and Jeff Gordon has the kind of clean-cut good looks that can send a young girl's heart all aflutter. Michael Waltrip is also a tall, handsome man. But then what? Not to be invidious or catty or anything, but Winston surely did not choose to sponsor the Jimmy Spencer car because that pudgy Pennsylvanian looks sharp in his pre-race interviews. Most Winston Cup drivers are reasonably good-looking guys, but few are potential GQ material; many are, well, plain-looking down-home men whose assets are not that they are handsome or well-spoken but that they know how to drive a race car as fast as it will go. A NASCAR calendar featuring drivers in Speedos might be feasible, but if you had that contract, you'd soon find yourself grateful that there are only twelve months in a year.

It is also easy to exaggerate the differences between today's drivers and those of the past, not all of whom were floppy-eared old hound dogs, not by any means. Harry Gant was known as "Handsome Harry" because he was a good-looking guy. In their prime, drivers like Richard Petty and Freddie Lorenzen also turned more than one girl's head. Standards of physical attractiveness, as all other elements of culture, evolve over the decades, but judged by the standards of the day, most of the drivers of the premodern era were reasonably good-looking fellows. Fact is, automobile racers have *always* had sex appeal, and whether you are talking Formula One tracks in exotic European cities or quarter-mile dirt tracks out in the American backwaters, women fans have always had eyes for the racers.

Not all of the legendary drivers were vulgar loudmouths either. "Race drivers used to talk like bootleggers because that's what they were." Well, that's what *some* of them were. "Now they talk like highly paid corporate PR men because that is what they have become. Junior Johnson has been replaced by Jeff Gordon. And a once-wild sport has become tame."[19] So says Peter Carlson in his NASCAR essay for the *Washington Post Magazine*. But ask yourself, just what relationship is there between the looks, demeanor, or salaries of the drivers and the "wildness" of the racing action? Race fans have vivid memories of the Rusty Wallace car flipping end-over-end ten or fifteen times as it careened out of control at 200 mph down the Daytona frontstretch. What difference does it make that Rusty is a good-looking, well-spoken, well-compensated man? Would the racing action be "wilder" if drivers were uglier or less well-spoken? In the May 1999 event at Charlotte, Jeff Burton dueled with Bobby Labonte for 600 miles and beat him to the finish line by a half-second. That's about as "wild" as competition gets. What does it matter that Burton and Labonte are both reasonably attractive guys?

Kyle Petty, himself quite a character, fears that big corporate money has driven all the "characters" out of the sport. A more realistic assessment is that the demands on today's drivers—from their fans, sponsors, and the sport itself—leave them with little time or reason to be "characters" in Petty's sense. Okay, the idea of sending Kyle's dad Richard to diction school was stupid (something that a Petty sponsor, Firestone Tire and Rubber, suggested back in the late sixties). But do currently active drivers such as Bill Elliott, Kenny Schrader, Rusty Wallace, Kyle Petty, or Michael Waltrip have any less "character" than, oh, Freddie Lorenzen or Marvin Panch or even David Pearson? Today's higher speeds and more evenly matched teams have, if anything, made Winston Cup racing even "wilder" than it once was. And it is corporate sponsorship that has made for faster speeds and more evenly matched teams.

Stock-car racing is part of popular culture and is by no means exempt from cultural trends. At one time, the "town drunk" was a comic figure exploited successfully by the likes of Red Skelton, Jackie Gleason, and other top comedians. Why don't today's comedians do "town drunk" routines? Because we no longer think drunkenness is all that funny. In the forties and fifties, someone who could drink prodigious amounts of alcohol without falling over was a "real man." Today, we'd consider him a fool. The top NASCAR drivers these days are not foul-mouthed, wild-eyed drunks and womanizers for the simple reason that we no longer consider these to be heroic or "manly" traits. To the contrary, the public image of many current drivers is that of the devoutly Christian family man—not because corporate sponsors demand it but because the larger culture does. Young boys who once adored the likes of moonshiners Curtis Turner or Fonty Flock now worship clean-cut family men like Jeff Gordon, Bobby Labonte, and Dale Jarrett. This is a step backward?

If there seem to be fewer drunks and hard-core party animals among today's Winston Cup drivers than there were three or four decades ago, it's because there are fewer drunks and party animals in society at large. Today's drivers are more sophisticated and media-savvy than drivers used to be because ours is a more sophisticated, media-conscious age. In these respects and others, NASCAR mirrors larger cultural trends more than it marches obediently to the orders of its corporate sponsors.

Very few of today's top drivers finished or even attended college, yet they have succeeded beyond most people's wildest dreams. Jeff Gordon barely completed high school, but he is a millionaire many times over. Dale Earnhardt dropped out of school in the tenth grade and got his start racing for grocery money; at the time of his death, his annual income was estimated at about $27 milllion. Thus, stock-car racers embody the uniquely American heroism of the self-made man, one reason major corporations find them attractive as pitchmen. Many take evident pains to project a pious public image and openly embrace Christian and family values. That is also appealing to the average marketing executive—and to the average American. I suppose there is some truth to the allegation that corporate sponsors demand well-mannered, well-spoken drivers, but the idea that this has somehow made stock-car racing less colorful or less interesting or tamer than it once was seems dumb.

Corporate sponsorship has made Winston Cup racing more "colorful" in at least one respect—the cars themselves. John Shelton Reed mentions the "vivid colors" as an important element in the sport's "visceral appeal." Howell remarks on the racing machines "brightly burnished with names, logos, decals and digits," an "overwhelming sensory experience." Even critics like Peter Carlson can't fail to notice the "gloriously gaudy colors" and "familiar American logos" that adorn today's Winston Cup cars. By comparison, cars in the premodern era were downright drab. Winston Cup cars start every race in pristine condition—fresh paint, new decals, with nary a dent or scratch. This costs a lot of money, money that the sponsors are happy to invest. The point, perhaps, of the fresh paint and decals is to project the most positive possible image for the car's corporate sponsors, but from the fan's perspective, the effect is a spectacular visual display. In all of sport, there is nothing quite like those forty-three "extremely mobile billboards" nosing down out of the fourth turn, awaiting the green flag, all fresh and shiny, awash in sponsor logos and colors, engines winding to get under way. And all of it is made possible by the marketing strategies of the nation's leading corporations. Surely there are worse things they could do with their money.

Has NASCAR Become Less Competitive?

I don't follow racing much anymore. It's gotten too glitzy and it's also gotten noncompetitive. It used to be that any driver in a 40 car field could win on any given Sunday. That's not really true anymore. Winston Cup racing has come to be dominated by somewhere between 3 and 5 drivers who always win. There are maybe 10 drivers in the field who even have an outside shot at winning. The rest of the field now fills the role that the Harlem Globetrotters' opponents were relegated to. They create the illusion of a competitive race. — Fetzer Mills, correspondence with author

Fetzer Mills is a good old boy from North Carolina, a country music enthusiast with a degree in Southern studies who grew up on stock-car racing and wrote pieces about the sport a decade ago. He writes, "We followed stock car racing and knew the drivers and had our favorites the way kids in cities with major league baseball teams followed baseball."[20] His lament—that Winston Cup racing has come to be dominated by a few top drivers and is no longer competitive or exciting—is a common one among racing fans these days. Fetzer blames "the massive influx of corporate sponsorship" for these developments.

Nostalgia for an often-mythical bygone era is hardly restricted to stock-car fans. Baseball fans complain there'll never be another Ted Williams and sit in the bars drinking beer and reminiscing about the "good old days" before the designated-hitter rule. Golf enthusiasts just know there'll never be another Bobby Jones or Sammy Snead; or if they are a bit younger, another Arnie Palmer; or, younger still, another Jack Nicklaus. Of course, in every sport where precise comparisons of performance are possible over long stretches of time (for example, in track and field), the record is invariably one of continuous, often dramatic improvement.

Is there any real evidence that Winston Cup racing is less competitive than it used to be? For that matter, how can we define "competitiveness" with sufficient precision to determine whether it has waxed or waned? Fetzer's notion seems clear enough: the more drivers who actually have a chance of winning, the more competitive the race. This is not the only idea of competitiveness I want to explore, but it is a fine place to begin.

Jeff Gordon has been the dominant driver in the Winston Cup Series since his first championship in 1995. In his championship run of 1998 (his third championship in four years), he won thirteen of the thirty-three races, which tied Richard Petty's modern-era record for wins in a single season. His winning Winston Cup points total (5,328) was the largest points total ever accumulated by a Winston Cup champion since the current scoring system was adopted in 1975. The runner-up, Mark Martin, won seven races in 1998, and his points total (4,964) was the highest ever recorded by a second-place finisher up to that time and would in fact have won the Winston Cup championship outright in all but two of the seasons since 1975. So, it is obvious that two drivers, Gordon and Martin, dominated the 1998 field.

Still, in that same 1998 season, eleven drivers won one or more races: Gordon notched thirteen wins; Mark Martin had seven; Dale Jarrett won three; Jeff Burton and Bobby Labonte each won two; and Rusty Wallace, Jeremy Mayfield, Dale Earnhardt, Terry Labonte, Bobby Hamilton, and Ricky Rudd all won one race apiece. So, despite the domination of the two top teams, nine additional teams were competitive enough to pull down at least one victory.

The number of drivers or teams who had "even an outside shot at winning," as Fetzer puts it, surely exceeds the number who actually won. Among the competitors who won no races in 1998 were twelve drivers who had had at least one points win to their credit sometime earlier in the 1990s: former Winston Cup champions Darrell Waltrip and Bill Elliott; veteran drivers Ernie Irvan, Kyle Petty, Sterling Marlin, Ken Schrader, Geoff Bodine, Derrick Cope, and Brett Bodine; and relative newcomers Jimmy Spencer, Ward Burton, and John Andretti. And there were two additional drivers who had never won a points race but who had won major exhibition events: Michael Waltrip, who had won The Winston in 1996, and Mike Skinner, who had won two postseason exhibition races in Japan.

It seems fair to suppose that drivers who have recently won (that is, who have at least one victory in the 1990s) must have at least *some* chance of winning again. If so, then the number of drivers in the 1998 competition who had "even an outside shot" at winning was not "somewhere between three and five," or even "maybe ten," but twenty-five: eleven who in fact did win in 1998 and fourteen who had no 1998 victories but had won races in previous (recent) years. To these tallies one would want to add a number of drivers who, while yet to win, seemed poised for a breakthrough and who must have had at least that outside shot at victory: Tony Stewart, who won three races the following year; Joe Nemechek, who also recorded his first victory in 1999; Steve Park, who broke through to a first win in 2000; Jerry Nadeau, whose first win also came in 2000; and Ricky Craven, Wally Dallenbach, and maybe others, depending on who you talk to.

Realistically, then, the number of teams with *some* chance at a victory in the 1998 season must have been closer to or thirty. For comparison, the usual Winston Cup starting field is made up of forty-three drivers; in all of 1998, sixty-eight drivers started at least one event. And if twenty-five or thirty of the forty-three starters have at least some chance at victory on any given weekend, well, that strikes me as pretty competitive. How many major league baseball teams start the season with "an outside shot" at making the playoffs? How many NFL teams have any real chance of getting to the Super Bowl? How many of the 20,000 runners in the Boston Marathon stand even a remote chance of being first across the finish line? And all this, mind you, in a season that was admittedly dominated by just two teams.

The 1999 season saw Dale Jarrett crowned as the Winston Cup champion. His year was not nearly as dominating as Gordon's 1998 season had been. En route to the championship, Jarrett won four races, but the remaining thirty victories were split among ten drivers: Gordon with seven, Jeff Burton with six, Bobby Labonte with five, Tony Stewart and Dale Earnhardt with three each, Mark Martin with two, and Terry Labonte, Joe Nemechek, John Andretti and Rusty Wallace with one apiece. So, in 1999 as well as in 1998, eleven drivers notched at least one win and at least another dozen must have had an outside shot at a victory.

How does 1998 or 1999 compare in these respects with previous years? Is the level of competitiveness higher or lower than it used to be? When Fetzer and I exchanged e-mails on this question, I asked, not rhetorically, "Truth be told, just how competitive was the Winston Cup back twenty years ago, when David Pearson and the Allison boys won nearly everything that Richard Petty didn't?" The domination of the series by a few top teams is hardly a new phenomenon. Or is it?

Although NASCAR itself dates to 1948 and champions have been crowned in every year since 1949, I'll focus here on the modern era. Since 1972 NASCAR's annual season has featured between twenty-eight and thirty-four events, each of them contested by forty-three of the forty-seven to fifty teams that travel around the country and attempt to qualify for every race. So what have been the patterns in the three decades of the modern era?

The thirty-three Winston Cup events in 1998 produced eleven winners, so the ratio of winners to races was .33. Table 4 shows the number of races, the number of different winners, and the ratio of winners to races

Table 4. Number of Separate Race Winners Each Season, 1972–1994

Year	No. of Races	Different Winners	Winners:Races
1972	31	6	0.19
1973	28	7	0.25
1974	30	5	0.17
1975	30	8	0.27
1976	30	8	0.27
1977	30	7	0.23
1978	30	7	0.23
1979	31	9	0.29
1980	31	10	0.32
1981	31	9	0.29
1982	30	8	0.27
1983	30	12	0.4
1984	30	12	0.4
1985	28	9	0.34
1986	29	13	0.45
1987	29	10	0.34
1988	29	14	0.48
1989	29	11	0.38
1990	29	14	0.48
1991	29	14	0.48
1992	29	12	0.41
1993	30	10	0.33
1994	31	12	0.39
1995	31	11	0.35
1996	31	11	0.35
1997	32	11	0.34
1998	33	11	0.33
1999	34	11	0.32

The table shows the number of races and the number of separate drivers who won at least one race in every season from the onset of the modern era to the present day. In the 1970s an average of 7.1 different drivers won a race each season; in the 1980s, that average increased to 10.8; and in the 1990s, to 11.7. If a "competitive" season is one in which many different drivers win at least one race, then each decade of the modern era has been more competitive than the last.

Table 5. Number of Top Five Finishers Finishing on the Lead Lap, Selected Races, 1972–1996

Year	Daytona 500	Dover Downs (Fall Race)	Bristol (Fall Race)	Atlanta (Second Race)
1972	1	1	1	2
1973	1	3	1	1
1974	4	1	2	2
1975	1	2	1	3
1976	1	2	1	4
1977	1	2	2	5
1978	2	2	2	3
1979	3	3	3	4
1980	2	3	3	2
1981	5	1	1	5
1982	3	4	3	4
1983	4	3	3	3
1984	5	2	2	4
1985	2	1	4	4
1986	4	3	2	1
1987	5	5	5	4
1988	5	5	2	5
1989	5	3	4	4
1990	5	3	5	4
1991	5	1	3	5
1992	5	3	4	5
1993	5	5	5	5
1994	5	5	5	5
1995	5	5	5	5
1996	5	5	5	5

The table shows the number of the top five finishers who finished on the lead lap in four selected events from 1972 to 1996. In the 1970s it was common for only one car to complete the entire event, and the average number of cars finishing on the lead lap in that decade (for these four events) was only 2.09. In the 1990s all five top five finishers usually ended the race on the lead lap; the average number doing so was 4.57. If the number of cars finishing on the lead lap is also an indicator of "competitiveness," then by this measure, too, each decade of the modern era has been more competitive than the one that preceded it.

Table 6. Points Margins in NASCAR Championship Seasons, 1975–1998

Year	Champion's Total	Runner-up Total	Difference	10th Place Total	Difference
1975	4783	4061	722	3182	1601
1976	4644	4449	195	3447	1197
1977	5000	4614	386	3294	1706
1978	4841	4367	474	3566	1275
1979	4830	4819	11	3615	1215
1980	4661	4642	19	3742	919
1981	4880	4827	53	3449	1431
1982	4489	4417	72	3451	1038
1983	4667	4620	47	3612	1055
1984	4508	4443	65	3643	865
1985	4292	4191	101	3507	785
1986	4468	4180	288	3537	931
1987	4696	4207	489	3405	1291
1988	4480	4464	24	3621	867
1989	4176	4164	12	3569	607
1990	4430	4404	26	3572	858
1991	4287	4092	195	3582	705
1992	4078	4068	10	3603	475
1993	4526	4446	80	3644	882
1994	4694	4250	444	3617	1077
1995	4614	4580	34	3718	896
1996	4657	4620	37	3632	1025
1997	4710	4696	14	3576	1134
1998	5328	4964	364	3786	1542

The competitiveness of a NASCAR season can also be charted according to the points margin by which the eventual champion bests his closest competitor. The table shows the champion's points total, the runner-up's points total, and (just for comparison) the tenth-place finisher's points total for each year since the current points system was adopted (1975). Judged by the winning points margins, the 1970s were the least competitive decade for the Winston Cup by a pretty wide margin.

for every Winston Cup season since 1972. In three seasons (1988, 1990, and 1991), twenty-nine races produced fourteen winners (a ratio of .48); by this measure, then, these were the three most competitive years for the series.

On average, the least competitive years for the Winston Cup have not been the recent years but the first years of the modern era. The thirty races of the 1974 season were won by just five drivers, for a ratio of .17, the lowest shown. In the eight seasons of the 1970s, the average number of winners per year was 7.1. In contrast, among the ten seasons of the 1980s, the average was 10.8; among the ten seasons of the 1990s, 11.7. By this criterion, the Winston Cup Series has grown more competitive, not less. And why? Because corporate sponsorship has given more teams the resources necessary to compete at the highest level.

Other trend series show similar patterns. *The Stock Car Racing Encyclopedia,* which bills itself as "the complete record of America's most popular sport," reports the number of laps completed by the top five finishers at each race each year. Although this is a crude measure, a race where all five top finishers finish on the lead lap is more competitive than one where only the winner completes the final lap. So this offers a second opportunity to see whether Winston Cup racing has gotten more or less competitive over the years.

Trying to calculate and present these data for every race in every year at every track is unwieldy. To simplify things, I've again focused just on the modern era and on four specific races that provide continuous records for the era: the Daytona 500, the fall race at Dover, the August race at Bristol, and the fall race at Atlanta. These comprise a reasonable sampling of current NASCAR venues. (Basic data are shown in table 5.)

How many Daytona 500 races ended with all five of the top five finishers on the same lap? Answer: In the 1970s, none of them. In the 1980s, about half of them. In the 1990s, all of them. How's that for a clear trend? There are thirty-two races from the 1970s shown in the table, and in those thirty-two races, sixty-seven top five finishers finished on the lead lap, so the average for the decade was 2.09 top five finishers on the lead lap at the race's end. Put another way, in the 1970s, at least at these four tracks, the average race came down to two guys. By this measure, the 1980s were more competitive than the 1970s, the average being 3.38 top five finishers ending on the lead lap, and the 1990s more competitive still, with an average of 4.57. "Back in the good old days," it was rare indeed to have more than a couple of cars still dueling at race's end; today, it is unusual to have *any* of the top five (or even top ten) racers finish off the lead lap.

Another indicator of seasonal competitiveness is how close the race for the Winston Cup championship is. In 1998, as I mentioned, Jeff Gordon won the championship with 5,328 points, while Mark Martin finished second with 4,964, a difference of 364 points. How does this margin compare to prior years? Table 6 shows the first, second, and tenth place points totals and the gap between them each year since 1975. As it happens, Gordon's dominant 1998 season ranks only sixth among the past twenty-four years in degree of domination. The gap between first and second place was wider in 1975, 1977, 1978, 1987, and 1994. By this measure, the all-time most dominating performance was Richard Petty's 1975 championship, with a winning margin of more than 700 points. Nothing else in the modern era even comes close.

Average points margins by decade again suggest that the 1970s were less competitive than more recent decades. Between 1975 and 1979, the gap between first and second place averaged 358 points; from 1980 to 1989, only 117 points; and from 1990 to 1998, 134 points. Given our metric, the seventeen-point difference between the 1980s and 1990s is not significant, but the much larger difference between either of these and the 1970s certainly is. Here, too, the evidence does not suggest that Winston Cup racing has somehow become less competitive.

Just for kicks, I also calculated the points difference between the first and tenth place finishers. The largest such difference, 1,706 points, was registered in 1977. The points gap between first and tenth averaged 1,399 in the 1970s; 979 in the 1980s; and 955 in the 1990s. Again, the 1970s are shown to be the least competitive decade of the modern era.

The number of first-time winners each decade is another indirect indicator of trends in competitiveness. In every year, most races are won by drivers who have won before, but from time to time, previous non-winners drive themselves into Victory Lane. Years where no new winners emerge are therefore "noncompetitive" in that they are completely dominated by the old hands. By implication, more competitive years are those that produce the most first-time winners.

The Insider's Guide to NASCAR Racing has a table showing "Modern Era First Time Winston Cup Winners—1972 to 1996."[21] I've added the

1997, 1998, and 1999 results to this table. The eight seasons of the 1970s produced only seven first-time winners, for an average of .875 new winners per year. In contrast, the ten seasons of the 1980s produced nineteen first-time winners (1.9 per year) and the ten seasons of the 1990s produced fifteen first-time winners (1.5 per year). Once again, the early years of the modern era were the least competitive.

Dale Earnhardt remarked in a 1999 interview, "The sport has changed tremendously over the years and the competition is the best it's ever been. Each week the field gets closer and closer when it comes to qualifying. When we started this tour twenty years ago, there were a couple of seconds [in qualifying lap time] between first and 40th; now it's down to hundredths of a second."[22] Unfortunately, none of my references shows qualifying times or speeds for each competitor, each race, each year, so we'll have to take Earnhardt's word on this. But the Intimidator was a top driver for a long time—he was Rookie of the Year and won his first race in 1979, is sixth on the all-time win list, and won seven Winston Cup championships—so his word ought to count for something.

One problem with the hypothesis that Winston Cup racing has become less competitive is that NASCAR goes to great lengths to keep the level of competition high and to assure a level playing field for all contenders. Every car is built to exacting specifications and is checked again and again before each race to ensure that these specifications are met. Any hint of "domination" is quickly investigated and corrected. For example, when Ford replaced its Thunderbird stock-car racing machine with the Taurus, the new car had aerodynamic advantages that put the Chevrolets and Pontiacs at a disadvantage. NASCAR quickly ordered small changes in the Fords' aerodynamics to level the playing field. (The same thing happened at the start of the 2000 season.) Midway through the 1998 season, Jeff Gordon's Chevrolet was so dominant that competitors alleged he had to be cheating on something; the speculation was that the Gordon team was illegally treating his tires to make them stick better in the corners. Although subsequent tests revealed nothing, still the tests were done.

NASCAR tests body shapes with a dozen different templates, never allowing variances of more than a half-inch from the standard; randomly selects cylinders for a pump test to determine the true overall displacement of the engine; removes and inspects every car's carburetor just before each race to make sure it meets the code; draws fuel samples from the top qualifiers and top finishers to make sure the fuel has not been doped; and completely tears down and inspects the engines of the top three finishers at every race. Since 1995, large fines have been imposed on teams breaking the rules. So when the engines fire up on race day, every chariot is essentially equal and is being pulled by much the same horse. What varies from car to car are the skill and courage of the driver, the cleverness of the crew chief, the talent of the crew—and Lady Luck. This must surely make for more competitive racing than back in the "good old days," when cheating was rampant and rules were rarely enforced.

There are some measures, however, according to which NASCAR has gotten less competitive over time. Over the half-century history of the sport, Buick, Chevrolet, Chrysler, Dodge, Ford, Hudson, Jaguar, Lincoln, Matador (American Motors), Mercury, Nash, Oldsmobile, Plymouth, Pontiac, and Studebaker automobiles have all won NASCAR championship races. Today, only Chevrolet, Ford, Pontiac, and Dodge compete. So, a few top makes have driven all other manufacturers out of the Winston Cup business. In the early years, the manufacturers' championship (determined by which make of car wins the most races) was a contested battle among a half-dozen makes. Today, it usually comes down to Ford versus Chevy. Most fans, I think, would welcome more models and manufacturers back into the series. The 2001 reentry of the Chrysler (now Daimler-Chrysler) Corporation into the Winston Cup was especially welcome, given Chrysler's historical association with stock-car racing and their prominent role in other motorsports, such as drag racing and even NASCAR's truck series.

Another significant trend is the rise and subsequent domination of the Winston Cup Series by multicar racing teams. Although the existence of these multicar teams is nothing new, it is now the rare competitor who has no teammates with him out on the track. Hendrick Motorsports fields three cars in nearly every event; Robert Yates Racing, Richard Childress Racing, and Joe Gibbs Racing all field two; Jack Roush Racing fields as many as six. Emblematic of the near-domination of the series by the multicar teams was the 1997 Daytona 500, where the three Rick Hendricks cars finished first (Jeff Gordon), second (Terry Labonte), and third (Ricky Craven). In the 1998 season, nine of the eleven cars that won at least one race were members of multicar teams. (The only one-car teams posting a victory in 1998 were Bobby Hamilton and Ricky Rudd. In 1999, there were none.)

The rise of multicar teams has occasioned much commentary among NASCAR aficionados, and there is a legitimate concern that they threaten the competitiveness of the series. Darrell Waltrip says, "These bigger teams are not only sucking up all the sponsors, but they're sucking up the help." Even Robert Yates, himself a multicar team owner, expresses concerns about this development: "When I'm sitting in the stands, I don't want to see multi-car teams. . . . I do go against monopolies." But he adds, no doubt correctly, "NASCAR will keep somebody from getting dominant."[23]

For now, the multicar team is the unmistakable wave of NASCAR's future. Winston Cup racing is expensive and multicar teams introduce essential economies of scale. Small, independent one-car teams—in particular teams for which the driver is also the owner (there were only four in 1999: Bill Elliott, Brett Bodine, Dave Marcis, and Ricky Rudd)—may fall by the wayside. And, in some important sense, perhaps, the competitiveness of the Winston Cup Series will fall with them.

On the other hand, fans have been expressing concerns throughout the modern era that corporate involvement in the Winston Cup would reduce the level of competition to the point where the series would be completely dominated by a small handful of the best-funded drivers. Three decades later, there is little evidence to suggest that this has happened and much evidence to suggest the opposite. Fans who complain that these days every race comes down to a contest among the same three, four, or five top drivers—"It is the same every week," laments fan Jeff Brock—have forgotten the early years of the modern era when this was almost literally the case.

The influx of corporate sponsorship has transformed NASCAR from a sport of mainly regional interest to a national phenomenon and a $2-billion-a-year business. Peter Carlson guesses that souvenir sales alone now top a billion dollars a year. Emblematic of the fact and scale of corporate influence was Humpy Wheeler's selling of the name of his speedway to Lowe's. Will the naming rights to other NASCAR venues also be auctioned off to the highest bidder? I'd count on it—the money is too good to turn down. One day in the not-too-distant future, perhaps we'll see the Home Depot car win the True Value Hardware 500 at the Lowe's Motor

Speedway, or maybe the Interstate Batteries car will win the Exide Batteries 400 at the Diehard Batteries International Raceway. But when these advertising oddities happen, you can be sure that the stands will be full of people, many of them direct beneficiaries of corporate sponsorship—and it will be a hard-fought, competitive race featuring the best drivers and the fastest cars. Critics and naysayers can whine all they want, but the overall effect of corporate influence in the Winston Cup has been that more fans enjoy more competitive and more interesting racing than ever before. Even if it gets to the point where there are thousands of sponsors and advertising space on Winston Cup cars has to be auctioned off by the square inch, the racing action will still be as wild as anything on the planet.

Grand Finale in Atlanta

By the time we headed to Atlanta for the season's final race, most of the important racing questions had been answered. Dale Jarrett had already nailed the 1999 championship, and Tony Stewart was Rookie of the Year. Most of the top ten finishing positions in the points race were also locked in. With nothing significant still to be decided, teams could throw caution to the winds and go all-out for a season-ending victory, something to leave a sweet taste in the mouth all winter. The NAPA 500 looked like it might be wild and wooly. And it was.

The *Fixin' to Git* entourage for Atlanta was Chris, Kelley, Denise, me, and our Florida relatives, Ed and Elaine (Elaine and Chris are sisters). We came with definite preferences about the outcome. There'd been eleven different winners so far in the season, and I was hoping Atlanta would produce a twelfth. That would break the four-year string of eleven-winner seasons and put 1999 above the average for the decade. So I was rooting for any of the thirty-two starters who had yet to win a race in 1999 — that is, three-quarters of the field.

My top choices were Ricky Rudd (to extend the streak) and Michael Waltrip (to end the streak — over 400 Winston Cup starts with no wins). A third first-time winner on the season or a first win by a single-car team were also high on my wish list. By season's end, Chris was a confirmed Tony Stewart fan; Brother Kelley was rooting for Stewart's team-mate Bobby Labonte. Denise declared herself bored with racing—this would be her fourth race in five months—and hoped only that the race was short. I hadn't seen Ed and Elaine in a while and could only assume that Ed would be backing his perennial favorites Bill Elliott and Jeff Gordon. An Elliott victory . . . yeah, that would do the trick, too.

I had ordered four tickets on the main stretch by phone a few months in advance, surprised again that any tickets, much less good tickets, were still available to the general public. These seats were in the Champions Grandstand right across from the pits—outstanding ducats at $100 a crack. I also had two NAPA hospitality-package tickets from my pal Jay. These freebies were in the North Turn Grandstand about where the fourth turn exits onto the front straight—good seats, yes, but not as good as the seats I had paid for. I took comfort in knowing that not all the great seats get gobbled up by corporate sponsors.

The Louisiana and Indiana contingents coalesced on Friday at the Suburban Lodge in Stockbridge, Georgia, a little burg halfway between downtown and the Atlanta Motor Speedway (located in the town of Hampton). Ed and Elaine were coming in later and would meet up with the rest of us at Sunday's race. The Suburban Lodge was twenty miles from the track, a clean but cheesy inn that charged top prices for motel-style rooms, but with no maid service, no clean towels or linens, not even a person at the front desk to complain to. We settled in, showered off the crud of a long road trip, and headed to a seafood buffet that was also mediocre. But we hadn't come to Atlanta for the food or accommodations.

The Suburban Lodge, we learned, was not a conventional motel. Most of the people there were long-term tenants renting rooms by the month. Still, you could tell there were race fans around as soon as you entered the parking lot. Out front was a Winston Cup show car built by Junie Donleavy and decorated with the insignia of the lodge. A Ricky Rudd show-car trailer was parked out back. There was no coffee shop or restaurant where fans could congregate, but the T-shirts and gimme hats suggested that maybe half the people there were race fans. The Lodge's long-term residents seemed befuddled by the Winston Cup hoopla. As for the race fans, they seemed a strange mix compared to the motel crowds in Darlington and Birmingham—insular keep-to-yourself types who sat in

Infield campers at the Atlanta Motor Speedway, November 1999. This photo was taken the day before the Winston Cup race, during Happy Hour. Note the scoring tower at the right of the photo. A similar tower will be found at every NASCAR venue. The tower's race-day function is to give fans an overview of which cars are running in the top twenty positions. Without a radio, this is the only way to know how your favorite drivers are doing. During Happy Hour, the tower shows the twenty drivers posting the fastest times. When this photo was taken, Eliot Sadler, driving the Number 21 car, had the fastest car and had just turned a lap at 187.323 mph.

their rooms, watched TV, and drank beer. Nothing about the lodge crowd felt anything like the NASCAR Family reunion to which I had become accustomed.

The NAPA hospitality packages included two tickets to Saturday's ARCA finale, so Kelley and I spent Saturday taking in the ARCA action, watching Happy Hour, and scouting track logistics. Our trip to the track uncovered no easy way to get there from the Suburban Lodge and no obvious place to park, either. Any attempt to park past the track and pointed south toward I-75 seemed certain to be ruled out by traffic control. So when we headed back to the motel after Happy Hour, we were still uncertain how best to attack the next day's parking problem.

We had arrived at the track early, in the middle of the morning's Winston Cup practice. From a distance, the track looks like a collection of luxury condos and was impressively clean, modern, attractive, and well-appointed. It was a sharp hike up the grade to the entrance and another steep climb to the grandstand seats, but the Champions Grandstand afforded a clear view of the entire 1.54-mile oval, as good a view as our seats at Daytona and Talladega. So we snuggled in to watch the ARCA boys bang into one another in the Georgia Boot 400.

Yes, the ARCA *boys:* regrettably, Shawna Robinson was not among the day's competitors. I was disappointed when the racing action proved tame in comparison to the ARCA carnage I'd witnessed at Charlotte and Talladega—perhaps by now the drivers had gotten a better feel for high-speed superspeedway racing. The most exciting moment in the race came on the last lap when Craftsman Truck regular Ron Hornaday had to drive around a wreck that developed right in front of him, but even with that distraction he beat second-place finisher and pole-sitter Derrick Gilchrist to the finish line by more than four seconds—a huge margin of victory by today's competitive standards. It was Hornaday's first-ever ARCA appearance, and he won in a car sponsored by NAPA—a welcome bonus for the auto-parts giant on its big race weekend. Hornaday made a cameo appearance later that evening at the big NAPA race party at the Marriott Marquis Hotel downtown—nice guy, a shy, retiring sort, not at all charismatic. But the NAPA bigwigs who accompanied him were beaming.

Our NAPA hospitality packages included two tickets to the Marquis event, so after the racing Chris and I got dressed up and went to hang out with the favored classes. This was my first sponsor's party. Most of the people in attendance, two or three thousand in number, had some affiliation with NAPA, its customers, or its suppliers. The party occupied all the hotel's ballrooms. One room was full of show cars, each sporting NAPA colors and logos. There were two giant halls filled with hundreds of tables for eight and immense buffet lines dispensing ham, chicken, salads, and a stunning variety of desserts—the kind of all-you-can-eat spread you'd expect to pay $15.99 a head for. There were stages for skits, a dee jay, a dance floor, and a dozen walk-up bars (beer, wine, and soft drinks were gratis, while mixed drinks could be purchased). We were togged out in dressy casual, and while we weren't underdressed, there were plenty of jackets, ties, and cocktail dresses—and not a single guest in a race T-shirt or gimme hat. The dee jay played classic rock and country favorites, and there were driver appearances, skits, and floor shows. The price tag for the gala had to run into the middle five figures, which seems like a lot but was no doubt small change in NAPA's total weekend outlay.

Overall, the ambience was subdued. A few couples danced, but most sat at their tables wolfing down free food, sipping glasses of wine, and

(I gathered) discussing the ups and downs of the auto-parts market. That wine and not beer appeared to be the beverage of choice was a sure sign that these were not hard-core NASCAR folks. I was expecting something less swank, more wild, and more drunken and was disappointed that the whole affair resembled a church social more than a gathering of the NASCAR clan. We left after an hour and a half, glad to have done the sponsor-party thing but not anxious to do another. The impromptu campfire party at Indy had been more fun—the people had been friendlier, more down to earth, and everyone had been a serious race fan.

We were up early the following morning and on our way to the track by 8:00; even then traffic was bumper-to-bumper for miles. Among the NASCAR venues I've visited, none manages the pre-race traffic more poorly than Atlanta's. We crept along until we hit the main gate about 9:00, and as I had expected, we were waved vigorously into the trackside parking lot. Once I had made the turn and was thus committed, I checked the rearview mirror and realized that braver souls behind me were simply ignoring traffic control and driving straight past the entrance to quick-getaway parking spots south of the track. Compounding our troubles was that all of us early birds were herded to the rear of the lot and slotted into parking spaces about as far from the exit as you could get. The price for my timidity was that we languished in parking-lot traffic for well over an hour after the race.

As we stepped from our cars we were approached by an older gentleman soliciting donations for disabled American veterans. Ten bucks got us three small plastic flags: one American, one Confederate, one checkered—the flags of NASCAR Nation. Between the parking lot and the track were the souvenir trailers where a season-ending fire sale was under way. As a NASCAR season nears its end, there is a musical-chairs rotation of drivers and teams (fans call it Silly Season), and a lot of racing merchandise is rendered obsolete. When Robert Yates ended his contract with driver Kenny Irwin and offered the ride in the Number 28 Havoline Ford to Ricky Rudd, all the Kenny Irwin goodies at the Yates souvenir trailer and everything in the Ricky Rudd Tide Performance Motorsports trailer were instantly out-of-date. So the crowds around the trailers were thick with fans hunting down bargains and collectibles. We stopped for a while at the Rudd trailer and picked up $20 gimme hats at two-for-five-dollars

Crowd scene at the souvenir trailers a few hours before the NAPA 500 in Atlanta. You can see five or six trailers in this shot, but, altogether, there are fifty or sixty souvenir trailers that show up for each Winston Cup race. Note the sign at the right of the photo: "End of Season Clearance Sale." Toward the end of each Winston Cup season, drivers, crew chiefs, and sponsors often switch teams; when this happens, a lot of souvenir merchandise is rendered obsolete. As the last race of the 1999 season, the NAPA 500 was the last chance to unload obsolete souvenir goods. Gimme hats that had sold for $20 apiece just a few weeks before could be bought at the bargain rate of two for $5.

and little matchbox replicas of the Number 10 Tide Ford at two-for-a-buck (pre-sale price: $5.99 apiece). Later we heard that all the souvenir trailers would be heading to Charlotte after the NAPA 500 to unload whatever 1999 merchandise remained. Apparently, if you motored up to Charlotte and bought $100 worth of stuff, you could take one lap at the Lowe's Motor Speedway in your own car for another $50. With my sporty new V-6 Sebring sitting in the parking lot, the deal sure was tempting. The Sebring's speedometer tops out at 150 mph. You don't suppose . . . ?

Friday's qualifying had been full of surprises and seemed, symbolically, to usher in a new NASCAR era. Kevin LePage, runner-up to Kenny Irwin for 1998 Rookie-of-the-Year honors, qualified on the pole for the first time in his career. Another 1998 rookie, Steve Park, sat on the outside of the front row, his best qualifying effort ever. Other newcomers

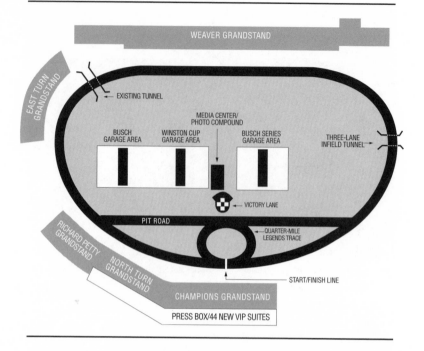

among the top qualifiers included Todd Bodine, the youngest of the Bodine brothers, who started fifth; Dave Blaney, eventually a contender
for Rookie-of-the-Year honors in 2000 (his first full Winston Cup season), who started seventh; Gary Bradberry, who rolled off in ninth; 1999
rookie Buckshot Jones, at eleventh; and 2000 rookie Dale Earnhardt Jr.,
at thirteenth — impressive qualifying efforts by the Winston Cup youngsters. Most of the circuit's old hands had qualified poorly. Perennial front-
runner Mark Martin rolled off in third and champion Jarrett started
in tenth, but Gordon started at sixteenth, Rusty Wallace at nineteenth,
Bill Elliott at twenty-seventh, Dale Earnhardt at thirty-sixth, and Bobby
Labonte at thirty-seventh. The contest was billed as "The Last Race of the
Century" and the qualifying motif — out with the old, in with the new —
seemed fitting.

Altogether, twelve of the fifteen fastest qualifiers had yet to score a 1999
win: the seven young'uns already noted plus my two top choices, Ricky
Rudd and Michael Waltrip, along with Geoff Bodine, Ward Burton, and
Chad Little. (The only 1999 race winners who qualified in the top fifteen

were Martin, Jarrett, and Jeff Burton). Nine of the fifteen fastest had never won a Winston Cup race. The odds on a twelfth winner of the season and perhaps even a third first-time winner seemed solid. When the green flag dropped, I was feeling smug.

And the race itself—oh my God, what a race! Between green flag and checkered, the lead changed hands *thirty-eight* times, the season's high. Relative youngsters LePage, Park, Johnny Benson, Jeremy Mayfield, Tony Stewart, Ward Burton, Dale Earnhardt Jr., and Eliot Sadler all took a hand at the front of the field, as did veterans Martin, Michael Waltrip, Dave Marcis, Kyle Petty, Bobby Labonte, Jeff Burton, and Jarrett. There were eight caution periods, which kept the field tightly bunched and guaranteed tight, competitive racing all over the track. There was so much going on you weren't sure what you should be watching: Bill Elliott dueling bumper-to-bumper with Kyle Petty and Kenny Schrader back around twentieth? Or Labonte, Jarrett, Mayfield, and Martin rubbing fenders up front? It was wild-assed racing excitement everywhere you looked.

My guys Waltrip and Rudd ran strong, and there were times when it looked like either one of them might bring home the bacon. Alas, it was not to be. Rudd hung around in the top ten for most of the day but never challenged for the lead and ultimately finished in seventh, his Tide sponsorship and sixteen-year winning streak both at an end. Waltrip, too, was among the front-runners most of the afternoon and even led twelve laps early in the race, but a tire failure slammed him hard into the wall at Lap 198. He had to be cut out of the mangled wreckage and helicoptered to an Atlanta hospital with a mild concussion. Released later that evening, he had finished the race in thirty-sixth place.

All the promising new faces had faded by the halfway point, although Park hung on to finish twelfth and Little E came in fourteenth, five positions behind his father. Two cautions in the final forty laps turned the race into a pair of feature dashes that saw only Bobby Labonte, Jarrett, Mayfield, Martin, and Jeff Burton seriously contending for the victory. Labonte had been strong all day on the short runs, and when the race was restarted for the final time with twenty laps to go, he drove away from the rest of the field to a comfortable victory. But Jarrett, Mayfield, and Martin put on a breathtaking display racing for second place. The three of them battled door-to-door through the final twenty laps, with Jarrett passing Mayfield one last time on the whiteflag lap to finish second. This three-car, twenty-lap, fender-rubbing blood duel for second place in a race that meant nothing in the season's points standings was some of the hardest-fought, most exciting on-track action I'd seen the whole season. That's NASCAR for you.

Among the *Fixin' to Git* contingent, only Brother Kelley had witnessed the outcome he was hoping for—a Bobby Labonte win. I hadn't seen a twelfth winner, a third first-time winner, or the season's first winner from a single-car team. My all-time favorite driver Bill Elliott finished twenty-second. Ricky Rudd failed to extend his winning streak, and Michael Waltrip was in the hospital when the checkered flag fell. The four drivers from the Indiana gang finished a mediocre fifteenth, twenty-ninth, thirty-third, and thirty-eighth. Judged against my pre-race preferences, there wasn't one thing about the outcome to be happy about. And yet I loved it all—every minute, every driver, every wreck, every fan I talked to, every cheap souvenir I bought.

It was near 4:30 when we got back to the car, past 5:30 by the time we cleared the parking lot, and creeping up on 6:30 before we were "south-bound and down" on I-75, headed for Orlando and a Thanksgiving Day family gathering. The 1999 *Fixin' to Git* Road Tour had come to an end. As we made our way to the car among the milling tens of thousands, I saw a fan walk past in what was, hands-down, the *Fixin' to Git* T-shirt of the race: "Racing: Because football, basketball, baseball, tennis, bowling, and golf only take one ball." Yeah, that's it. No bat and glove, no pig-skin, no woods and irons, no glandular freaks. Just balls and race cars. NASCAR: Because everything else is just a game.

7

We Are Family

The 1999 Winston Cup season began in February at Daytona and ended in November at Atlanta. For the fifth season in a row, 1999 gave us eleven different winners, just below the decade's average (11.7) but still better than the averages for the 1970s and 1980s. (The 2000 season was even better, featuring thirteen separate winners, and 2001 better still, with nineteen.) Jeff Gordon led all drivers with seven wins (but only finished sixth in the standings), while Jeff Burton had six and Bobby Labonte had five. Champion Dale Jarrett finished with only four wins, making 1999 the fifteenth season out of twenty-five since the current scoring system was adopted in which the champion was not the driver with the most victories.

Among the eleven winning drivers were three Yankees—Gordon, Rookie-of-the-Year Tony Stewart, and John Andretti, all from Indiana. The three Hoosiers scored eleven total victories to lead all states. North Carolinians Jarrett and Dale Earnhardt wracked up seven wins; Texans Bobby and Terry Labonte accounted for six. Other states in Victory Lane during 1999 were Virginia (Jeff Burton with six wins), Arkansas (Mark Martin with two wins), Florida (Joe Nemechek with one win), and Missouri (Rusty Wallace with one win). The strong performance of the Indiana Gang showed the continuing vigor of the Yankee Resurgence; at the same time, Southern fans could relish the return of the Winston Cup championship to North Carolina, considered by many to be its natural home.

Nineteen ninety-nine was the first year in stock-car racing's modern era in which all the year's winners were from multicar teams. The Hendrick Motorsports, Roush Racing, and Joe Gibbs Racing teams each had eight victories; Robert Yates Racing had four; Richard Childress Racing had three; Teams Penske, Petty, and Sabco scored one win apiece. Buckling to the trends, two of the remaining independent owner-drivers, Brett Bodine and Ricky Rudd, sold their single-car race teams at the end of the season, leaving Bill Elliott and Dave Marcis as the only owner-drivers to compete in 2000.

Jarrett's championship points total of 5,262 was the second strongest of the decade (table 6, 247) and marked only the third time that a Winston Cup champion had amassed as many as 5,000 points. That Jarrett scored so many points with only four victories shows the value of consistently strong finishes even if you're not winning many races. Jarrett led the points battle for the final twenty-four weeks of the season and wrapped up the championship in Miami, a week before the season finale — the third time in the 1990s that the championship was not decided at the final race. Jarrett and his father, Ned, joined Lee and Richard Petty as the only father-son duos to bring home NASCAR's top championship honors. At forty-two, Jarrett is also one of the oldest drivers ever to have won the championship.

Bobby Labonte's second place points total of 5061 was the best ever for a runner-up and would have won him the championship in all but one of the previous seasons of the modern era. Still, the difference between first and second (201 points) was above the average for the decade (134 points). (Labonte went on to win the 2000 championship, making him and brother Terry the only siblings to have both won NASCAR's top honors.)

Sixty-nine drivers started at least one of the thirty-four races, up one from 1998. Among the top fifty finishers were twenty-four who hailed from non-Southern states, up from twenty-one the previous year and the best Yankee showing in the modern era (table 1, 192). There were also three non-Southerners who finished in the top ten (Stewart, Gordon, and Californian Mike Skinner), the best showing since 1990. The Yankee Resurgence proceeds apace.

The 1999 season gave fans two first-time winners, Stewart and Nemechek, whose September victories brought the total number of NASCAR Grand National or Winston Cup winners to 153. Another bonus: these two up-and-comers got their first wins on back-to-back weekends, the first time that's happened since 1970. Stewart's three wins were the most ever by a rookie. (The 2000 season featured four first-time winners—rookie Dale Earnhardt Jr., rookie Matt Kenseth, Steve Park, and Jerry Nadeau—bringing the total number of Winston Cup race winners to 157 by the end of 2000. The 2001 season added five more.)

The theme throughout the 1990s, one that has carried over to the new century, was growth and more growth: more fans, more venues, more winners, more sponsors, more money. Can NASCAR's fabulous growth continue indefinitely? What does the future have in store for competitors, sponsors, promoters, and fans?

Multicar Teams

The easiest prediction for NASCAR's coming decade is that multicar teams will continue to thrive and one-car independents will disappear. The independents are practically gone already; the economies of scale in present-day championship stock-car racing are too seductive. Not only did no single-car team post a win in 1999, only one, the Bill Davis Pontiac driven by Ward Burton, was able to crack into the season's top ten. Davis, seeing the writing on the wall, added a second car to his team for 2000.

Many fans mourn the passing of the one-car independents and worry about the effects of multicar teams on the level of competition and racing excitement. I'm not sure the concern is warranted. Multicar teams share information, testing dates, production facilities, engine-building programs, and even some staff, but once the green flag drops it's every man for himself. Some of the most electrifying racing in 1999 saw teammates Bobby Labonte and Tony Stewart rubbing fenders and banging up against one another. Their tight-fought duels in the Exide 400 at Richmond and in the Pennzoil 400 at Miami-Homestead were particularly memorable. I was on the lookout throughout 1999 and 2000 for on-track examples of drivers going out of their way to help teammates, and I can only recall a couple instances of racing altruism that went beyond the normal courtesies one driver extends to another. I think it may even add to the overall excitement as team members butt heads for the distinction of being the team's alpha male—more of those "races within the race" that so please a discerning fan.

New Teams

There'll be fresh faces among the Winston Cup teams and sponsors in 2000 and more fresh faces in 2001. Despite a rocky 2000 season, one new team to watch is the A. J. Foyt entry sponsored by Conseco Financial Services. Foyt had a stellar Winston Cup career: seven victories and thirty-six top ten finishes in 128 races from 1963 to 1994; but his main claim to racing fame is his reputation as Mr. Indianapolis 500—the Brickyard's most dominating driver of all time. Conseco put a $12 million sponsorship package on the table to fuel the team's entry into the Winston Cup. That kind of money coupled with Foyt's racing savvy and his indomitable will to win will make the new team fun to watch over the coming years.

(I was a little disappointed when Craftsman Truck regular Mike Bliss was initially named as the driver of Foyt's Pontiac, although by season's end, Bliss had ceded the reins to veteran Rick Mast. Given Conseco's business, I would have thought that David *Green* was the obvious choice. *Green.* Greenbacks. Money. Get it? Or maybe *Rich* Bickle. Then I heard that Pfizer, makers of Viagra, would be sponsoring a car in 2000 driven by Jeff *Fuller.* Not bad—it called to mind novelist William H. Gass's metaphor for male sexuality: "full up, erect, and on the charge." But wouldn't Ron *Hornaday* be a better choice to pilot the Viagra car? "Viagra: It helps you grow a Horn-a-Day"—now there's a marketing slogan your average NASCAR guy can relate to. As it turned out, Bliss ended the season driving the Viagra car—which certainly seems appropriate. Or *Buckshot* Jones at the helm of the Remington Arms entry. And why stop there? How about *Rusty* Wallace behind the wheel of the WD-40 car, Kevin Le*Page* in command of the Amazon.com entry, *Sterling* Marlin in a car sponsored by Zale's Jewelers, either of the *Grubb* brothers [Kevin and Wayne] in a Picadilly Cafeteria machine, Derricke *Cope* in a car hawking PMS medications, or Elton *Sawyer* in the Weyerhauser Lumber machine? Shouldn't *Dick Trickle* be at the wheel of a Depends Adult Diapers entry? Sorry, I couldn't resist.)

In conjunction with their sponsorship of the Number 27 Pontiac, the

The Pfizer walk-in men's health station at the 2001 Pepsi 400 at Daytona. Pfizer's best-known product is Viagra, used in the treatment of "erectile dysfunction." The company's "men's health initiative" came to NASCAR in 2000 and has been surprisingly popular, as evidenced by the size of the crowd. Inside the tent, you could have your blood pressure checked and pick up brochures discussing a variety of men's health issues, but you could not score free samples of Pfizer's wonder drug.

makers of Viagra also announced a men's health initiative for the 2000 racing season. Good grief! Pfizer partnered with NASCAR and established stars Rusty Wallace, Mark Martin, and Bobby Labonte to encourage male fans to get regular health check-ups and to educate men about health issues, including erectile dysfunction. Pfizer staffed walk-in men's health stations at all the 2000 Winston Cup events. Will there soon be "Viagra girls" working the Winston Cup crowds, passing out glassine packets of the miracle drug? If they do, will the parking lot traffic *ever* clear? Now that NASCAR has embraced a Men's Health initiative, can soup-and-salad concessions be far behind?

A number of minority race teams will also be vying for space in the Winston Cup starting grid in 2000 and beyond. None of these teams has a lock on building a competitive program, and none yet has the kind of financial backing that Conseco has showered on Foyt, but given NASCAR's Diversity Management Council, its apparently earnest efforts to encourage minority participation, and the number of new minority teams being formed, fans can anticipate a more diverse Winston Cup field to develop over the next decade. Adequate sponsorship is, of course, the key. The white male monopoly of Winston Cup competition and the thin scattering of minority fans grow more embarrassing each year.

Manufacturers

The manufacturers' championship also promises to heat up in the new century. For most of the 1990s, the only real competition was between Chevy and Ford, with Pontiac a distant third. But the Pontiacs found a niche in the 1999 season, when they proved well-nigh unbeatable on the relatively flat mile-and-a-half ovals. And now Dodge is back in the competition, too. The inside word (I heard it from Brother Kelley, who works for Chrysler) is that the decision to get back into the Winston Cup was made by Daimler and was part of the agreement that led to the 1999 merger between the two automotive giants. (Daimler-Benz is a heavy hitter in European racing.) Chrysler products were a dominant force in Grand National racing in the fifties, sixties, and seventies, and all serious stock-car fans are thrilled to see them back in.

The Chrysler-Daimler entry is the Dodge Intrepid. Jeff Gordon's former crew chief Ray Evernham was hired to run the Dodge racing program and there are already nine or ten Dodge teams in the competition, including Bill Elliott, Team Petty (three cars), and the Bill Davis team (two cars). Chrysler-Daimler invested big bucks in the program and with Evernham at the controls, Buddy Baker said we should "look for them to be up to speed pretty quick." (Confirming the prediction, the Dodge teams notched four victories in the 2001 season.) Baker, who drove Dodge entries during part of his own career, added, "More car makes means more competition, more competition means better racing. It couldn't be a better thing for the sport."[1]

New Venues

The NASCAR family of racing venues is also in the middle of a growth spurt. The schedule for 2000 was identical to 1999, but 2001 witnessed new Winston Cup events in Kansas City and Chicago (the France-controlled International Speedway Corporation is heavily involved in both these tracks) and further expansion later in the decade seems inevitable. About midway through the 2001 season I started hearing talk about a possible thirty-eight-event season in 2002. The Kentucky Speedway in Sparta (near Cincinnati), the track at Fontana (California), and even a new speedway planned for New Jersey have all been mentioned as possible expansion sites. There are dozens of other U.S. cities, many with world-class short tracks already in place, who would jump at the chance to host a Winston Cup weekend.

If further expansion is in the offing, as it certainly seems to be, then two questions arise: What kinds of tracks will the new venues be? And where will NASCAR find dates for them in its already crowded racing schedule?

Five of the six most recent additions to the Winston Cup schedule are mile-and-a-half ovals, and all of these but one are also relatively flat. (This includes the new tracks in Kansas City and Chicago.) The flat mile-and-a-half oval has become something of a NASCAR cliché. Why? Flat tracks are easier and cheaper to build than high-banked superspeedways, and you can squeeze plenty of grandstands around a 1.5-mile perimeter. Never mind that many fans find the racing on these tracks boring—they tend to be one-groove tracks whose flat corners rule out two- and three-wide racing.

Much of the charm of Winston Cup racing over the decades is that every venue has been unique. This, sad to say, is less true today than at any previous point in NASCAR's history. The new tracks remind me of the bland, homogenized major league baseball stadiums erected in city after city in the 1970s and 1980s, many now being abandoned in favor of new venues built along classic lines, of which Baltimore's Camden Yards is the premier example. Surely, there's room in the Winston Cup expansion for some variety. Does every new track have to be a cookie-cutter replica of Las Vegas or Miami?

A surprising number of fans who have been to many different Winston Cup venues will tell you that Bristol is their favorite—a short track, barely a half-mile around, but steeply banked to enhance speeds and completely enclosed by towering grandstands that seat a hundred fifty thousand. With only three short tracks left on the Winston Cup schedule, a Bristol clone would be a welcome addition.

The problem with dates is that there are only fifty-two weekends in a year. Between the start of the 2000 season in mid-February and its conclusion in mid-November, the teams competed in thirty-four points races; that number increased to thirty-six in 2001 and might increase again, to thirty-eight in 2002 or later. Adding the annual all-star event at Charlotte and the Speed Week's events leading up to the Daytona 500, that's thirty-eight to forty weekends of racing. In 1999 and 2000, there were five open weekends in the Winston Cup calendar with no races scheduled. In 2001, the two new events reduced the number of open dates to three; adding two more events would, all else equal, reduce the number to one. Open weekends give drivers, teams, and families some time off. They are also used for testing sessions and for rescheduling events that were canceled because of bad weather or other contingencies. With only three open weekends remaining in 2001 and possibly only one in later years, NASCAR will have to look elsewhere for new expansion dates.

Since it is difficult to extend the season on either end (as it is, there is only an eleven- or twelve-week break between seasons, which is barely enough time to get new cars and motors built and tested), impossible to run more than one event per week, and probably unwise to nibble away at the remaining open dates, adding races at some tracks will, sooner or later, require canceling events at others. One easy target: the all-star event at Charlotte the weekend before the Coke 600. Move the all-star race to the Thursday or Friday night before the Sunday of Memorial Day weekend and you free up the previous weekend to race elsewhere. Since most of the teams are headquartered in and around Charlotte, the current scheduling of The Winston and the Coke 600 is NASCAR's equivalent of a home-stand; still, as the pressure for new dates intensifies, it will be increasingly difficult to justify wasting an entire weekend on a seventy-lap curiosity piece.

If more new dates prove necessary, then some existing events will probably have to be discontinued. Legendary tracks such as Daytona, Bristol, Charlotte, and Talladega will almost certainly continue to host their two events each year, but less-venerated tracks may have to sacrifice one of their annual events to fuel the expansion. There has already been some talk of moving one of the two annual races at Rockingham, Darlington, and Atlanta to more "weather-friendly" sites or dates. Also, despite the France family's interests in the road course at Watkins Glen, the days of Winston Cup road racing must be numbered. At present, every team must maintain a road-racing program to compete in just two events: the June race at Sears Point and the August race at Watkins Glen. In contrast, there are four restrictor-plate races (two each at Daytona and Talladega) and six short-track races (two each at the three short-track venues) on the annual schedule. Nearly all the teams complain about the enormous costs involved in racing in the Winston Cup. NASCAR could achieve a substantial reduction in these costs and simultaneously open up two race dates by calling a halt to road racing in the Winston Cup. Many fans despise the road races anyway.

There is also some discussion of expanding internationally. The precedent exists: as I mentioned earlier, Richard Petty made his Grand National debut in Toronto. The Japanese have built an outstanding Winston Cup track, and a number of Japanese drivers have competed in November exhibition races at that facility. And you can bet the Germans have started thinking about a NASCAR-style track to showcase the Daimler-Chrysler racing program in Europe. Automobile racing is already wildly popular there—it would prove fertile soil for even further NASCAR expansion, maybe not in the first decade of the new century but perhaps in the second.

Television Coverage

In addition to new teams, sponsors, manufacturers, and venues, the NASCAR Family also has new television coverage for the 2001 season and beyond. CBS, whose live broadcast of the 1979 Daytona 500 got this whole NASCAR thing going, is out. ESPN and TNN, whose coverage fueled NASCAR's rapidly expanding popularity from the mid-1980s to the present day, are also out. The new TV deal, worth more than $400 million a year for the next ten years, will give the first half of each season to Fox Sports and the second half to NBC-Time Warner and TBS. There are lots more fans who follow the Winston Cup on TV than are able to get to the tracks, so the shift in TV coverage is consequential.

Fox debuted its Winston Cup coverage with the 2001 Daytona 500, the race that saw Dale Earnhardt killed. Former driver Darrell Waltrip and crew chief Larry McReynolds were hired as color commentators and most fans seem to feel that the Fox team has done an excellent job. Sure, Darrell, Larry, and the other Fox commentators spend too much time talking to each other, but with that exception, the Fox Winston Cup coverage earns high marks.

NBC debuted its coverage of Winston Cup racing at the inaugural running of the Pennzoil 400 at Miami-Homestead (the next-to-last race of the 1999 season), and it stunk. That's not just my opinion, either. The ratings were the lowest of the season—actually, the lowest for *any* race broadcast on network TV since NASCAR started keeping track in 1996. I'm sure Dick Ebersol, chairman of NBC Sports, looked at the ratings and the $2.4 billion, ten-year contract he had just signed with NASCAR and wondered, "Good Lord, what have we done?"

The loyalty of NASCAR fans to their sport is legendary. What could NBC have possibly done to drive fans away from their TV sets in record numbers? Here's what: The network kept cutting away from the racing action to run human-interest stories about the drivers and other fluff that they had in the can and were obviously anxious to get on the air, race or no race. Much of this was the sort of musically choreographed, slow-motion, voice-over pseudo-dramaturgy that one has come to expect of the major networks' coverage of big-time sporting events—the annoying filler that you sit through for three or four hours while you're waiting for the Super Bowl to start. Hey, if you want to run some of this stuff as part of the pre-race show, fine. CBS and ABC have been doing it for years. And if you've got a rain delay or a lengthy caution period that you want to fill with something other than commercials, well, that's okay too. But when you have Rookie-of-the-Year Tony Stewart contending for a record-breaking third win of the season, his teammate Bobby Labonte doing his damnedest to deny Stewart the victory, and Dale Jarrett wrapping up the Winston Cup championship all on the same day, then you'll keep fans in front of the TV by keeping the cameras on the race.

Apparently chastened by its 1999 ratings, the NBC broadcast of the 2000 race at Miami-Homestead was commendably filler-free, and veteran broadcasters Alan Bestwick and Benny Parsons provided snappy expert commentary. (Bestwick and Parsons were selected to anchor the network's 2001 race coverage also and by all accounts did a fine job.) Gone, too, was the pompous Brian Williams, whose 1999 race commentary was vacuous only when it was not inane.

Alas, neither Fox nor NBC has shown much interest in the old hands and familiar faces from the CBS, TNN, and ESPN days—announcers and commentators like Ned and Glenn Jarrett, Buddy Baker, Ken Squier, the Doctors Dick Berggren and Jerry Punch—guys who to your average Winston Cup couch potato were as comfortable as an old pair of shoes and as much a part of the Winston Cup weekend as a six-pack and a bag of pork rinds. I miss in particular the "delightfully undecipherable" Buddy Baker, whose incisive race commentary was always served up with an aw-shucks down-home manner and a thick Carolina drawl that would charm the pants off anyone, even a Yankee.

New Money

The TV deal brings a lot of new money into a sport that never seems to have enough of it. NASCAR gets 10 percent of the new revenue, the tracks get the lion's share of sixty-five percent (this is a fine time to own a Winston Cup race facility), and the remaining quarter goes to the drivers and teams in the form of enhanced purses. Once the dust settles, the new TV deal promises to *double* the average purse for a Winston Cup race. Winning a million dollars in a single season was once a big deal, but in 1999 thirty-eight drivers won a million bucks or more. (Jeff Gordon again led the way with winnings of nearly $5.3 million.) With even bigger purses in 2001 and beyond, the million-dollar season will become ho-hum.

Good thing, too. Costs escalate every year and will go up even more when new dates and races are added to the schedule. The more these costs can be recouped through team performance, the less the pressure on corporate sponsors to up the ante. Team owner Bill Davis was recently quoted in the *Charlotte Observer*, "I don't care how big a company is, how much money it has in an advertising budget, how well this sport works for them, how much they believe in this sport and how well it sells their product, there's a limit to what they can justify spending."[2] As the going rate for primary team sponsorship trends upward past $5 million per year, there is concern that Winston Cup racing is near, at, or possibly already past that limit. New TV revenues will ease the pressure on sponsors and may also help to slow the ever-increasing price of tickets, which go up, it seems, five or ten bucks per race every year.

During NASCAR's early years, the rule of thumb that Bill France Sr. followed was to keep racing cheap enough that anyone who could afford a good bass boat could also afford to race stock cars. Granted, the price of a decent fishing boat has also gone up these past fifty years, but it is nowhere near the millions of dollars necessary to compete in a Winston Cup season. Fans and commentators fear that if the costs continue to rise, sponsors will balk and we'll be left with just a handful of adequately funded teams who will then beat up on everyone else week in and week out—a return to the pattern of the premodern era. Not knowing the minds of sponsors, I can't say how close Winston Cup racing is or will soon be to their spending limits, but it does seem that the concern is more urgent these days than ever before. But, then, people have been saying that for the past twenty-five years. So we'll grant Bill France the younger the final word on the matter. "This is America. That's what you get with a market-driven economy. It's plain and simple. It's just America." Take that.

The Minor Leagues

As the pressure for new race dates attests, there's just not enough Winston Cup racing to go around. But there's plenty of other stock-car racing out there, and the sport's minor leagues are well positioned to feed off the Winston Cup's success. NASCAR surveys show that the Busch Series is already more popular than drag racing or IRL contests. A Busch car is basically a Winston Cup car with a slightly lower compression ratio. Many of today's top Busch drivers are destined for Winston Cup greatness a few years hence. Also, when the Winston Cup and Busch Series are at the same track on the same weekend, some Winston Cup stars also compete in the Busch race. The point: even now, Busch races are often as exciting as Winston Cup races, the drivers are nearly as talented, the competition is just as keen, and the tickets are half the price. The Busch Series already sells out in a few of its smaller venues. As the fan base grows, the series will start selling out everywhere, just like the Winston Cup, and that will be followed by lucrative new TV deals, more and better-heeled sponsors, and a further influx of fans.

Can you feel the possibilities? Soon stock-car fans will have an older, more established league, the Winston Cup, that is being challenged for supremacy by an upstart, the Busch Series. This calls to mind baseball's American and National Leagues or football's American and National Conferences, does it not? Why not a season-ending, three-day, three-race showdown featuring the top twenty drivers from each division—a World

Series or Super Bowl of stock-car racing to determine not the champion driver but the year's championship league? How about a Friday night contest in identically-prepared IROC-style race cars, then a Saturday race in cars conforming to the Busch configuration, followed by the Sunday climax featuring Winston Cup cars? Score each race just like you score Winston Cup races now, accumulate points over the three events, and whichever league ends the three-race series with the most points wins. I'd be there for the weekend and so would hundreds of thousands of other fans. The TV rights alone might go for—what?—$20 million?

Fifty or sixty thousand fans showed up for the 1999 ARCA race at Talladega and there were nearly as many at the ARCA event in Atlanta. The ARCA races I attended in 1999 featured some of the wildest racing action I've ever witnessed. So, there's plenty of growth in store for ARCA, too. Ditto the American Speed Association (ASA), based in Indiana and popular throughout the Midwest. When TNN lost out in its bid to retain broadcast rights to some of the Winston Cup events, it promptly purchased an equity partnership in ASA and began broadcasting ASA races in 2000. Winston Cup fans are fiercely loyal to TNN Motorsports (always voted number 1 by fans for the best race coverage), and ASA will see those loyalties broaden its own fan base. ESPN, ESPN2, Speedvision, and other cable networks must also be shopping for race-related programming, and that, too, will be a boon to the stock-car minor leagues.

NASCAR's short-track feeder program, the NASCAR Winston Racing Series, took a hit in 1999 when, as part of the tobacco settlement with the Feds, Winston agreed to drop its sponsorship of the series. The NWRS runs on about a hundred tracks all over the country, some dirt, some asphalt, ranging in size from .25 to .63 miles. These are tracks where younger drivers gain the seasoning they need to move up to the sport's higher echelons; as such, the competitors are often only sixteen or seventeen years old. The tobacco settlement prohibits Winston from being involved in any sport where persons under age eighteen are allowed to compete. So, the choices were either to change sponsors or to change the rules by raising the NWRS minimum age to eighteen—given the nature of the series, changing sponsors was felt to be less detrimental. Within the week, the Exide Corporation stepped up with a short-track sponsorship package for 2000 and beyond.

It is a strange world in which we live. The feds have no problem with sixteen-year-old boys being allowed to drive hot rods around a half-mile dirt track at ninety miles an hour but not, by God, if the activity is sponsored by the tobacco companies. Is that Winston logo over in the fourth turn the biggest hazard to the health of these young men? Please.

The twenty-first century racing boom will even extend to little local dirt tracks that are springing up all over the country, tracks like those my father and his friends raced on a half-century ago. The *Fixin' to Git* Road Tour included a Saturday night at the Westbank Speedway, just over the Huey P. Long Bridge from New Orleans. This is about as raggedy a racing venue as can be imagined — the parking lot is an open dirt field, the track little more than a bulldozer scar on the side of a bayou, the grandstand a rickety wooden structure that looks like it would topple in a strong breeze. But several hundred fans turned out for a night of dirt-track action, and everyone was having a good time. Tickets were ten bucks a head, beers were a buck-fifty a pop, the concession stand goodies were passable, and you could even buy souvenir pins featuring photos of the night's competitors and cars.

The competition ranged from Pro Stock to Bomber Class, with three or four divisions in between. We spent more of the night than we wanted watching the wrecker pull cars out of the swamp, as the only restraining wall was along the frontstretch and all that otherwise stood between the cars and the marshland was driving skill. Also, as we were near the bayou on a muggy night in September, the insect problem proved extreme. Still, I had as much fun as I would have had anywhere else in New Orleans on a September Saturday night, and that's saying a lot.

Only three cars were entered in the Bomber competition, two of them driven by a father and son, the third being an old Chevy station wagon that looked like a refugee from the demolition derby. The ex-wife/mother of the father-son duo sat right behind us, a rough, foul-mouthed woman with homemade tattoos on both arms and a boyfriend who got stumped trying to figure how much money he'd need if he wanted to buy four beers. (He went to the concession stand with a twenty just to be sure.) But she beamed with a mother's pride when the son (I believe his name was Danny) bested "that fuckin' bastard," his father, and when Danny joined his mother in the stands with his victor's trophy, she proudly introduced him to everyone. He turned out to be a polite, soft-spoken young lad. I thought, if the Winston Cup is the Rockefeller of stock-car racing, these folks are the Joads. But I had a blast at the Westbank Speedway that Saturday night, and oddly enough, so did the other academic types who had agreed, somewhat reluctantly, to tag along with me for the evening.

An article on local dirt tracks in the New Orleans paper (22 December 1999) emphasized the strong family base that makes dirt-track racing the sport that it is. "The competitive racing generally fills the stands every Saturday night. It is not unusual to see three or four generations of a family sitting in the stands cheering on their clan's driver." These dilapidated little speedways "might not hold 100,000 screaming fans, but [they] hold the same family virtues and competitive racing that has made the sport what it is today."[3] Race fans: We Are Family. And that sense of family, of clan, was as strong at the Westbank Speedway as it was at Daytona or Richmond. I had nothing in common socially, intellectually, financially, or culturally with most of the people at the Westbank Speedway, except that I, too, was a race fan. And — this is the glory of the NASCAR Family — that was enough.

The Skeleton in the Family Closet

Stock-car racing drips with Americana — with traditional values, unquestioning patriotism, a finely-honed sense of fair play. NASCAR *is* America, and increasingly, America *is* NASCAR. Among the Winston Cup competitors over the years have been namesakes of Presidents (Bill Clinton, George Bush, John Kennedy — even a Jeff Davis) and other prominent politicos (Bob Kennedy, Ted Kennedy, John Lindsay, Bill Bennett). There's been a Dizzy Dean, a Banjo Matthews, a Cotton Farmer, two men named Crash (Bond and Carson), and two named Lucky (Walters and Long). We've had a William Faulkner, a Jack Anderson, a Bobby Fisher, a Henry Ford, a Rambo, a George Gallup (plus three men named Samples and one named Poling), a Jim Stewart, a Jim Jones, a Jim Wright (no relation). Over the decades, NASCAR's championship series has featured seventeen Millers; eleven Bakers; six Cooks; four Skinners, Porters, and Potters; three Farmers and Carvers; two Ropers, Carpenters, Hunters, and Hookers; and a Goldsmith, a Clothier, and a Painter. Competitors have been Petty, Mean(s), Moody, Coy, Frank, Wimpy, Good, Mello, Bright, Craven, Handy, Hurt, and Sage. We've had Possums, Skunks, Lambs, Bass, Doves, Foxes, and Minx out on the track. There've been six

Kings, two Princes, a Baron, a Bishop, a Castle, a Duke, a Nobel, and one Gaylord. There's been a Klutz, Frank Lies, and Tru Cheek. Some men were born to racing: Lake Speed, Nolan Swift, Bill Champion, and three drivers named Rush. We've had a Joel Million, a Worth McMillion, a Johnny Dollar, and a Bill Poor; one Christ, two Christians, two Elders, one Angel, and four Parsons; a man named England, one named Ireland, one Dutch, one French, one Swede. Bobby Brewer, Earl Beer, Augie Pabst, Larry Bock, George Cork, Charles Muscatel, Johnny Walker, and Dick Allwine have sipped at NASCAR's cup. There've been four or five Pee Wees, a number of Cox, Dick Burns, Dick Passwater, Dick Trickle, and Bill Butts — nearly everything from A (Paul Aars) to Z (Ralph Zrimsek). Is this a hoot or what?

We stand on the cusp between the past century and the next and seek metaphors that make sense of the transition. The NASCAR Family is a good one. The fervid popularity of a purported anachronism like stock-car racing is a useful reminder that much of the twentieth century will persist into the twenty-first. Millenial fever has struck the chattering classes; their leading conceit, centuries old, is that we stand, even now, on the brink of the Great Transformation. So, the pages of our learned journals are filled with shrill announcements that the postmodern, post-industrial, post-affluent society is about to arrive. You think? These folks need to get to the track for a Winston Cup weekend, where people still eat animal flesh with gusto and junk food like there's no tomorrow, smoke cigarettes one after another, guzzle beer by the buckets, pinch their women on the ass, and take a child's delight in watching big, powerful, American V-8 gas-hogs run around a race track at 200 mph. There's not much that's postmodern or postindustrial about a stock-car race. But I learned more about America, who she is, and where she's headed from a season at the tracks than I ever learned from the *New York Review of Books*. And had lots more fun while I was at it.

The new century saw, reviled, and then quickly dismissed its first "atavar," Atlanta Braves relief pitcher John Rocker, who in the 3 January 2000 issue of *Sports Illustrated* unleashed a torrent of politically incorrect invective so bilious it had commentators editorializing for weeks. This slanderous diatribe covered "queers with AIDS," "black dudes," welfare mothers, women in general, Asians, foreigners in general, New Yorkers, and just about everybody else who was not a white male from Macon,

The "atavar" John Rocker shown in the photograph that accompanied his now-famous interview in *Sports Illustrated*. Note the head gear. Courtesy of Ronald C. Modra/*Sports Illustrated*.

Georgia.[4] Major League baseball ordered Rocker to undergo psychiatric evaluation, and pundits like *Newsweek*'s Anna Quindlen had a field day ranting about Rocker's deep "pool of prejudice." Quindlen at least had the sense to ask in print, "Why in the world does anyone think this man is worth listening to, much less worth excoriating?"[5]

And just what is the relevance of the John Rocker fiasco for us? The photograph accompanying the *Sports Illustrated* interview showed Big John togged out in his camouflage hunting gear, rifle at the ready, looking to bag a deer somewhere out in the woods of his native Georgia. Surely, the point of the photo was to tweak liberal sensibilities with an outfit and pose as politically incorrect as the interview itself — Good Lord, the man's a Bambi killer, too! And right there on top of Rocker's head, plain as day, an exclamation point for the overall ensemble, was a NASCAR gimme hat. The implied association of NASCAR with bigotry, although tacit and probably unintentional, was palpable—it cut like a sharp knife. And it reminded me again that race is the skeleton in the NASCAR Family closet. On the tracks and in the stands, stock-car racing remains a white person's sport. Surely, I'm not the only fan hoping for some progress on this front early in the new century.

Early in the 2000 season, the Winston Cup bad boys headed back to Darlington for their annual spring race. Darlington has always been the most Confederate of the NASCAR venues: the spring event was the Rebel 300, 400, or 500 in the 1960s and 1970s and the TranSouth 400 or 500 since; the fall event has been the Southern 500 since its inception. But in 2000 our lads revved it up for the Mall.com 400 @ Darlington Raceway. According to the Associated Press, Dale Earnhardt's victory the previous weekend had Darlington's phones ringing and tickets were just jumping off the track's online ticket outlet. The Mall.com 400 @ Darlington? A Darlington ticket outlet on the Internet? Now we're talking social change.

Or maybe not. There can be no better ending for this book than *Sports Illustrated*'s "This Week's Sign of the Apocalypse" for 30 October 2000, which read (verbatim): "Eugene Fleener of Gosport, Indiana, was charged with murder in the shooting death of Daniel Hutchison. The two had allegedly gotten into an argument in a bar because Hutchison was wearing a Jeff Gordon cap and Fleener is a Dale Earnhardt fan." *La plus ça change.* . . .

Prelude: On the Road to Charlotte

1   "Goodbye, Sweet Charlotte: Famed Track Sells Its Identity," *Sports Illustrated* (22 February 1999): 66.

2   As a matter of fact, there is a Museum of the New South located in Charlotte, one that "explores the history and economic, social, and cultural changes that have transformed Charlotte, NC, and its 13 surrounding communities into a New South epicenter." See U.S. Airways's *Attaché* (November 2001): 24.

1   Car Culture and the American Dream

1   Steve Rushin, "A Fun Ride, I Reckon," *Sports Illustrated* (22 February 1999): 22.

2   You can learn much more about Indiana small towns than you ever wanted to know in my essay "Small Towns, Mass Society, and the Twenty-first Century," *Society* 38, no. 1(November–December 2000): 3–10.

3   If you are unsure about the difference between drag racing and stock-car racing, or about any of the other more or less technical aspects of the sport as I describe them here, not to worry. Chapter 3 will tell you everything you need to know.

4   For readers unaware of the terminology, the Winston Cup is NASCAR's premier competition—it is to stock-car racing what the NBA is to basketball. NASCAR is the National Association of Stock Car Automobile Racing, the sanctioning body for Winston Cup racing and for a number of other series as well, among them the Busch Grand National Series and the Craftsman Truck Series, both of which are minor-league stepping-stones with large and growing fan followings. (You're not surprised that NASCAR drivers also race pickup trucks now, are you?) NASCAR

also sponsors regional stock-car competition with its Busch North and Winston West Series, and sanctions modified races and a number of others — in all, twelve racing series bear the NASCAR imprimatur. Finally, NASCAR is only one of several sanctioning bodies that sponsor and promote motor sports events. Chapter 3 fills in the details.

5 Small detail: Daytona is one of two NASCAR tracks (Talladega is the other) where the Winston Cup cars run with "restrictor plates" that dampen horsepower and reduce speed. So, when they fire engines at these tracks, the motors are actually putting out about 450 horsepower, not the 750 they put out without restrictor plates. Again, see chapter 3. (In 2000 NASCAR added restrictor plates to the race at Loudon, New Hampshire, in an effort to hold down speeds — this in the aftermath of the deaths of Adam Petty and Kenny Irwin.)

6 James Bryant and Mary McElroy, *Sociological Dynamics of Sport and Exercise* (Englewood, Colo.: Morton Publishing, 1997), 1.

7 Richard Huff, *The Insider's Guide to Stock Car Racing: NASCAR Racing, America's Fastest Growing Sport* (Chicago: Bonus Books, 1997).

8 My gratitude to John Shelton Reed, Director of the Institute for Research in Social Science at the University of North Carolina, Chapel Hill, for making the Southern Focus poll data available to me.

9 Bill Colson, "We Get Letters," *Sports Illustrated* (19 March 2001): 14.

10 Huff, *Insider's Guide,* 4.

11 For one example see John McKinney and Linda Bourque, "The Changing South: National Incorporation of a Region," *American Sociological Review* 36, no. 3 (June 1971): 399–412. "The paper attempts to demonstrate . . . the rapidity with which the South is becoming an integral part of American society."

12 See Wright, "Small Towns, Mass Society."

13 These highway factoids come from a little book by Wendell Cox and Jean Love entitled *40 Years of the Interstate Highway System, The Best Investment a Nation Ever Made: A Tribute to the Dwight D. Eisenhower System of Interstate & Defense Highways* (Washington, D.C.: American Highway Users Alliance, June, 1996). One wonders, do people elsewhere in the world write tributes to highways?

14 Peter Golenbock and Greg Fielden, eds., *The Stock Car Racing Encyclopedia* (New York: Macmillan, 1997). The encyclopedia ends with the 1996 season, so I augmented their information with the results from the 1997, 1998, and 1999 seasons. Keller had two victories in twenty-nine starts in his six-year NASCAR career, the other victory in a Hudson. He was killed racing Indy cars at Phoenix in 1961.

15 Racing hometown is missing from the driver listings in a number of cases, and many times, it is missing for drivers with suspiciously foreign-sounding names: Derhaag, de Stafano, Gallulo, Genove, Jaemar, Kalajainen, McCorkindale, Micka, Poalillo, Stolarcyk. So, the actual number of foreigners who have driven in NASCAR may be higher than I report.

16 1974 was also Ross's rookie season, making him one of very few Winston Cup
    drivers to win a race in his rookie year. Tony Stewart, NASCAR's 1999 Rookie of
    the Year, won three races in his rookie season, the all-time record. (The first of his
    three victories came at Richmond, a race I attended.) Since Stewart's feat, Dale
    Earnhardt Jr., Matt Kenseth, and Kevin Harvick have all posted rookie-season
    wins. (Another notable item from the 1999 season: Canadian Ron Fellows fin-
    ished second to Jeff Gordon in the road race at Watkins Glen, the best showing
    for a non-American in decades.)

17 Both John Andretti and Tony Stewart have raced in the Indianapolis 500 and
    the Charlotte 600 *on the same day*. In 1999 Stewart finished ninth at Indianapo-
    lis, then hopped on a private plane and made the green flag at Charlotte, where
    he finished fourth despite being made to start at the back of the field because
    he missed the morning drivers' meeting. (He was, ahem, busy.) In 2001 Stewart
    pulled off the two-fer again, this time finishing sixth at Indy and third at Char-
    lotte. Eleven hundred miles of competition racing on a single day is a remark-
    able feat, rather like running a competitive marathon, then turning around and
    running back.

18 Bob Schaller, *Top Stars of NASCAR,* vol. 1 (Grand Island, Nebr.: Cross Training
    Publishers, 1999), 8.

19 Robert Hagstrom, *The NASCAR Way: The Business that Drives the Sport* (New
    York: Wiley, 1998), 154.

20 Mark D. Howell, *From Moonshine to Madison Avenue: A Cultural History of the
    NASCAR Winston Cup Series* (Bowling Green, Ohio: Bowling Green State Uni-
    versity Popular Press, 1997), 91.

21 Quoted in Hagstrom, *The NASCAR Way,* 149.

22 Ibid., 153–54.

23 John Shelton Reed and Dale Volberg Reed, *1001 Things Everyone Should Know
    about the South* (New York: Doubleday, 1996), 259.

24 One of the first in the genre was by NASCAR writer Richard Huff, whose *Behind
    the Wall: A Season on the NASCAR Circuit* (Chicago: Bonus Books) appeared
    in 1991. Other examples include Paul Hemphill, *Wheels: A Season on NASCAR's
    Winston Cup Circuit* (New York: Simon and Schuster, 1997); Shaun Assael, *Wide
    Open: Days and Nights on the NASCAR Tour* (New York: Ballantine, 1998); and
    Scott Huler, *A Little Bit Sideways: One Week inside a NASCAR Winston Cup Team*
    (Osceola, Wis.: MBI Publishing, 1999).

Daytona Pilgrimage

1   Wallace quotes from David Poole, "Jarrett Has Just Enough of Everything to
    Win," *Charlotte Observer,* 4 July 1999, sports sec., p. 1.

2 Deconstructing NASCAR

1 See, for example, Steve Lopez, "Babes, Bordeaux, and Billy Bobs: How I Learned to Love NASCAR and Not to Hate Superstar Jeff Gordon," *Time* (31 May 1999): 76. Lopez describes the passage as "the line Bill France says he stole from Hemingway." I have been unsuccessful in my efforts to locate the source of the passage or to confirm that Hemingway actually wrote it, and apparently I am not alone. Mark Wilson of the Hemingway Resource Center responded to my query by writing, "That quote has been a source of speculation and frustration around here for quite some time. We get quite a few emails asking for the source of it, but like you, have been unable to attribute it to Hemingway. If he did say it, it was probably from a news article, but we haven't been able to track it down. It certainly sounds like something Hemingway would have said. . . . That same question came up on our message board recently, and no one else out there was able to come up with anything either."

2 Steve Rushin, "A Fun Ride, I Reckon," *Sports Illustrated* (22 February 1999): 22; Steve Lopez, "Babes, Bordeaux, and Billy Bobs," 70–76.

3 Just so you know, "STP" stands for Super-Treated Petroleum, an engine additive invented by Andy Granatelli. The STP corporation has a long history of involvement in all kinds of automobile racing and was the primary sponsor of Richard Petty's race team until the middle of the 2000 season.

4 See "Goodby, Sweet Charlotte," *Sports Illustrated* (22 February 1999): 66.

5 Lopez, "Babes, Bordeaux, and Billy Bobs," 74.

6 Peter Golenbock, "Introduction," *Stock Car Racing Encyclopedia* (New York: Macmillan), xi.

7 Paul Hemphill, "Haulin' Whiskey, Haulin' Ass," in *Wheels: A Season on NASCAR's Winston Cup Circuit,* (New York: Simon and Schuster, 1997), 84–85.

8 Richard Huff, *The Insider's Guide to Stock Car Racing: NASCAR Racing, America's Fastest Growing Sport,* (Chicago: Bonus Books, 1997), 5. A student of Southern history would pause on this passage and wonder whether the argument described here is more likely to lead to a car race or to a fistfight followed by a shooting.

9 Mark D. Howell, *From Moonshine to Madison Avenue: A Cultural History of the NASCAR Winston Cup Series,* (Bowling Green, Ohio: Bowling Green State University Popular Press, 1997), 177.

10 Ibid., my emphasis.

11 In its first season, the NASCAR championship series was called the Strictly Stock Series. This was changed in 1950 to the NASCAR Grand National Championship series, then changed again in 1972 to the Winston Cup Grand National Series and ultimately shortened to the Winston Cup Series. For more details, see chapter 6.

12 Hemphill, *Wheels,* 189.

13 "Drafting" is a subtle trick of aerodynamics that allows two cars running nose

to tail to go considerably faster than either could go on its own. Skill at drafting is especially critical on NASCAR's superspeedways, where the cars often run in large packs for an entire race.

14 Howell, *From Moonshine to Madison Avenue*, 115.

15 In his book *American Zoom: Stock Car Racing—From the Dirt Tracks to Daytona* (New York: Macmillan, 1993), Peter Golenbock quotes old-timer Bob Tomlinson: "Richard's daddy Lee was a great racer, but he was not accepted by the other racers because he wasn't a bootlegger. He says he was, but he only says that because he wanted to be one of the boys with Junior Johnson and Curtis Turner and all the rest of them [Who were all the rest of them?] 'cause at the time the true racers were the ones who were drinking and hauling the moon" (165).

16 As quoted in Golenbock, *American Zoom*, 55.

17 Dunnaway may not have known that the car had been modified and has never been mentioned as a whiskey hauler in any of my sources. Jim Roper started in two of the eight races in 1949, then never raced in the NASCAR championship series again.

18 Golenbock, "Introduction," *American Zoom*, xiv.

19 John Shelton Reed, "The South: What Is It? *Where* Is It?" in *My Tears Spoiled My Aim, and Other Reflections on Southern Culture* (San Diego: Harcourt Brace, 1994).

20 NASCAR's modern era began in 1972 with the adoption of the present-day seasonal format of twenty-eight to thirty-six races each year, not more than one per week, and each involving all the top Winston Cup teams. In earlier years, NASCAR would run as many as sixty races a season, a number of them short races on small tracks in the middle of the week, and usually pitting a few of the top teams against local competition. Because of the starkly differing seasonal formats, comparisons between the premodern and modern eras are usually meaningless.

21 Lopez, "Babes, Bordeaux, and Billy Bobs," 75.

22 Tom Wolfe, "The Last American Hero Is Junior Johnson," *Esquire* (March 1965): 74, 138.

23 James Bryant and Mary McElroy, *Sociological Dynamics of Sport and Exercise* (Englewood, Colo.: Morton Publishing, 1997), 77–78.

24 Mike Harris, "Two NASCAR Drivers Fire Employees," an Associated Press wire story that appeared in the *New Orleans Times-Picayune*, 11 August 1999, sports sec., p. 1.

25 Russell Ash, *The Top Ten of Everything, 1998* (New York: DK Publishing, 1997). The table showing "Top 10 Movies with Sports Themes" lists *Days of Thunder* first, followed in order by *Rocky IV, Rocky III, Rocky, A League of Their Own, Rocky II, Tin Cup, White Men Can't Jump, Field of Dreams,* and *Chariots of Fire,* just in case you were wondering about the competition.

26 It is rare, although not unheard of, for a rookie to win a race in his first season. But Trickle then goes on to win four of his next five contests, which is patently absurd.

27 Quoted in Dave Hager, "Thunder Row," *Entertainment Weekly* (10 August 1990): 50.

3 Racin' Basics

1 Not so with my brother-in-law Neil Maller, an engineer and also an instructor at a fast-driving school whose idea of a great weekend is to get his BMW out on a road course and drive the hell out of it. Neil was gracious enough to review an earlier draft of this chapter for technical accuracy, and he made a number of useful suggestions.

2 In 1999 Winston Cup races were held in Florida, North Carolina, Nevada, Georgia, South Carolina, Texas, Tennessee, Virginia, Alabama, California, Delaware, Michigan, Pennsylvania, New Hampshire, New York, Indiana, and Arizona—eight Southern states and nine states outside the South. Since 1999, venues have been added in Illinois and Missouri.

3 A common human eye-blink keeps the eyes closed for about one-tenth of a second. At 200 mph, a race car would travel 29.3 feet in one-tenth of a second, which, given a wheel-base of 110 inches, amounts to roughly three car-lengths in "the blink of an eye."

4 A recent illustration: Wildfires near Daytona caused the 1998 Pepsi 400 to be rescheduled to a later date. The only open date available was the weekend before the October race at Talladega. For the first time in NASCAR's history, the teams were forced to run at the two restrictor-plate tracks on back-to-back weekends. Most teams would normally have only two restrictor-plate cars in the stable. If one of them was damaged at Daytona, there'd be only one left to take to Talladega, so, soon after the July Fourth cancelation, most teams built (or converted) a third restrictor-plate car.

5 "Some teams have several cars and a couple of employees on staff whose main duty is to haul the show cars by trailer from site to site. These guys can be on the road more than two hundred days a year, logging sixty thousand miles or more" (*The Official NASCAR Handbook: Everything You Want to Know about the Winston Cup NASCAR Series,* [New York: HarperHorizon, 1998], 143). Usually, show cars are former racing machines that have been wrecked or have otherwise outlived their usefulness and that are dolled up with a little bodywork and paint so they look just like the real thing sitting out in front of the local Home Depot. It's the stock-car equivalent of being put out to pasture.

6 Quoted in *USA Today,* 18 February 2000, sports sec., p. 1.

7 V. Gregory Payne and Larry D. Isaacs, "Age and Peak Performance in Adulthood," in *Human Motor Development: A Lifespan Approach,* ed. V. Gregory Payne and

Larry D. Isaacs, 3d ed. (Mountain View, Calif.: Mayfield Publishers, 1995). Data are for "selected" sports; there are certainly some sports — for example, women's gymnastics — whose top athletes peak even earlier.

8   Earnhardt secured the 1994 championship with one race to go. Jeff Gordon's 1998 Winston Cup championship was locked up at Rockingham with the Atlanta race still to go. And the 1999 championship was decided at Miami-Homestead the week before the season finale at Atlanta. All the other championships of the 1990s were decided in the last race of the season.

9   Tom Wolfe, "The Last American Hero Is Junior Johnson," *Esquire* (March 1965): 142.

10 Quoted in Richard Huff, *The Insider's Guide to Stock Car Racing: NASCAR Racing, America's Fastest Growing Sport,* (Chicago: Bonus Books, 1997), 62.

Lost in the Land of Cotton

1   Stroker Ace, *Stand on It* (Boston: Little, Brown, 1973), 58.

2   Smokey Yunick, quoted in Peter Golenbock, *American Zoom: Stock Car Racing — From the Dirt Tracks to Daytona* (New York: Macmillan, 1993), 55.

3   Ace, *Stand on It,* 59.

4   The NASCAR Subculture

1   John Shelton Reed, *Kicking Back: Further Dispatches from the South* (Columbia: University of Missouri Press, 1995), 162.

2   Stroker Ace, *Stand on It* (Boston: Little, Brown, 1973), 58.

3   Peter Golenbock, *American Zoom: Stock Car Racing — From the Dirt Tracks to Daytona* (New York: Macmillan, 1993), 4.

4   Mark Howell, *From Moonshine to Madison Avenue: A Cultural History of the NASCAR Winston Cup Series* (Bowling Green, Ohio: Bowling Green State University Popular Press, 1997), 3.

5   The .625-mile short track at North Wilkesboro was one of eight venues in NASCAR's inaugural 1949 season and hosted two championship events a year through September 1996. The track was purchased in 1996 by Bruton Smith and Bob Bahre specifically to gain control of these two Winston Cup dates, one of which went to Smith's new track in Texas and the other to Bahre's new track in New Hampshire. This sale established the idea that "a Winston Cup *date* has marketable value, separate from the assets of a racetrack itself" (Robert Hagstrom, *The NASCAR Way: The Business that Drives the Sport* [New York: Wiley, 1998], 125).

6   Steve Rushin, "A Fun Ride, I Reckon," *Sports Illustrated* (18 February 1999): 22.

7   Ibid.

8   Ibid.

9   *The Official NASCAR Handbook* has a seven-page "Racing Glossary" focused

mainly on technical *arcania*. Huff's *Insider's Guide* has a seven-page glossary of "Words to Race By" and a two-page explanation of the flag system. Golenbock's *American Zoom* includes a two-page "Glossary of Racing Terms." Mark Howell's *From Moonshine to Madison Avenue* contains a four-page "Glossary."

10   Reed, *Kicking Back,* 156–57.

11   NASCAR insider Peter Golenbock says that if you score a comp ticket to a tower suite, you'll see "thousands of well-dressed middle-management types in slacks and sports shirts, and even a few in shirts and ties" (*American Zoom,* 7). It makes those cheap seats on the back stretch sound pretty good after all.

12   As for Evernham, he is now a team owner and chief technical consultant to the Dodge racing operation which re-entered the Winston Cup competition at the beginning of the 2001 season. The new Dodges qualified well and ran competitively, but it wasn't until the November race that Evernham's team won a race. So much for the idea that "anyone could win with an Evernham-prepared race car."

13   Quoted in Steve Lopez, "Babes, Bordeaux, and Billy Bobs: How I Learned to Love NASCAR and Not to Hate Superstar Jeff Gordon," *Time* (31 may 1999): 76.

14   Reed, *Kicking Back,* 161.

15   A handy summary of my thoughts on the topic is "Ten Essential Observations on Guns in America," *Society* 32:3 (March–April 1995): 63–68, on the off chance you're interested.

16   Tom Wolfe, "The Last American Hero Is Junior Johnson," *Esquire* (March 1965): 138.

17   Reed, *Kicking Back,* 162.

18   Golenbock, *American Zoom,* 3.

19   People who said they had been to a NASCAR race at least once in their lives were then asked if they had "been to one in the last five years." About half of both Southerners and non-Southerners said yes. Those who had been at least once in the past five years were then asked if they'd been to a NASCAR race in the past twelve months: 55 percent of Southerners (who had been at least once in the last five years) had done so, and ditto almost 70 percent of the non-Southerners. So there are obviously large differences in the numbers of casual fans (who may go to a race or two every five or ten years) vs. the truly hard-core fans (who go to multiple races every year).

20   Among those who ever watched, 15 percent of Southerners and 19 percent of non-Southerners said they watched televised NASCAR events "almost every week"; an additional 26 percent and 24 percent watched at least "once or twice a month."

21   The gender differences in both surveys are smaller than one would expect given informal impressions and observations at the tracks. Reed's guess at the 1992 Southern 500 was that "male fans outnumbered female ones by seven or eight to one." Based on the GSS result, the expected differential would be more like 2:1. The explanation for the discrepancy may simply be that women race fans at-

tend fewer races than men, so that at any given race, the predominance of men is larger.

5 The Yankee Invasion

1   If you're still reading, you may already know about professional bass fishing and the Southern origins of the top anglers, but if not, see Aaron Kuriloff's story for the *New Orleans Times-Picayune*, "South's Hold on Classic Remains Firm: Yankee Anglers Remain Oddity on Fishing Circuit," 29 July 1999, D-6. In the 1999 BASS Master's Classic, the Super Bowl of professional fishing, thirty-one of the forty-five competitors hailed from Dixie.

2   My source for everything reported in this chapter is the *Stock Car Racing Encyclopedia*. (ed. Peter Golenbock and Greg Fielden [New York: Macmillan, 1997]).The encyclopedia ends in 1996 so where appropriate, I've supplemented with race outcomes from the 1997, 1998, and 1999 seasons, which I get from newspapers or from *www.thatsracing.com*, a *Charlotte Observer* website.

3   For example, Peter Golenbock in *American Zoom: Stock Car Racing—From the Dirt Track to Daytona* (New York: Macmillan, 1993): "Big Bill France had been a controversial figure; the autocratic way in which he ran NASCAR at times angered both car owners and drivers, who accused him of unfairness and self-interest. But if you look at the Big Picture, one thing is very clear: The vision of Big Bill France made NASCAR stock car racing the immensely popular sport it is today" (77).

4   Steve Lopez, "Babes, Bordeaux, and Billy Bobs: How I Learned to Love NASCAR and Not to Hate Superstar Jeff Gordon," *Time* (31 May 1999): 75.

5   Ralph Moody was from Massachusetts, but during the winters he headed south to race in Virginia, the Carolinas, Georgia, and Florida; he settled permanently in Charlotte in 1956. Kirk Shelmerdine was born and raised around Philadelphia but is a NASCAR legend because of his work with Richard Childress Racing and his role as crew chief to Dale Earnhardt during Earnhardt's glory years. Tim Richmond was an Ohio native but broke into NASCAR driving for Rick Hendrick's Charlotte-based team. Finally, Felix Sabates is a Cuban émigré who fled Castro's regime in 1959; he bounced around America but settled finally in North Carolina where, in addition to his other sporting and business interests, he built a NASCAR team around Kyle Petty and Robin Pemberton.

6   Golenbock, *American Zoom*, 130, 154, 164.

7   Mark Howell, *From Moonshine to Madison Avenue: A Cultural History of the NASCAR Winston Cup Series* (Bowling Green, Ohio: Bowling Green State University Popular Press, 1997), 67.

8   Golenbock, *American Zoom*, 142.

9   Ibid., 67.

10 Ibid., 64.

11 The first truly Southern professional sports team (outside of racing) was the

Atlanta Braves, who moved to Atlanta from Milwaukee for the 1966 season. The Houston Astros (né Colt .45s) began playing in 1962 but were never a *Southern* team in the way that the Atlanta teams have been. Most Southern professional sports teams date to the 1970s or even the 1980s.

12   John Shelton Reed, *Kicking Back: Further Dispatches from the South* (Columbia: University of Missouri Press, 1995), 161.

13   See John Shelton Reed, *Whistling Dixie: Dispatches from the South* (New York: Harcourt Brace, 1990), 13.

6   Alcohol, Tobacco, and Firearms

1   Steve Rushin, "A Fun Ride, I Reckon," *Sports Illustrated* (18 February 1999): 22.

2   I say "nearly every car" because sometimes a car's primary or associate sponsors are direct competitors to the corporation sponsoring a particular award. For example, Exide Batteries sponsors a "hard charger" award, which goes to the driver who most improves his position between the start and finish of the race, but it certainly wouldn't do to have an Exide Batteries decal on a car sponsored primarily by Interstate Batteries. Usually, when a sponsor disallows the display of a competitor's decal, the sponsor also agrees to pay the same bonus to the team if they would otherwise have won the award.

3   Correspondence with the author.

4   Peter Golenbock, *American Zoom: Stock Car Racing — From the Dirt Track to Daytona* (New York: Macmillan, 1993), 109.

5   Ibid., 43.

6   Ibid., 84.

7   Six Petty championships (three of Lee's and three of Richard's) are represented in the table, and in five of the six, Team Petty also led (or was tied for the lead) in total races entered. Contrast that with the three David Pearson championships, where Pearson was fifth, fifth, and fourth in total races run. I'll leave it to readers to ponder the significance of this interesting difference.

8   Mark Howell, *From Moonshine to Madison Avenue: A Cultural History of the NASCAR Winston Cup Series* (Bowling Green, Ohio: Bowling Green State University Popular Press, 1997), 61.

9   This is known in marketing circles as "saturation advertising," where every conceivable consumer of your product is constantly exposed to your brand name, corporate logo, or advertising slogans. To be clear, the point (in the case of Budweiser) is not to drive beer drinkers into the bars; the point is to make beer drinkers who are in the bars think of Budweiser when they tender their order. On marketing in the beer industry, see Peter Hernon and Terry Ganey, *Under the Influence: The Unauthorized Story of the Anheuser-Busch Dynasty* (New York: Avon Books, 1991).

10 Richard Huff, *The Insider's Guide to Stock Car Racing: NASCAR Racing, America's Fastest Growing Sport* (Chicago: Bonus Books, 1997), 108.

11 Ibid., 102.

12 Robert Hagstrom, *The NASCAR Way: The Business that Drives the Sport* (New York: Wiley, 1998), 47–73.

13 Peter Carlson, "Red Necks, White Lightning and Blue Suits: the Changing Culture of NASCAR," *Washington Post Magazine* (12 September 1999): 10–17, 24–25, 28.

14 Ibid., 28.

15 Hagstrom, *The NASCAR Way,* 68,

16 Ibid., 52–53.

17 Ibid., 59.

18 Huff, *Insider's Guide,* 95.

19 Carlson, "Red Necks, White Lightning," 28.

20 Correspondence with author.

21 Huff, *Insider's Guide,* 193–94.

22 Quoted in Bob Schaller, *Top Stars of NASCAR,* vol. 1 (Grand Isle, Nebr.: Cross Training Publishing, 1999), 51.

23 Huff, *Insider's Guide,* 66–67.

7 We Are Family

1 Quoted in Jim Utter, "Baker Says Chrysler's Return Good for the Sport," *Charlotte Observer,* 9 October 1999.

2 Quoted in David Poole, "More Than Ever, Money Is Driving NASCAR's Boom," *Charlotte Observer,* 16 November 1999.

3 Sanford Myers, "A Muddy Good Time," *New Orleans Times-Picayune,* 22 December 1999, D-7.

4 Jeff Pearlman, "At Full Blast," *Sports Illustrated* (3 January 200): 60–64.

5 Anna Quindlen, "Ignore Them Off the Field," *Newsweek* (21 January 2000): 68.

Ace, Stroker, 145; *Stand on It*, 18, 59, 287
  n.1
Adams, Rebecca, 18
Addiction, imagery of, 145
Advertising, saturation, 290 n.9
African Americans in NASCAR, 80–84.
  See also Diversity in NASCAR
Alberts, Trev, 203
Allison, Bobby, 40, 95, 223; Coca-Cola
  sponsorship of, 223
Allison, Cliff, 40
Allison, Davey, 40, 51, 125, 150
Allison, Donnie, 40
American Basketball Association, 68
American Broadcasting Company
  (ABC), 42
American Dairy Association, 10, 211
American Motor Sports Club, 89–90
American Sociological Association, 82,
  97
American Sociological Review, 97, 282
  n.11

American Speed Association, 84, 129,
  275; future of, 275
America Remembers, 160
Andretti, John, 5, 24, 40, 93, 94, 138, 176,
  195, 243, 244, 263, 283 n.17; hometown
  of, 93, 176
Andretti, Mario, 40, 199
ARCA. *See* Automobile Racing Club of
  America (ARCA)
ARCA cars, 3, 128, 131; photo, 128
ARCA races, 3, 41, 147, 209–11, 230, 256–
  57, 275; argot of race fans, 148–50;
  at Atlanta, 256–57; at Charlotte, 3;
  interest in, 210; at Talledega, 210
Ash, Russell, 285 n.25
Assael, Shaun, 56, 283 n.24
Atlanta Journal-Constitution, 12
Atlanta Motor Speedway, 37, 104, 105,
  126, 130, 162, 190, 248, 254–62, 287
  n.8; diagram, 260; fastest lap at, 105;
  gate 13 (photo), 162; infield campers
  (photo), 256; lead lap finishers at,

Atlanta Motor Speedway (*continued*)
248; opening, 190; start-finish line
(photo), 130; traffic control, 258
Autographs, 38–39, 238
Automobile Racing Club of America
(ARCA), 3, 96, 129, 275

Backup cars, need for, 108–9
Bahre, Bob, 287
Baker, Buck, 40, 68, 183, 199
Baker, Buddy, 40, 61, 62, 106, 183, 268,
273, 291 n.1; and 200 mph lap, 62, 106
Baker, E. G. ("Cannonball"), 71
Banking (of race tracks): aid to fans'
view, 94; defined, 99; effect on speeds,
105
Baseball, 58, 104, 108
Basketball, 61
Beer, 134, 161, 258; companies as
sponsors, 161; price of, 161
Benson, Johnny, 153, 195, 229
Berrier, Ed, 108
Bestwick, Alan, 272
Betty Crocker Racing Family, 135–36
Bickle, Rich, 195, 232
Blaney, Dave, 195, 260
Bliss, Mike, 135
Blue Angels. *See* Fly-by
Bodine, Brett, 39, 243, 252, 264
Bodine, Geoff, 39, 40, 105, 198, 243, 260
Bodine, Todd, 39, 260
Bootleggers. *See* Moonshine
Bootlegger's turn, 66
Bourque, Linda, 282 n.11
Bown, Chuck, 40
Bown, Dick, 40
Bown, Jim, 40
Boys, Buddie, 40
Boys, Trevor, 34, 40
Bradberry, Gary, 260
Brakes, 110

Brasington, Harold, 189
Brickyard 400 at Indianapolis, 55, 56, 82,
87–97; difficulty of obtaining tickets
to, 90; inaugural race, 88; in 1994, 150;
in 1999, 87–97; racist comments of
fans at, 82; seats at, 93–94; view at, 94
Bristol Speedway, 48, 50, 105, 150, 173,
179, 190, 248, 269; banking, 50; fans'
favorite, 269; fastest lap, 105; lead lap
finishers at, 248; night racing at, 48;
opening, 190
Broadcasting rights, cost of, 42, 235,
271–73
Bryant, James, 75, 77, 282 n.6, 285 n.23
Budweiser beer, 161, 227, 237, 290 n.9
Burdick, Bob, 203
Bureau of Alcohol, Tobacco, and Firearms, 217
Burger King, 46–47, 237
Burton, Jeff, 5, 39, 134, 140, 177, 178, 195,
239, 243, 244, 263; Rookie of the Year
(1994), 195; winner of 1999 Southern
500, 140
Burton, Ward, 39, 140, 177, 178, 243, 260,
261, 265
Busch Grand National Series, 39, 41, 42,
91, 96, 129, 147, 148, 161, 171, 230, 274–
75, 281; cars, technical specifications
of, 274; future of, 274–75; popularity
of, 147
Byron, Red, 67, 68

Cable TV coverage of NASCAR, 41–42
Car God, 33
Carlson, Peter, 231, 239, 241, 252, 291 n.19
Cars, 32–33; American love affair with,
33; and American values, 33; invention
of, 64; winning Winston Cup races,
251. *See also* Winston Cup: cars
CART-IRL dispute, 127, 148
Caution period, defined, 3, 121

Championship Auto Racing Teams (CART), 127, 147

Charlotte, NC, 1–15, 29, 65, 71, 83, 85, 146, 179, 205–8; association with NASCAR, 14; as epicenter of stock-car racing, 2; as headquarters of NASCAR teams, 13; the "New South," 14–15, 281 n.2; population of, 14; Speed Week, 1

Charlotte Motor Speedway. *See* Lowe's Motor Speedway

Charlotte Observer, 21, 273, 283 n.1, 289 n.2

Chevrolet, 10, 34

Chicago, 82, 87, 96, 97, 190, 268

Christian, Sarah, 69, 79; photo, 69

Chrysler Corporation: 1964 dispute with NASCAR, 222; re-entry into Winston Cup competition, 251, 268, 271, 288 n.12, 291 n.1

Cigarettes, 220–22; ban on advertising of, 220; Surgeon General's Report, 220. *See also* Winston cigarettes

Civil War, 30, 201; Winston Cup races as allegorical replay of, 200

Class. *See* Social class

Clemson University, 202

Clinton, Bill: at Darlington, 159–60

Coca-Cola, 184, 223, 228

Coca-Cola 600 (Charlotte 600), 1, 9, 35, 120, 122, 231, 270, 283 n.17; and Jeff Gordon, 122; NASCAR's longest race, 120

Columbia Broadcasting System (CBS), 41, 271

Competitiveness, 241–53; definitions of, 242, 248, 249; indicated in Championship points system, 247, 249, 264; multi-car teams as threat to, 251–52, 265–66; NASCAR's role in maintaining, 250–51; trends in, 244–50

Complimentary tickets, 236, 288 n.11

Confederate flag, 12, 30, 35, 36, 54, 81, 83, 84, 96, 141–43, 151, 181, 182, 202, 258; cartoon featuring, 12; in Charlotte at 2001 race, 83; in Darlington, 141; in *Days of Thunder*, 84; in Daytona infield, 83; photo of, at track, 182

Conseco Financial Services, 135, 266, 267

Contingency awards, 109, 218, 232, 290 n.2

Contracts (of drivers), 120

Coolers, size limits on, 161, 162

Cope, Derrike, 82, 196–97, 243

Corporatization (and NASCAR), 43, 62, 109, 182, 184, 217–42; and competition, 219, 224, 227, 241–42; and drivers, 238–40; and fans, 235–41; and racing, 223–24, 237, 240; and regional parochialism, 182, 223–24; illlustration of, 109

Country-western music, 31, 46, 50, 157, 168

Cox, Wendell, 282 n.13

Craftsmen Truck Series, 42, 147, 171, 230, 281 n.4

Craven, Ricky, 153, 195, 243, 251

Crew chiefs, 115–16

Cruise, Tom, 59, 84–85, 180

Cultural tensions in NASCAR, 15. *See also* Confederate flag; Diversity in NASCAR

Dallenbach, Wally, 243

Darlington Speedway, 56, 82, 97, 108, 113, 122, 132–43, 150, 151, 157, 159, 181, 188, 189, 190, 197, 201, 209, 223, 280; capacity of, 138; Coca-Cola affiliation with, 223; Confederate track, 141–42, 280; diagram of, 139; first NASCAR super-speedway, 132, 188, 189; in-field, 151; opening of, 141, 188, 190;

Darlington Speedway (*continued*)
ownership of, 138; pits, 138; primitive appearance of, 138; reconfiguration of, 139–40; and Strom Thurmond, 142; track nickname, 113, 132; and Darrell Waltrip, 122

Davis, Bill, 265, 268, 273

Days of Thunder, 34, 59, 84–86, 118, 180, 197, 207, 285 n.25, 286 n.27

Daytona 500, 5, 21, 36, 41, 60, 80, 88, 89, 104, 147, 148–50, 153, 196, 198, 248, 251, 271; economic impact of, 147; and Tiny Lund, 198

Daytona Beach, FL, 14, 40, 46–47, 55, 70, 286 n.4; founding of NASCAR at, 70

Daytona International Speedway, 24, 49–50, 87, 106–7, 117, 146, 178, 188–89, 190, 216; banking, 50; building of, 188–89; capacity of, 49–50, 146; comparison to Indianapolis Motor Speedway, 87; diagram of, 50; France family interest in, 188–89; history of, 188, 189; night racing at, 48–49; opening, 189; photo, 117; restrictor plates, 107

Daytona USA Theme Park, 50, 231

Deaths: from alcohol, tobacco, firearms, 217, 221; of drivers, 20–21

Deconstructionism, 57

Dieringer, Darel, 199, 200

Dirt tracks, 18, 43, 183, 187, 188, 276–77; future of, 276–77

Diversity in NASCAR, 54–55, 79–84, 96, 267–68, 278–79; Diversity Management Council, 54, 80, 267

Donahue, Mark, 199

Donleavy, Junie, 109, 255

Dover, Delaware (NASCAR track at), 150, 182, 190, 248; lead lap finishers at, 248; nickname, 150; opening of, 182, 190

Drag racing, 21–22, 100, 127, 274, 281 n.3

Drafting, 67, 107, 215, 284–85 n.13

Drivers, 34, 39–41, 101, 161, 238–41; accessibility to fans, 38, 238; ages of, 114–15; as "All-American," 35; Canadian, 34, 191, 283; contracts, 120; families of, 36–37, 39, 40; names of, 33, 266, 277–78; nationality of, 34; regional origins of, 73, 191–201; safety, 21; salaries and earnings of, 119; sex appeal of, 239

Dunnaway, Glenn, 72, 285

Duvall, Robert, 34, 84–85, 180

Earnhardt, Dale Jr., 27, 39, 178, 196, 260, 261, 265, 283 n.16; first Winston Cup win, 265, 283

Earnhardt, Dale Sr., 2, 5, 38, 39, 52, 53, 78, 85, 91–94, 119, 134–35, 136, 140, 149, 150, 151, 155, 156, 163, 176–77, 178, 195, 197, 202, 213, 215, 216, 240–41, 243, 244, 250, 260, 263, 271, 280, 287 n.8, 289 n.5; career, 52, 119, 155, 250; death of, 20, 26–29, 271; education, 240; fans of, 53, 135, 156, 176–77, 213, 216; income, 241; and Labonte incident at Bristol (1999), 134–35, 140, 163, 177; photo, 157; products endorsed by, 119; souvenir sales, 29, 119

Earnhardt, Ralph, 39

Easley, Hank, 23

EasyCare 100 (ARCA race), 3

Ebersol, Dick, 272

Economaki, Chris, 22

Economics of racing, 129–31

Eel River, 55, 56

Elliott, Bill, 10, 48, 53, 106, 125, 152–53, 238, 240, 243, 252, 255, 260, 264, 268; career of, 152; photo, 153

Engines (of Winston Cup cars), 110, 112; cost of, 112

Erickson, Ray, 69

Erving, Julius, 68, 82

ESPN, 42, 271

ESPN2, 26, 42

Evernham, Ray, 38, 115, 155–56, 203, 206, 212, 268, 288 n.12

Exide Batteries 400 at Richmond, 133, 174–78, 265

Fans: argot, 148–50; as amateur poets, 29; as a subculture, 144–69; camaraderie, 147–48; coveted by marketers, 234; drunkenness of, 6–7, 51, 177; female fans, 80, 151, 177, 223, 234; gesticulations of, during races, 177; Gordon-haters, 155–56, 207; gun ownership among, 159–60; loyalty of, 234–35, 272; outdoorsmanship of, 156–57; product loyalties of, 54, 234–35; regalia, 134, 150–52; regional chauvinism, 201–2; regional differences, 26, 165, 166–67, 180–81; social characteristics of, 166–68, 233–34; working class origins of, 75–79, 137. *See also* Winston Cup: attendance

Favre, Bret, 148

Federation Internationale de l'Automobile, 127

Fellows, Ron, 283 n.16

Fielden, Greg, 282, 289 n.2

Firecracker 400, 46. *See also* Pepsi 400 at Daytona

Fishing, 58–59, 181, 289 n.1

Fixin' to Git Road Tour (1999): as a family affair, 44; Atlanta, 254–62; Charlotte, 1–15, 205–8; Daytona, 47–56; Darlington, 132–43; expense of, 44, 146; funding of, 89–90; idea for, 13, 17–18, 25, 44; Indianapolis, 87–97; pit tour, 174–76; Richmond, 170–79; Talledega, 208–16; Westbank Speedway, 276–77. *See also* T-shirts

Flock brothers (Bob, Fonty, Tim), 40, 67, 74, 200, 240

Fly-by, 24, 35, 50, 176, 213

Ford, Henry, 32

Ford Motor: dispute with NASCAR, 222

Formula One, 33, 88, 127

Fort Wayne, IN, 87, 89

Fox Broadcasting, 41, 42, 235, 271–72

Foxworthy, Jeff, 168–69

Foyt, A. J., 24, 55, 135, 266, 267; career, 266; formation of Winston Cup team, 135, 266

France, William H. G. ("Big Bill"), 70–71, 72, 124, 183, 184, 187–90, 221, 223, 273, 289 n.3; statue outside Daytona, 70

France, William Jr. ("Bill"), 54, 184, 274

Ganey, Terry, 290 n.9

Gant, Harry, 115, 239

General Motors, 10, 222

General Social Survey, 26, 164–65, 167–68

Georgia Boot 400 (ARCA race), 257

Gibbs, Joe, 37, 38, 154, 251, 264

Gilchrist, Derrick, 257

"Gimme" hats, 89: as subcultural regalia, 150, 279

Goldsmith, Paul ("Goldy"), 198, 199

Golf, 61, 108

Golenbock, Peter, 59, 63, 72, 145, 164, 165, 196, 197, 221, 282 n.14, 284 n.6, 285 n.15, 287 n.2, 288 n.18, 289 n.8, 290 n.4

Gordon, Jeff, 5, 10, 11, 38, 51–52, 53, 62, 74, 78, 90, 93, 94, 97, 115, 118, 119, 122, 125, 126, 128, 131, 149, 150, 151, 154, 155–56, 160, 173–74, 176, 177, 181, 184, 195–98, 202, 203, 206, 207, 211, 212, 216, 218, 238–44, 249, 250, 251, 255, 260, 263, 264, 273, 280, 283 n.16, 287 n.8; career of, 155–56, 174; dislike of,

Gordon, Jeff (*continued*)
155–56, 207; and Evernham, 206, 212; fans, 93, 151, 156, 173–74, 176; photo, 157, 174; nickname, 195; products endorsed by, 10, 211; Rookie of the Year, 115, 155, 195; souvenir trailer (photo), 174
Gosselin, Mario, 3
Granatelli, Andy, 199, 284
Green, David, 39
Green, Jeff, 39
Gumbel, Bryant, 81
Guns, 136–37, 217
Gurney, Dan, 199
Guthrie, Janet, 79–80

Hager, Dave, 286
Hagstrom, Robert, 36, 59, 230–31, 233, 234–35, 283, 287, 291 n.15
Hall, Roy, 67
Hamilton, Bobby, 40, 243, 252
Happy Hour, 47, 91, 147, 159, 166, 211, 256
Harris, Mike, 285
Harvick, Kevin, 283 n.16
Hemingway, Ernest, 59, 284 n.1
Hemphill, Paul, 63, 67, 283 n.24, 284 n.7
Hendrick, Rick, 84, 119, 289 n.5; and Hendrick Motor Sports, 118, 130, 131, 251, 264
Hensley, Jimmy, 115
Hernon, Peter, 290 n.9
Home Depot, 4, 177, 227, 236
Hornaday, Ron, 257
Hospitality packages, 174–75, 229–30, 256, 257
Howell, Mark, 37, 59, 64, 66, 67, 119, 145, 198, 203, 227, 241, 283 n.20, 284 n.9, 285 n.14, 287 n.4, 288 n.9, 289n. 7, 290 n.8
Hubert, Tom, 82

Huff, Richard, 26, 41, 64, 114, 120, 131, 165, 171, 228, 229, 236, 249, 282 n.7, 283 n.24, 284 n.8, 287 n.10, 288 n.9, 291 n.18
Huler, Scott, 283 n.24
Hunter, Jim, 189
Hurtubise, Jim, 199
Hutcherson, Dick, 183, 198
Hyde, Harry, 84

Indiana Gang, 93, 94, 154, 206–7, 262
Indianapolis 500, 4, 22–23, 35, 41, 56, 80, 87, 93, 127, 266, 283 n.17
Indianapolis Motor Speedway, 87–89, 146, 150, 158, 178, 188; diagram of, 88; seats at, 93–94
Indy cars, 34–35, 127, 128; photo, 128
Indy Racing League, 33, 89, 91, 96, 127, 147, 208, 274
Infield campers, 7, 38, 160, 214, 256; photos, 7, 38, 214, 256
Inside NASCAR (magazine), 10
Institute for Research in Social Science, 165, 282 n.8
Interstate highway system, 32, 33, 282 n.13
International Hot Rod Association, 126, 147
International Race of Champions, 91–92, 147, 275
International Speedway Corporation, 96, 189, 268
Irvan, Ernie, 135, 154, 171, 243
Irwin, Kenny, 21, 41, 93, 94, 150, 195, 206–7, 258, 259, 282 n.5; death of, 21, 41; and Tony Stewart, 206–7
Isaacs, Larry D., 286–87 n.7

Jarrett, Dale, 5, 10, 11, 39, 51, 52, 53, 55, 93, 94–95, 113, 126, 138, 212, 215, 232,

240, 243, 244, 254, 263, 264, 272, 283
n.1; photo, 95
Jarrett, Glenn, 38, 40, 273
Jarrett, Jason, 40
Jarrett, Ned, 40, 89, 183, 264, 273
John Deere, 49, 157
Johnson, Junior, 66–67, 78, 125, 127, 181,
220–21, 222, 239, 285 n.15, 287 n.9;
career of, 66, 67
Jones, Buckshot, 196, 260
Jones, Parnelli, 199
Joyner, Jay, 230, 236
Joyner-Kersee Racing, 82

Kansas Speedway Corporation, 96, 268
Keller, Al, 34, 282
Kellogg's Corn Flakes, 151, 232, 236, 237
Kendall, Don, 188
Kenseth, Matt, 195, 265; first Winston
Cup win, 265, 283 n.16
Kentucky Speedway, 269
Kidman, Nicole, 84
Kimmel, Frank, 128
Ku Klux Klan, 61, 81
Kulwicki, Alan, 85, 86, 125, 150, 181, 186,
195, 196
Kuriloff, Aaron, 289 n.1

Labonte, Bobby, 11, 37, 38, 39, 52, 53,
93, 94, 154, 207, 212, 215, 239, 240,
243, 244, 255, 260–65, 267, 272; and
Earnhardt incident at Bristol, 134–
35; victories in 1999, 263; victory at
Atlanta, 1999, 261
Labonte, Terry, 5, 11, 39, 40, 82, 125, 134–
35, 140, 151, 160, 186, 232, 243, 244, 251,
263, 264
Latford, Bob, 124, 218
Lead lap finishers, 246, 248
Legends cars, 3, 129

Lepage, Kevin, 140, 195, 215, 259
Linder, Dick, 69
Little, Chad, 49, 238, 259
Logansport, IN, 18, 23, 55–56, 87
Lopez, Steve, 60–63, 74, 81, 83, 196, 217,
284 nn.1, 2, 5, 285 n.21, 288 n.13, 289
n.4
Lorenzen, Freddie, 197–98, 201, 239, 240;
career, 197
Loudon, New Hampshire (NASCAR track
at), 41, 82, 179, 189, 190, 202, 282 n.5
Love, Jean, 282 n.13
Lowe's Home Improvement stores, 2, 4,
177, 207–8; bombing of, 207–8
Lowe's Motor Speedway (Charlotte
Motor Speedway), 1–15, 41, 104, 190,
205–8, 259; bomb threat at 1999 race,
207–8; capacity of, 2, 146; sale of
naming rights, 2, 15, 208, 252
Luckovich, Mike, 12, 142; cartoon by, 12
Lund, "Tiny," 20, 198; legend of, 198
Luzerne Community College, 202

Marbles (racing debris), 103
Marcis, Dave, 115, 119–20, 196, 252, 264
Mardi Gras, 10, 61
Marlin, Coo Coo, 40
Marlin, Sterling, 26, 40, 157, 203, 243
Martin, Mark, 5, 10, 90, 91, 92, 140,
242–43, 244, 249, 260, 261, 263, 267
Martin brothers (Otis and PeeWee), 67
Martinsville Speedway, 34, 93, 101, 104,
110, 120, 122, 156, 173, 179, 190, 204,
206–7; fastest lap at, 101
Mast, Rick, 177, 178
Mayfield, Jeremy, 92, 140, 196, 243
McElroy, Mary, 75, 77, 282 n.6, 285 n.23
McGriff, Herschel, 115, 199; career of, 199
McKinney, John, 282
McReynolds, Larry, 115-16, 271

Megaspeedways (Daytona, Talledega), 105, 106–7, 110

Michigan International Speedway, 82, 122, 135, 182, 189, 190; designer, 189; opening of, 182, 190

Miller beer, 92, 161, 237

Mills, Fetzer, 219, 242, 243, 244

Minor leagues (stock car), future of, 274–77

Minority race teams, 82, 96, 267–68

Modern era of NASCAR, 182–84, 190, 285 n.20

Modifieds, 24, 92, 128, 282 n.4; photo, 128

Moneypenny, Charles, 189

Monster trucks, 50

Montgomery, John Michael, 50, 157

Moody, Ralph, 289

Moonshine, 63–72, 85, 285 n.15

Moore, Bud, 198, 222

Moroso, Rob, 37, 115

Motor Racing Network, 8, 22, 140

Motor Racing Outreach, 37

Multi-car teams, 251–52, 264, 265–66

Murchison, Clint, 188

Musgrave, Ted, 153, 160

Myers, Sanford, 291

Nadeau, Jerry, 153, 154, 195, 243, 265; first Winston Cup victory, 154, 243, 265

Nantahala Gorge, NC, 204, 208; and Eric Robert Rudolph, 208

NAPA 300 (1999), 148

NAPA 500 (1999), 38, 104, 109, 158, 230, 236, 254–62; outcomes, 261–62; photo, 259; qualifying, 259–60; souvenir trailers, sponsor party at, 257–58

NASCAR: 14, 30–31, 33–35, 38–41, 70, 72–74, 88, 108–14, 129, 174–76, 182–91, 214, 224–26, 230–31, 238, 250–51, 281 n.4; books about, 44, 56, 59, 283; champions by state and region, 195; Christian fellowship in, 36, 37–38; class origins of NASCAR fans, 75–79; fans, 36, 38, 174–76; first race at Charlotte, 12–13, 34, 71–72, 179, 218; founding of, 70–72; gender issues and, 79–80; as gun culture, 159–60, 161; and hippies, 211; and homosexuals, 163; identification with the Old South, 181, 186; Japan event, 124, 243, 271; legends of, 15, 30, 37, 196–201; paradox, 31, 41–43; races, 120–24; racism in, 54–55, 80–84; records, 183–84; regional parochialism, 182–83, 185–91, 196, 224; rival sanctioning organizations, 71; rules, 163; sexism, 79–80; Southern origins of, 72–75; subculture, 35, 43, 144–69; teams, 114–20; tracks, 103–8, 190–91, 268–71; values, 35–36, 163–64, 241, 277; venues, 184–92, 268–71; winners, 191–92, 193, 265; women, 3, 69, 79–80. *See also* Competitiveness; Diversity in NASCAR: Diversity Management Council; Drivers; Moonshine; Television coverage of NASCAR; Winston Cup: attendance; Winston Cup teams

NASCAR family, 36–37, 55–56, 134, 212, 213, 277, 278; as author's family, 56

NASCAR weekends: economic impacts of, 147; events that take place during, 146–47

NASCAR Winston Cup Illustrated (magazine), 10, 219

NASCAR Winston Racing Series (short-track program), 275–76

Nashville Network, The (TNN), 26, 42, 271, 275

National Association for the Advancement of Colored People (NAACP), 96, 142

National Broadcasting Corporation
(NBC), 42, 271, 272
National Hot Rod Association (NHRA),
127, 147
National Opinion Research Center
(University of Chicago), 26, 164
Nemechek, Joe, 51, 52, 153, 154, 212, 213,
216, 232, 243, 244, 263, 265
Newsweek (magazine), 12, 279
Newton's Laws of Motion, 100
Night racing, 6, 48
North Carolina, 30, 193–95, 265; drivers
from, 13, 193–95; NASCAR race shops
in, 165
North Wilkesboro, NC, 37, 148, 179, 189,
190, 287 n.5

Orlando, FL, 24, 70, 262

Panch, Marvin, 183, 198, 203, 240; career,
198
Park, Steve, 195, 243, 259, 265
Parks, Raymond, 68
Parsons, Benny, 41, 272
Payne, V. Gregory, 286–87 n.7
Pearlman, Jeff, 291 n.4
Pearson, David, 197, 240, 244, 290 n.7
Pemberton, Robin, 289 n.5
Pennzoil Corporation, 229, 237, 265
Penske Motorsports, 189, 264
Pepsi 400 at Daytona, 10, 24–25, 35, 49,
116, 177; in 1992, 115–16; in 1999, 35,
46–56, 146; in 2001, 27–28, 48, 83, 152,
182, 267
Pepsi-Cola, 10, 138, 188, 230; and Day-
tona International Speedway, 188
Performance Research (marketing study),
234–35
Periodicals on racing, 60–62
Petty, Adam, 41, 150; career of, 41; death
of, 21, 41, 282 n.5

Petty family, as racing's First Family,
40–41
Petty, Judson, 68
Petty, Kyle, 40–41, 114, 135, 156, 239, 240,
243, 289 n.5; career of, 40
Petty, Lee, 40, 68, 183, 264, 285, 290;
career records, 40; death of, 40
Petty, Maurice, 40
Petty, Richard, 24, 39, 40, 52, 54, 68, 81,
95, 115, 116, 119, 135, 138–39, 150, 152,
176, 181, 183–84, 185, 195, 201, 239, 240,
242, 244, 249, 264, 271, 285 n.15, 290
n.7; career records, 39, 40, 183–84;
championships, 195; final race at Darlington, 159; final race at Daytona, 24,
115–16, 150; nickname, 39, 40; photo,
39; records set by, 183–84, 242; STP
sponsorship, 284 n.3
Pit crews, 116–17
Pit road: at Richmond, 174–76; rules of,
123, 175
Pit stops: adjustments made during, 5,
112–13; green flag, 121; need for, 121;
speed of, 116–17; strategies, 121–22;
yellow flag, 121
Pocono, PA (NASCAR track), 82, 190
Points, championship, 124–26, 247, 249,
264; alternative systems, 126; bonus,
124–25; problems with, 124–26
Polaris All-Terrain Vehicles, 157, 158; as
sponsor with a country theme, 157;
photo, 158
Pole position, 51
Poole, David, 283, 291
Powell, Colin (General), 11
Pre-race festivities and ceremonies, 35,
50–51, 136–37, 162, 173–74, 212, 213;
photo, 137
Prohibition, 63–65; repeal of, 65. *See also*
Moonshine
Prole sports, 75–79; culture of, 75–77

Provisional starting positions, 95
Pryor, Richard, 59
Purdue University, 23
Purses, 3, 52, 88–89, 92, 178

Quaid, Randy, 84, 180
Qualification, 111–12
Quindlen, Anna, 279, 291 n.5

Race weekends, 8, 171–72, 205, 209, 213,
    256, 258
Racing, 17, 32–35, 64–65, 72–79, 99–101;
    books about, 13; conditions, 111–12;
    cost of, 78; dangers of, 21; strategies,
    121–23. *See also* NASCAR; Winston Cup
Racing basics, 98–131
Racism, 54–55, 80–84, 278–79
Rathmann brothers (Dick and Jim), 74,
    199
Rear-end differential, 110–11
Recreational Vehicle (RV) villages at
    Winston Cup races, 1, 15, 55, 92–93,
    147, 151, 157–59, 168, 209; display of
    flags and banners at, 55; gemeinshaft
    in, 158; photos, 7, 159
Reed, Dale Volberg, 283 n.23
Reed, John Shelton, 72, 145, 151, 159, 164,
    181, 201, 202–3, 219, 241, 282 n.8, 283
    n.23, 285 n.19, 287 n.1, 288 n.21, 290
    n.12
Regalia (of fans), 150–52
Regional differences: among drivers,
    191–201; among fans, 26, 165, 166–67,
    180–81; in race locations, 184–91
Regional fables, 72–75
Remington Firearms, 157, 160
Restrictor plate racing, 53, 148, 214–16
Restrictor plates, 107, 282, 286
Rexford, Bill, 69, 73, 181, 195
Ribbs, Willy T., 80, 81

Richard Childress Racing, 251, 264, 289
    n.5
Richard Petty Driving Experience, 78–79
Richmond, VA, 6, 44, 147, 154
Richmond International Raceway, 48,
    108, 133, 135, 170–79, 189, 190, 216,
    283 n.16; designer, 189; diagram, 172;
    opening, 190
Richmond, Tim, 37, 84, 199, 289 n.5
Riverside Park (Agawam, MA), 24, 171
R. J. Reynolds Tobacco Co., 184, 220–23,
    230
Road racing, 30, 106, 110, 127, 270–71;
    tracks, 104, 105
Roberts, Glenn ("Fireball"), 20, 68, 197,
    199; death of, 20, 197
Robinson, Shawna, 3, 79, 210–11, 257;
    photo, 211
Rocker, John, 278–79; photo, 279
Rockingham, NC (NASCAR track), 190,
    204, 287 n.8; opening, 190
Rollins, Shorty, 114
Rookie of the Year, 37, 51, 53, 93, 114–
    15, 157, 195, 254, 259, 260, 283 n.16;
    average age when won, 115
Roper, Jim, 69, 72, 73, 285 n.17
Ross, Earl, 34, 283 n.16
Roush, Jack, 251, 264
Rudd, Ricky, 11–12, 51, 52, 53–54, 109,
    114, 153, 154, 171, 177, 178, 184, 212–13,
    216, 243, 252, 254, 255, 258–59, 260,
    261, 262, 264; sale of race team, 109,
    264; sixteen-season winning streak,
    51, 171, 184, 213, 254, 262; youngest
    Rookie of the Year, 114
Rudolph, Eric Robert, 208
Rushin, Steve, 17, 60–63, 148–50, 218, 281
    n.1, 284 n.2, 287 n.6, 290 n.1
RV Villages. *See* Recreational Vehicle
    (RV) Villages

Sabates, Felix, 131, 289 n.5

Sadler, Eliot, 196, 256

Salaries: crew, 116, 120; drivers, 119–20

Sanctioning organizations for motor sports, 126–29, 281–82 n.4

Schaller, Bob, 283 n.18, 291 n.22

Schrader, Ken, 92, 153, 240, 243

Scott, Wendell, 59–60, 67, 80–81, 183; career of, 80; photo, 81

Seagraves, Ralph, 220, 222

Sears Point, CA (NASCAR road track), 30, 104, 120, 190

Sellers, Shane, 29

Shelmerdine, Kirk, 289

Short tracks, 105, 178–79, 269, 275–76; racing at, 110, 148, 177–79

Show cars, 109, 79, 255, 286 n.5; photo, 79, 109

Silly Season, 258–59

Simpson, Bill, 26

Skinner, Mike, 4, 40, 52, 153, 177, 195, 207, 237, 243, 264

Smith, Bob, 67

Smith, Bruton, 189, 287 n.5

Social class, 75–79, 137–38

Sosebee, Gober, 68

South Carolina, 132–43

South of the Border, 170

South, 30–31, 61, 72–75, 141, 180–203; literacy in, 200; NASCAR's identification with, 181–82; new, 14–15, 281 n.2; old, 30, 181; and pro sports, 200, 289–90 n.11; rural poverty in, 141; storytelling as a tradition in, 200–201

Southern 500 at Darlington, 56, 132–43, 159

Southern Focus Poll, 26, 165–67

Southern Sociological Society, 18

Souvenirs: sales, 119, 258–59; trailers, 28–29, 47–48, 173–74, 259; trailers (photos), 48, 174, 259

Speedvision, 26, 42

Spencer, Jimmy, 24, 40, 161, 231, 238, 243

Sponsors, 228–30, 232, 257–58; beer companies, 223, 227; car and tire companies, 222; Coca-Cola, 223, 228; Gatorade, 218, 228; Pepsi-Cola, 223, 230; R. J. Reynolds Tobacco Co. (Winston cigarettes), 220–22, 230–31. See also Corporatization

Sponsorship, 222, 227–35, 266, 273. See also Corporatization

Sponsors Report, 231–32

Sports, 57–59, 62, 75–79, 98; in American culture, 25–26; books about, 58–59

Sports car racing, 127–28

Sports Car Club of America, 33

Sports Illustrated (magazine), 2, 17, 29, 60, 62, 82, 148, 278, 279, 281 n.1, 282 n.9, 284 n.4, 290 n.1; advertising in, 62

Sprint cars, 128; photo, 128

Staley, Enoch, 189

Stewart, Tony, 4, 11, 37, 51, 52, 53, 93, 94, 101, 151–54, 174, 177, 195, 206–7, 212, 216, 218, 227, 236, 243, 244, 254, 255, 263, 264, 265, 272, 283 n.17; record for wins in a rookie season, 177, 265, 272, 283 n.16; Rookie of the Year (1999), 195, 254, 263; in Stock Car Racing Encyclopedia, 34, 248, 282, 289; in Stock Car Racing Magazine, 10, 11, 39, 160

Stop-and-go penalty, 123

STP, 135, 136, 184, 224, 284 n.3

Strait, Bob, 210–11

Superspeedways, 105–6

Talledega, 44, 50, 61, 81, 82, 104, 106–7, 122, 159, 188–90, 202, 204, 205, 208–16, 286 n.4; building of, 188, 189–90;

Talledega (*continued*)
capacity of, 213; designer, 189; diagram, 209; restrictor plates, 107
Team Petty, 40, 54, 264, 268
Television coverage of NASCAR, 26, 41–43, 228, 235, 271–73
Texas Motor Speedway, 11, 41, 104, 179
Texas World Speedway, 191
Thigpen, David, 80
Thomas, Herb, 68, 69, 74, 199
Thompson, Fred, 85
Thurmond, Strom, 61, 142
Tichener, George, 22
Tickets: prices, 8–9, 49, 90, 91, 133, 166, 174, 209, 212, 230; scalpers, 9, 133–34, 212
Tide laundry detergent, 11, 53, 228, 236
Time magazine, 60, 62, 80
TNN. *See* Nashville Network, The
Tobacco Road, 500, 202, 203
Tomlinson, Bob, 285 n.15
Tracks, 99–103; challenges of asymmetry, 113; characteristics of, 103–8; food at, 138, 173; maximum steerable speed, 99–101; as shrines, 33. *See also* Winston Cup: tracks
Traffic jams, 9, 90
TransSouth, 400, 140, 280
Transporters, 112, 129, 130, 218; photo, 130
Trickle, Dick, 114, 115
Triplett, Kevin, 82
Tritt, Travis, 29
T-shirts, 28, 49, 50–51, 55, 150–51; Atlanta (NAPA 500), 262; Charlotte (UAW-GM Quality 500), 208; Darlington (Southern 500), 137; Daytona (Pepsi 400), 50–51; Richmond (Exide Batteries 400), 178; Talledega (Winston 500), 211
Turner Broadcasting System, 42

Turner, Curtis, 67, 68, 69, 189, 197, 199, 201, 240, 285 n.15; and Freddie Lorenzen, 197
Tuthill, Bill, 71

UAW-GM Quality 500 (1999), 205–8
United States Auto Club (USAC), 128
University of Nebraska, 203
University of North Carolina, Chapel Hill, 26, 165, 202, 203, 282 n.8
University of North Carolina, Charlotte, 9, 202
University of Tennessee, 203
University of Virginia, 170–71, 203
Unser, Al Jr., 91
USAR Hooters ProCup series, 3, 35, 129
Utter, Jim, 291

Wallace, George C., 188
Wallace, Kenny, 39, 153
Wallace, Mike, 39
Wallace, Rusty, 5, 11, 39, 52–53, 85, 92, 105, 110, 126, 134, 146, 155, 160, 186, 232, 239, 240, 243, 244, 260, 263, 267; Daytona jinx, 52; Winchester rifle honoring, 160
Walton, Izaak, 58
Waltrip, Darrell, 39, 95–96, 115, 122–23, 138, 146, 152–53, 155, 159, 197, 206, 243, 252, 271; career of, 95–96; photo, 95; retirement of, 95, 115
Waltrip, Michael, 39, 92, 153, 154, 238, 240, 243, 254, 260, 261, 262; wreck at Atlanta (1999), 261
Watkins Glen, NY (NASCAR road track), 104, 108, 189, 190, 223, 283 n.16
Weatherly, Joe, 20, 67, 197, 199
WELCOME RACE FANS banners, 14, 92, 147, 151, 212, 229
Westmoreland, Hubert, 68, 72
Wheeler, Humpy, 2, 189, 222, 252

Whiskey Rebellion, 63, 64

Whiskey runners. *See* Moonshiners

White, Jack, 69

Whitesell, Brian, 206

Wide World of Sports (ABC), 41

Will, George, 57, 58

Williams, Brian, 272

Wilson, Mark, 284 n.1

Wilson, Waddell, 197

Winston cigarettes, 161, 184, 221, 222, 238; and NASCAR, 184, 231

Winston Cup, 24–25, 37, 120–26, 157–58, 191, 193, 264; attendance, 9, 25–26, 145–46, 165, 179, 213, 233; cars, 33–34, 79, 108–14, 116, 128, 218, 241, 251; costs of racing in, 78, 129–31; expansion, 96; future of, 263–80; points, 124–26; renaming, 184, 222, 284 n.11; schedule, 269–70; season, 36, 104, 124, 190, 244, 248, 262; tracks, 103–8, 190–91, 268–71. *See also* Cars; Competitiveness; Corporatization; Fans; Moonshine; Periodicals on racing; Points, championship; Purses; Silly Season; Winston Cup teams

Winston Cup teams, 114–20, 183, 264, 266; formation of new, 266; one-car independents, 252, 264; owner-driver teams, 252. *See also* Multi-car teams

Winston Open, 3, 4

Winston, The, 1–15, 93, 243, 270; format of race, 5; rules for setting the field, 3–4

Wolfe, Tom, 66–67, 75, 127, 163, 285 n.22, 287 n.9, 288 n.16

Wood, Leonard, 198

Wright, James (author): books by, 17–18; career, 23–24; childhood, 18–19, 87; driver preferences, 152–55; education, 23; family, 55–56; photo, 214

Wright, Jim (author's father), 18–19, 20; photo, 19, 20

Yankee Hiatus (from NASCAR), 186–90, 203; and corporatization, 223

Yankee Invasion (of NASCAR), 180–203; drivers, 191–96; venues, 184–91

Yankee Resurgence, 186, 190–91, 196, 263

Yarborough, Cale, 106

Yates, Robert, 11, 51, 112, 251, 252, 258, 264

Yunick, Smokey, 68, 132, 198, 199, 287 n.2

JIM WRIGHT is the Provost Distinguished Research
Professor of Sociology at the University of Central
Florida. His many publications include (with Beth
A. Rubin and Joel A. Devine) *Beside the Golden Door:
Policy, Politics, and the Homeless* (1998); (with Joseph
F. Sheley) *In the Line of Fire: Youths, Guns, and Violence
in Urban America* (1995); and (with Joseph F. Sheley
and Zina T. McGee) *Weapon-Related Victimization
in Selected Inner-City High School Samples* (1995).

The Library of Congress has cataloged the hardcover edition as follows:
Wright, Jim.
Fixin' to git : one fan's love affair with NASCAR's
Winston Cup / by Jim Wright.
p. cm.   Includes index.
ISBN 0-8223-2926-3 (cloth : alk. paper)
1. Stock-car racing—United States.   2. NASCAR (Association)
3. Winston Cup.   I. Title.
GV1029.9.S74 W75   2002   796.72′0973—dc21   2002000485

ISBN 0-8223-3220-5 (pbk. : alk. paper)